SULTANS in SPLENDOR

Alas, the Western lands have become the daysprings of knowledge.
Nothing remains of the fame of Rum and Arab, of Egypt and Herat.
The time is a time of progress, the world is a world of science.
Is the survival of societies compatible with ignorance?

Sadullah Pasha, *The Nineteenth Century*

SULTANS in SPLENDOR

Philip Mansel

THE VENDOME PRESS
New York and Paris

Other works by Philip Mansel

Louis XVIII
Pillars of Monarchy: Royal Guards in History
The Eagle in Splendour: Napoleon I and His Court
The Court of France 1789—1830

First published in the United States of America by
The Vendome Press, 515 Madison Avenue, N.Y., N.Y. 10022
Distributed in the United States by
Rizzoli International Publications
597 Fifth Avenue, N.Y., N.Y. 10017

Library of Congress Cataloging-in-Publication Data

Mansel, Philip.
    Sultans in splendor.

    1. Middle East—Court and courtiers—Pictorial
works. 2. Middle East—Kings and rulers—Pictorial
works. I. Title.
DS44.5.M36   1988   956'.01'0922   88–20674
ISBN 0–86565–109–4

Printed and bound in Italy

Contents

To Mohammed and Fouad

THE MONARCHIES OF THE MIDDLE EAST 1869

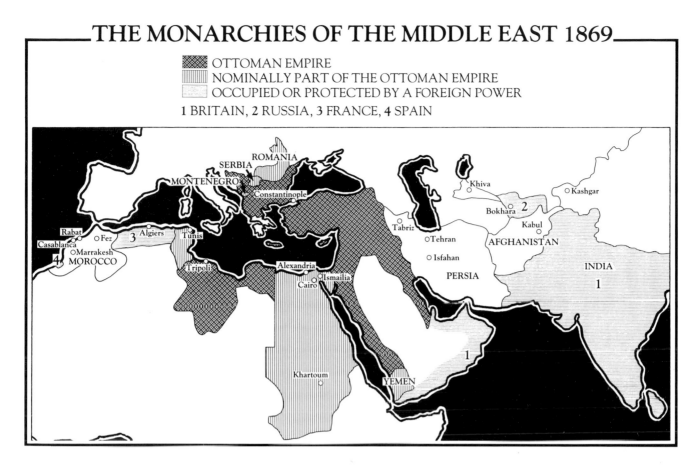

OTTOMAN EMPIRE
NOMINALLY PART OF THE OTTOMAN EMPIRE
OCCUPIED OR PROTECTED BY A FOREIGN POWER
1 BRITAIN, 2 RUSSIA, 3 FRANCE, 4 SPAIN

Author's Note

Proper names have been rendered in the European, usually French, form used at the time by the individuals concerned when writing in European languages: hence Fouad King of Egypt, and so on. Family trees show only the most important members of the dynasty. The term Middle East is used to describe the area between Morocco and Afghanistan.

Acknowledgments

The author wishes to acknowledge all those who provided him with hospitality, information or photographs during his research for this book. In particular he would like to thank: Professor Rauf Abbas, Princess Widjdan Ali, Gaston d'Angélis, Mme Arkash, Youmna Asseily, Professor Nurhan Atasoy, Izzealdine Atif, Princess Rebia Ayyub, Shahla Basharat, M. Ben Mansour, Mrs I. Bowler, Mr and Mrs John Brinton, Mme F. Charles-Roux, Lody Cordahi, Dr Leslie Croxford, Mme Hasna Dauda, Caroline Davidson, Fouad Debbas, H.W.Y.P. Dickson, General and Mrs Djam, Leila Doss, Nancy Hatch Dupree, Rana Eldem, Seddam Eldem, Mahpeyker Enver, Ahmad Faroughy, Princess S. Firouz, Sir Brinsley Ford, Sir Edward Ford, Gerald de Gaury, Nedjla Gerrmann, James and Hyatt Graham, Elizabeth Gruninger, Ara Güler, Çelek Gülersoy, Badr al-Hajj, Princess Ayesha Hassan, Prince Hassan Hassan, Prince Abbas Hilmi, Ezzat M. Jaafar, Sue and Ossama Kaoukgi, M. Karkagi, Farid Kioumgi, Zenan Kuneralp, Princess Malekeh Mansur, Captain Mallouba, Suleiman Mousa, Mr Naim, Ruth Niknejad, Princess Fevsi Osmanoglu, Prince Nazim Osmanoglu, Princess Nazim Osmanoglu, Prince Osman Nami Osmanoglu, Prince Osman Vassib Osmanoglu, John Papasyan, Jacques Perot, Professor Julian Pitt-Rivers, Leon B. Poullada, Prince Ali Qajar, Prince Hamid Qajar, King Reshad of the Tunisians, Max Rodenbeck, Paul Rolo, Alan Rush, Nasir Saberi, Major Y. Salim, Adel Sabit, Mme Sabit, Professor George Scanlon, Mrs I. Taymurtash, Robert Tignor, Taha Toros, Prince and Princess Aziz Toussoun, Michael Weinstein, Bridget Westenra, Professor Nur Yulman, Princess Fahrelnissa Zeid, Prince Ra'ad bin Zeid, Nolly Zervudachi, Virginia Zervudachi, Mme I. Zulficar-Mohsen.

He is especially grateful to Professor Albert Hourani and the Hon. Sir Steven Runciman for taking the trouble to read an earlier version of the manuscript.

Introduction
The Opening of the Suez Canal

Official Tribune at the opening of the Suez Canal
*Europeans are clearly in the majority among the Khedive's
guests, as they were among the canal company's shareholders.
The number of European ladies present shows how accessible
Egypt had become by 1869.*

THE Khedive Ismail was a magnificent host. He had organised an endless round of entertainments for the guests who had come to Egypt in the autumn of 1869 for the opening of the Suez Canal: journeys up the Nile, visits to the Pyramids, reviews, weddings, operas (*Rigoletto* was performed instead of *Aida*, which Verdi failed to deliver on time). The climax took place in November in Ismailia, the city he had founded on the edge of the canal. A palace for the Khedive and an encampment of tents for his guests had been erected in a few months. Parties never stopped: there were whirling dervishes, screaming dervishes and *almées* or dancing girls to entertain the guests.

The Khedive Ismail (1863–79)
He acquired the title of Khedive (meaning master) from the Ottoman Sultan in 1867, in recognition of his unique status as a semi-independent vassal of the Ottoman Empire. He is wearing the fez and the special Ottoman frock-coat known as the stambouline, *which was standard dress for the Ottoman ruling class in the second half of the nineteenth century.*

The Khedive's ball on 18 November was particularly memorable. As the Emperor Francis Joseph of Austria wrote to his wife: 'Several thousand people had been invited to the ball but many more came . . . so the company was very mixed.' He found the pushing crowds and the wait for supper so painful that he longed to leave. Less pompous guests, however, were fascinated by the mixture of people and costumes – desert chieftains prowling round young women in plunging dresses, Indian rajahs next to Levantine merchants and European diplomats, the Empress Eugénie of the French, wearing a beautiful scarlet dress covered with diamonds, in the same room as Garibaldi's son and 'very many vulgar people'. One journalist described the ball as 'the most astonishing mixture of costumes, uniforms, faces and decorations in the entire world'.[1]

The ball was not merely a sign of the Khedive's generosity as a host; it was also part of the celebrations to inaugurate the Suez Canal, which were intended to display the Khedive's power and progressiveness. The presence of such guests as the Empress of the French, the Emperor of Austria, the Crown Prince of Prussia and Prince Henry of the Netherlands enabled the Khedive to repay the hospitality which he had received in Europe and to prove that he was as royal as they were. The journalists and businessmen invited – who repaid his hospitality by ceaseless complaints and threats to leave early – were meant to be impressed by the extent of Egypt's modernisation. The celebrations were intended to inaugurate not only the canal but also a new age for Egypt and the Middle East.

However, the inauguration brought problems as well as triumphs for the Khedive Ismail; and these problems dominated all the monarchs of the Middle East after 1869, although not always at the same time or in the same way. Although it had been dug by Egyptians, the Suez Canal could not have been completed without European technical skills. But such skills were increasing the technological gap between Europe and the Middle East, and making it more difficult for the armies and economies of the Middle East to compete with those of Europe.

The Suez Canal was also a triumph for European finance. It was the idea of a cousin of the Empress Eugénie, Ferdinand de Lesseps. Through his friendship with Ismail's predecessor, Said Pasha, his relationship with the Empress and years of intrigue in London, Paris and Constantinople, he had finally obtained permission to start work on the canal. Even Britain, which had long been opposed to the Frenchman's scheme –

The Emperor of Austria's yacht steaming through the canal
Although the canal had been a French project, by 1880 80% of the tonnage using it was British.

Palmerston had declared that it was 'physically impracticable' – had dropped its opposition.

The success of the canal, however, revealed the dangers of dealing with European financiers. Ferdinand de Lesseps unloaded surplus shares in the canal company onto Said and Ismail, while depriving them of the control of the company to which the number of their shares entitled them. Loans were equally hazardous. Between 1854 and 1881 the rulers of Egypt borrowed £94 million abroad but received only £45 million. The consequent loss of financial independence, as well as the widening technological gap, could lead to a loss of political independence.

The religion of Europe also threatened the monarchs of the Middle East. They were all Muslim rulers of Muslim countries; and for the Ottoman Sultan and the Sultan of Morocco, who both called themselves 'Caliph' (that is to say successor of the Prophet Mohammed as leader of the Muslims), their religious role was as important as their political position. However, at the celebrations of inauguration, a Catholic bishop, Monseigneur Bauer, spoke of

Christianity 'raising its voice opposite the crescent' in the Middle East. This new confidence might provide a pretext for European powers to intervene to 'protect' the Christian minorities (now including European businessmen) which inhabited the territory of almost every Middle Eastern monarchy.

France, whose Empress's yacht led the procession of ships steaming down the Suez Canal the day it was opened, had established itself as the 'protector' of the Catholic minorities of the Middle East. Russia assumed a similar attitude towards the Orthodox populations, and both had already intervened in Lebanon and the Balkans respectively. For European imperialism was entering its golden age – as was shown by the presence at the celebrations of the Emir Abd el-Kader, the unsuccessful leader of Algerian resistance to the French thirty years before.

1869 saw other moves in Europe's advance on the Middle East. France established a commission to manage Tunisian finances – the Bey of Tunis had spent recklessly in an effort to improve his army. Two months before the opening of the canal, the British and

Russian Foreign Ministers met in Heidelberg to regulate the progress of each other's empires in central Asia.[2] The Russian Empire was also advancing in the Caucasus, and the British Empire had signed treaties with the rulers of the Gulf and Aden in order to 'protect' its route to India. The British Empire might decide to take over other countries more directly on the route to India, such as Egypt. A *Times* correspondent in Egypt, Moberly Bell, wrote: 'We must either hold Egypt or lose India.'

Thus the monarchs of the Middle East had entered a bewildering new epoch, dominated by unprecedented dangers from Europe. Some reacted by clinging to their own traditions and refusing, when possible, any contact with Europe or attempt at modernisation. Others believed that the best way to meet the threat from Europe was to modernise their power-base. The Ottoman Empire, which had once been the greatest power in Europe, was still the greatest power in the Middle East. It stretched from the Danube to the Gulf and from Tripoli to Trebizond. The Ottoman Sultan Abdul Aziz (1861–76) was suzerain of Egypt and it had been necessary to obtain his permission before digging the Suez Canal. Nevertheless, in 1869 a former Grand Vizir, Fouad Pasha, wrote from Nice to Sultan Abdul Aziz: 'The Empire of the Sultans is in danger. We must change all our institutions, political and military, and adopt the new laws and the new appliances invented by Europe.'[3]

There was nothing in Islam to stop rulers adopting new laws and appliances. For example, representation of the human form was thought to be impious only by a minority of Muslims. Photography had been demonstrated to the great Mohammed Ali, grandfather of the Khedive Ismail and founder of his dynasty, at Alexandria in 1839, within a few months of its invention in Europe; and it had since been adopted with enthusiasm in the courts of the Middle East. It appealed to monarchs' desire to learn what was happening in their own dominions, as well as to their need to be commemorated. In 1862 the Shah of Persia, and in 1867 the Ottoman Sultan, appointed a court photographer. Thus the history of the Middle East in this period can be related through photographs, many of them taken by specially appointed court photographers and preserved in the dynasties' own collections. They show the monarchs and their courts as they saw themselves.

Although inventions such as photography could be adapted to the needs of Middle Eastern monarchs, new institutions were, at least in theory, opposed to their traditions. All European monarchs except the Tsar of Russia had accepted constitutions by 1869. But there had never been representative assemblies in the Middle East. Subjects traditionally made their views known to their monarchs through the *ulema* (the interpreters of Islam to Muslims), the court, the Royal Guard or by shouting in the street. A monarch in the Middle East was in theory absolute, as is shown in innumerable manuals of kingship, known as *Mirrors for Princes* (the last of which was written for the Shah of Persia in 1909). They exalt the monarch in the belief that 'the prosperity and ruin of the world are both from kings'. Monarchs on earth were the equivalent of angels in heaven: the main safeguard for a monarch's subjects came from his sense of self-interest.

According to an old Persian saying often quoted in *Mirrors for Princes*, there was 'No sultan without soldiers, no soldiers without money, no money without prosperity, and no prosperity without justice and good administration.' The word sultan itself, which was used for almost every ruler in the Middle East (even the Shah of Persia called himself a sultan), implied unlimited power. Respect for monarchs was so great that, according to most Muslim writers, obedience to the sultan, the shadow of God upon earth, was a duty for his subjects. Only if he gave a command contrary to the *Sharia*, the Muslim law, and that command was a novelty, was rebellion permissible.[4] These traditions of absolute kingship, often inherited from the pre-Islamic Persian Empire, provided some of the assumptions which governed the lives of the monarchs of the Middle East.

By 1869, however, it was clear that many of these assumptions were no longer valid. The sultans were under attack from the kings and emperors of Europe. Already their Muslim fellow-monarchs in India and Indonesia had fallen under European domination. Perhaps if the surviving independent Muslim rulers, in the belt stretching from Morocco to Afghanistan, tried to model themselves on European monarchs, they would become more secure. Thus the monarchs of the Middle East and North Africa were united by a need to modernise as well as by geography and Islam. They were also united by admiration for the greatest surviving Muslim power: the Ottoman Empire.

~I~
Long Live Our Padishah!

Abdul Hamid II
Abdul Hamid, who reigned from 1876 to 1909, is regarded by some as the last of the great Sultans, by others as a bloodthirsty tyrant. This photograph was taken before he became Sultan, when he grew a beard as a sign of his newly acquired authority.

'IF you want riches, go to India. If you want learning, go to Europe. But if you want imperial splendour, come to the Ottoman Empire.' There was still truth in this ancient proverb in the second half of the nineteenth century. For the Ottoman Padishah (great king) or Sultan had a unique position. In the Ottoman Empire the monarchy was so important that its inhabitants were called Ottomans, after the name of the dynasty (as if the inhabitants of the Austrian Empire had been called Habsburgs). It was a dynastic empire, defined not by geography or national identity but by the extent of the Sultans' conquests. Most Ottomans were proud of their name, since they were convinced of the incomparable grandeur and antiquity of their empire. The Ottoman dynasty had been powerful sovereigns, in both Europe and Asia, since the second half of the fourteenth century, when the Bourbons and the Habsburgs were still minor princes.

The Ottoman Sultan possessed unique authority over his subjects. He was not only Sultan, but also Caliph, 'servant of the two holy places' (Mecca and Medina) and owner of the relics of the Prophet and his companions which can still be seen in the Sultan's traditional residence, Topkapi palace. In the mid-nineteenth century the Sultan had left Topkapi for the great Italianate palace of Dolmabahçe on the Bosphorus. It is a massive assertion of imperial splendour and self-confidence and contains what is probably the largest throne-room in Europe. The veneration with which the Sultan was surrounded was shown by his ministers' and courtiers' obsequious behaviour in his presence. When the Princess of Wales

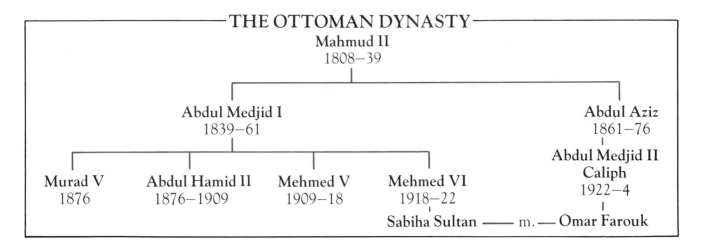

THE OTTOMAN DYNASTY

Mahmud II
1808–39

Abdul Medjid I
1839–61

Abdul Aziz
1861–76

Abdul Medjid II
Caliph
1922–4

Murad V
1876

Abdul Hamid II
1876–1909

Mehmed V
1909–18

Mehmed VI
1918–22

Sabiha Sultan —— m. —— Omar Farouk

came on a visit to Sultan Abdul Aziz in 1869, her lady-in-waiting, Mrs William Grey, noticed in the throne-room of Dolmabahçe guard officers 'all standing in attitudes of deepest humility, their eyes cast down, their arms crossed and taking care always to face the Sultan in whatever part of the hall he might be'.

His ministers were (or pretended to be) so afraid of him that even the Grand Vizir, the second person in the empire, who enjoyed a combination of power and rank without parallel in Europe, would almost prostrate himself in front of Abdul Aziz. Whereas in other countries it was the custom to kiss the monarch's hand, in the Ottoman Empire, at the great receptions held every year in the throne-room at Dolmabahçe after the fast of Ramadan, the Sultan's officials, officers and courtiers, after three reverences, made the gesture of kissing his feet. This slavishness was encouraged by the

absence, except in remote provinces like Albania, of a hereditary landowning ruling class, whose birth and wealth could, as in other monarchies, lead to a certain independence of attitude. There were not even inherited family names. A son of a shopkeeper, like Aali Pasha, could rise to become a liberal, reforming Grand Vizir under Abdul Aziz.[1]

Since 1826 a series of radical reforms had been introduced, modernising the army and navy and

Panorama of Constantinople, 1870

In 1870 Constantinople was one of the largest and most cosmopolitan cities in the world, and the political, commercial and cultural capital of the Balkans and the Middle East. In the middle of the photograph, surrounded by trees, is Topkapi palace, which contained the relics of the Prophet and the imperial jewels, as it still does.

Throne-room, Dolmabahçe
A lady-in-waiting of the Princess of Wales called this room 'one of the largest and most beautiful rooms in the world'. The chandelier, one of the largest ever made, was a present from Queen Victoria.

Dolmabahçe palace

Dolmabahçe, built in European style by an Armenian, Krikor Balyan, between 1843 and 1856, is over 900 feet long and has 285 rooms. The tall central block contains the throne-room. It is followed by the harem quarters and the apartment of the heir to the throne. Above the palace are ministries and the houses of senior officials.

The Sultan's bathroom, Dolmabahçe

Dolmabahçe was described by the Emperor Francis Joseph, who stayed there on his way to the opening of the Suez Canal, as 'magically beautiful and senselessly luxurious'. This bathroom, which can still be seen today, is made of translucent pink alabaster.

creating modern ministries and a new legal code. The pace of change increased after the Ottoman victory, with France and Britain, in the Crimean War. But these reforms did not solve the main problem of the empire: its dynastic character. In an age of nationalism how could the Ottoman Sultan continue to rule not only Muslim Arabs, Kurds, Albanians and Turks, but also the Greek, Serbian, Bulgarian, Armenian and Arab Christians who comprised 35% of the population of about thirty-two million?

The solution adopted by the Sultan's government was to assert that the common quality of Ottoman was more important than differences of race and religion. After 1868 there was usually at least one Christian minister. A circle of senior Christian officials and courtiers, with names like Karatheodory and Mavroyennis, continued to serve the Ottoman Sultans until the fall of the empire as ministers, personal doctors and Princes of Samos (a title invented simply to satisfy their vanity). The Ottoman Empire was so powerful and lucrative that a small, lawless country like Greece held few attractions for the Greeks living in the Ottoman capital, Constantinople.

In 1868, the same year as the appointment of the first Christian minister, the Lycée Impérial de Galataseray was opened in Pera, the 'European' quarter of Constantinople, on a hill above the Golden Horn. It provided a modern education for the sons of the Ottoman elite. The first pupils were as cosmopolitan as the *Almanach du Levant*, the indispensable yearbook published in Constantinople, which contained information in Turkish, French, Bulgarian, Armenian and Ladino (the language spoken by the Sephardic Jews who had fled to the Ottoman Empire from persecution in Spain after 1494). There were Muslims, Armenians, Greeks, Jews, Bulgarians, Roman Catholics and Armenian Catholics. No school in Britain or Russia, the two powers most insistent on the necessity for better treatment of minorities in the Ottoman Empire, was as cosmopolitan.

Constantinople was also the largest city in Islam and a cultural, religious and political centre for Arabs, Persians and the Muslims of the Russian Empire. King Abdullah of Jordan wrote in his memoirs: 'It contains Muslims of every walk of life, of all fashions and tongues, yet nobody and nothing seems strange and you can find anything you want from any country.'[2]

Like the Ottoman Empire itself, Constantinople was at a crossroads of history. It was a mixture of Europe and Islam, past and present. After 1888 the Orient Express connected it to the other capitals of Europe by rail, but slaves were still for sale in certain districts of the city. The latest fashions from Paris and Vienna could be seen beside the traditional costumes of the Balkans and the Caucasus. Half the Turkish population was dressed in the turbans and flowing robes of the past. The others wore the fez and the *stambouline*. Five different calendars were in use at the same time: the Muslim calendar; a special 'financial' calendar devised by the Sublime Porte (as the office of the Grand Vizir was called until the fall of the empire); the 'old style' Christian calendar used by eastern orthodox Christians and Armenians; the 'new style' Christian calendar used by western Europeans and local Catholics; and the Jewish calendar.

Omar Pasha
Omar Pasha, who was born in Croatia, was one of the many Europeans who went to the Ottoman Empire, converted to Islam and rose to high office. He was Commander-in-Chief of the Ottoman army during the Crimean War.

The cosmopolitan and tolerant character of the Ottoman Empire was emphasised by the most convincing compliment a country can receive, namely foreign immigration. Many foreigners rose high in the Sultan's service, such as Murad Pasha, formerly the Polish general Bem, and the English Woods Pasha who 'donned the fez' — obligatory for all in the Sultan's service — in 1869 and served in the Ottoman navy.[3] At that time the Ottoman Empire's determination to modernise and to provide equal opportunities for its subjects seemed to ensure its survival.

However, after the death of two exceptionally honest and intelligent ministers, Aali Pasha and Fouad Pasha, in 1869 and 1871 respectively, the personality of the Sultan became all-important. Abdul Aziz, who

Sultan Abdul Aziz
The Sultan liked wrestling, painting and playing Turkish music which he had composed himself. His extravagance and autocracy alienated his ministers and he was deposed in 1876.

had ascended the throne in 1861, had been intelligent enough to let himself be guided by two such able ministers. One official describes him as 'in many respects a sober man and of great personal dignity'.[4] Foreigners were impressed by the sight of the Sultan going to mosque on Friday (the ceremony known as the *Selamlik*, which was also the occasion for a dazzling military review). He was rowed in a barge by forty oarsmen in gold-embroidered jackets, 'a proud, haughty-looking man with lowered brows and a sombre expression upon his somewhat dark visage, looking straight before him, not deigning to notice the cheering of the spectators afloat'. Nor did he deign to speak more than a few words on the rare occasions when he attended a ball or dinner.

Abdul Aziz was determined to compete with the power and splendour of European monarchies: he had visited Paris, London and Vienna in 1867. He spent lavishly on the army and the navy, and on his own court. One estimate is that he had 5,500 courtiers and servants (excluding the courtiers' servants), 600 horses, 200 carriages and a harem of 1,000 to 1,500 women. He built two new palaces on the Bosphorus, Çirağan and Beylerbey. Beylerbey deeply impressed Mrs William Grey. She wrote: 'I don't think I ever in my life saw anything more beautiful, indeed no description of mine could convey any idea of its situation, the magnificent views over the Bosphorus, the richness and splendour, and at the same time the perfect taste in which it is filled up.'[5]

Sultan Abdul Aziz was eccentric as well as extravagant. It is rare for accurate contemporary information to be provided about the private life of an Ottoman Sultan, as he spent so much time in the harem. However, from the reports written in the 1870s by the British ambassador and Abraham Bey, an Armenian agent of the Khedive Ismail of Egypt, it is clear that the Sultan was becoming, in the former's expression, 'over-excited'. He developed a passion for presents of parrots, pheasants, beautiful cows of various colours and white hens with black heads. In addition, the Sultan, like his ambitious and influential chamberlains, appreciated presents of money.[6] In 1871 Abraham Bey wrote: 'General discontent reigns in the Ministries. There is no money. It is the Palace that rules.' In 1874 over half of government expenditure went on servicing the external debt. The Ottoman government issued a declaration of bankruptcy in 1875.[7]

The international situation of the empire was also

Beylerbey palace
Beylerbey, built on the site of a previous palace between 1861 and 1864, was so well designed that the Empress Eugénie, who stayed there in 1869, had its windows copied in the Tuileries palace in Paris.

Staircase in Beylerbey
Sultan Abdul Aziz himself planned the decoration of Beylerbey, with frescoes of Ottoman battleships and neo-Islamic patterns and calligraphy.

The last dwarves disappeared from the courts of Europe at the beginning of the nineteenth century; but they remained at the Ottoman court, making jokes and serving at table, until the fall of the empire.

deteriorating. Its traditional enemy, Russia, was recovering from defeat in the Crimean War and had not forgotten its mission to 'protect' the Slav subjects of the Ottoman Sultan in the Balkans. Austria, expelled from both Italy and Germany by 1866, was also turning to the Balkans as an area for expansion. The empire's weak finances and aggressive neighbours increased the threat from its minorities. Life was less agreeable, and careers were less available, for non-Muslims in the provinces than in the capital. Provincial administration was as corrupt and unjust as the minorities' own community organisations. Reforms were often enacted by what were known as 'watery commands' — orders which need not be obeyed.

In 1874 Midhat Pasha, an exceptionally able reforming governor or *vali*, first in Bulgaria and then in Baghdad, wrote to the Sultan's Grand Chamberlain: '. . . our finances are in a hopeless condition, the military administration is utterly disgraced . . . the non-Muslim element loudly proclaims the intention it long ago formed of placing itself under foreign protection'. In any other Middle Eastern monarchy, such a combination of European ambitions, government indebtedness, restless minorities and an 'over-excited' Sultan would have been fatal.[8]

Despite the apparent veneration which surrounded him, deposing the Sultan was one of the oldest traditions of the Ottoman Empire. In 1807–8 a cousin and an uncle of Abdul Aziz, Selim III and Mustafa IV,

had been deposed and killed by their own troops. Such a fate might await Abdul Aziz. A French journalist employed by Aali Pasha noticed that, in Constantinople, 'Behind the servility of the official world . . . was hidden a freedom of language and behaviour which was only revealed in intimacy.'

Already there was a group of discontented intellectuals in Constantinople called — since they spoke French so well — *Jeune Turquie* (Young Turks). They were led by the exiled Prince Mustafa Fazil of Egypt, a royal radical infuriated by being deprived of his property and his place in the succession by his brother the Khedive Ismail. In 1869, in an open letter to Abdul Aziz, he had denounced the Ottoman government's weakness, corruption and treatment of Christians, and had urged him to imitate the Emperor of Austria and the King of Sardinia, and save the empire by granting a constitution. Some of their subjects were beginning to expect Middle Eastern monarchs to follow European models in the exercise of sovereignty, as well as in the organisation of their armies and the appearance of their courts.[9]

In May 1876 there were riots in Constantinople in favour of a constitution. They were led by religious students known as *softas* and perhaps encouraged by Midhat and the ambitious, liberal heir to the throne, Murad Effendi. Midhat was independent, forceful and convinced that the empire could be saved by giving it a constitution. On 30 May, armed with a *fetva* (ruling) from the Sheikh al-Islam, the supreme religious official of the empire, authorising the Sultan's deposition on the grounds of his insanity and his 'diversion of public revenue to private expenditure, and conduct generally injurious to state and community', the ministers went to see the Sultan. Dolmabahçe was surrounded by troops and ships. Abdul Aziz could offer no resistance and signed a letter of abdication.

In accordance with Ottoman dynastic tradition, he was succeeded not by his eldest son, but by the eldest male of the dynasty, his nephew Murad. Murad V wanted to be a constitutional monarch. He described his accession as due to 'the favour of the almighty *and the will of my subjects*' (author's italics), and proposed a reduction in his own civil list. At his first *Selamlik*,

Midhat Pasha
Midhat Pasha was the leading advocate of constitutional reforms, as a minister and, from 1876 to 1877, as Grand Vizir. He was killed on the orders of Abdul Hamid in 1883, when he was living in exile in the Yemen.

instead of looking imperiously ahead like Abdul Aziz, he could be seen bowing right and left to the enthusiastic crowds. Already mentally unstable, he soon grew wilder, particularly after the murder of the War Minister and Abdul Aziz's mysterious death. The latter could not accustom himself to his deposition, and felt humiliated by the soldiers who were guarding him. On the morning of 3 June he asked his mother for a pair of scissors to trim his beard; he opened his veins instead, and bled to death.

Although nineteen doctors were satisfied that it was suicide, some people, including members of his own family, were convinced Abdul Aziz had been murdered on Midhat's orders. Soon Midhat and the ministers decided to depose Murad V also, much against his will. On 31 August Shevket Pasha, Marshal of the Palace, a very strong man, was obliged to take him in his arms and push him into his carriage. In the autocratic Ottoman Empire two sultans had been forcibly deposed in the same year.[10]

Murad V
Liberal and French-speaking, Murad V was deposed after a reign of three months in 1876 as he was alleged to be mad. He was immured with his family in the palace of Çirağan and remained there, a source of hope to Ottoman constitutionalists and of fear to his brother Abdul Hamid, until his death in 1904.

early 1876 by Ottoman irregular troops known as bashi-bazouks outraged European, and especially British, opinion: Gladstone stormed back to politics with the cry for the Turks to leave 'the province they have desolated and profaned . . . bag and baggage'. It was no justification that some Christians were just as brutal and believed in what a British consul called 'the unhappy theory, responsible for so much bloodshed, that the best way of attracting the attention of the Christian powers is to provoke the Turks to commit atrocities'. The great powers used the massacres as an excuse to press for further reforms.[11]

On 23 December 1876, thirty years before the Tsar of Russia, Sultan Abdul Hamid allowed a constitution to be proclaimed; a parliament met (with interruptions) from March 1877 to February 1878. However, even in this moment of weakness, he was determined — like other monarchs in a revolutionary situation — to retain control of his own household. Thus he resisted his ministers' attempts to keep Sadullah Pasha — a prominent liberal and author of a poem lamenting that 'the western lands have become the daysprings of knowledge' — in the key position of head of the palace secretariat.

In April 1877 Russia finally attacked in the Balkans and the Caucasus. Ottoman armies fought bravely, particularly at the siege of Plevna in Bulgaria, but by January 1878 Russian troops were camped on the shores of the Sea of Marmara, only ten miles from Constantinople. Syria was seething with discontent, and it seemed as if the Ottoman Empire would collapse.[12] Luckily for the empire, however, the British government was determined to preserve it as a barrier against Russian expansion. Queen Victoria was so pro-Turkish that she sent bandages to Turkish troops and danced — for the first time since Prince Albert's death — when Russia agreed to attend a peace congress in Berlin.

In 1878 treaties were signed which halved the empire's territory in Europe and ceded the province of Kars in eastern Anatolia to Russia, and Cyprus to Britain (110 years later Cyprus is the last country in the Middle East to contain British bases). The Ottoman

Murad V was succeeded by the third Sultan in 1876, his brother Abdul Hamid II. At the ceremony of the girding of the Sword of Othman (the founder of the dynasty in the thirteenth century), which was an indispensable part of the inauguration of an Ottoman Sultan, an onlooker described Abdul Hamid's pale, thin face, with dark rings surrounding great black eyes, as 'the countenance of a ruler capable of good or evil, but knowing his own mind and determined to have his own way'. At first, however, the ministers were too powerful, and the empire's situation was too desperate, for the Sultan to show his hand.

In 1875 the ambitions of the great powers and Balkan nationalists led to violence. A rising in Bosnia, encouraged by Austrian officers, could not be suppressed. The 'Bulgarian massacres' committed in

Empire remained the greatest power in the Balkans as well as the Middle East, but it was British hostility to Russia, and European concern for the balance of power, rather than its own armies, which had preserved it from disintegration.

Peace enabled Abdul Hamid to assert his authority. In 1878 he told a committee of senators and deputies that, instead of trying to enact reforms 'by persuasion and by liberal institutions', he now understood that 'it is only by force that I can move the peoples with whose protection God has entrusted me'. Parliament was dissolved. Midhat Pasha, whom he suspected of arranging the death of Abdul Aziz, had already been exiled in February 1877: the yacht taking him away waited in the Sea of Marmara for twenty-four hours in case popular reaction was so violent he would have to be recalled. Nothing happened. The Sultan was now supreme.[13]

Abdul Hamid II had such a powerful personality that it dominated the life of a generation. Like the Khedive Ismail, or the late Shah of Iran, he obsessed contemporaries in Europe and the Middle East almost as much as he himself was obsessed with his reputation among them. A sign of his concern for public opinion was that he gave more audiences and, at the beginning of his reign, appeared more frequently in public than his predecessors. When granted an audience or invited to dinner by the Sultan, few people could resist his charm. Anna M. Dodds, an American journalist who wrote an ecstatic book about his court called *In the Palaces of the Sultan*, appreciated his 'unexpectedly keen sense and enjoyment of humour' and beautiful manners, and described him as 'a reader of men and their thoughts'.

The German Crown Prince Wilhelm adored dining with Abdul Hamid, and afterwards playing Schumann with one of the Sultan's sons. He described his meeting with the Sultan as 'one of the most interesting encounters that I have ever had with foreign princes'. In 1877–8, when the empire needed Britain, Lady Layard, wife of the British ambassador — the great archaeologist Layard 'of Nineveh' — only had to utter a wish for it to be granted. After admiring the Sultan's bread, milk and song-birds, she received fresh bread from the imperial bakery every day, three cows and thirty cages of birds. She wrote: 'He seemed full of intelligence and the desire to do right, and every now and then his eyes flashed with merriment . . . a dear little man.' Arminius Vambéry, a Hungarian scholar and British agent who became one of the Sultan's protégés

after travels in Persia and central Asia, wrote, even after a fall from favour, that he was 'one of the greatest charmers that ever was'.[14]

Abdul Hamid was intelligent as well as charming. One of his officials, Ismail Kemal Bey, later an opponent of the Sultan and a leader of the movement for Albanian independence, remarked that he 'studied all the political and social questions which were presented to him and accepted suggestions with great amiability'. During his reign, his palace of Yildiz was 'the rendezvous of the best minds of the Empire', in particular of important religious leaders such as Sayyid Jamal al-din 'al-Afghani', who urged Muslims not to be afraid to face the challenges of the modern world; Sheikh Abul Huda from Aleppo, instructor in doctrine and tradition at the court; and Sheikh Mohammed Zafir from Tunisia, a member of the Sultan's secret religious committee.

Their presence was a sign that the Sultan used his position as Caliph — which, he told Layard, was 'even more sacred than that . . . [of] Sovereign of the Ottoman Empire' — as a political weapon. He subsidised religious orders and travelling preachers, who reminded foreign Muslims that the Ottoman Empire was the last great Islamic empire (Morocco and Persia were too weak to be rivals). The High Commission for Muslim Refugees, under the Sultan's presidency, resettled over a million refugees from the Caucasus and the Balkans in Anatolia and Syria between 1876 and 1905. In 1883 it was reported that the name of the Ottoman Sultan was 'now venerated in India as it had not formerly been'. From Nigeria to Sumatra Muslims invoked the aid of the Ottoman Caliph. In Egypt and Tunisia the Sultan had increasing prestige, particularly among the poor. An outward symbol of Abdul Hamid's policy was the Hejaz railway, built to carry pilgrims to the holy cities of Medina and Mecca and begun in 1900. It was paid for by non-Ottoman as well as Ottoman Muslims. The Shah of Persia and Indian princes made particularly generous donations.[15]

In addition to influential religious leaders, Abdul Hamid gathered round him as aides-de-camp or chamberlains bright young men chosen for their ability, such as his powerful First Secretary, Soraya Pasha (one of whose duties was to maintain the supply of beautiful and healthy Circassian girls for the palace). Abdul Hamid was particularly proud of what he did for education, which he had proclaimed to be a major concern at his accession. During his reign the Ottoman Empire, and Ottoman princes, began to catch up with

Egypt and its princes in the quality of their education. The Sultan founded a School of Civil Administration and dictated its regulations himself. By the end of his reign it supplied relatively well-trained administrators for all important provincial posts. He also carried out many useful practical reforms, such as improving the water supply of Constantinople and the agricultural yield of Anatolia.[16] An Agricultural Bank was established in 1888 and an Agricultural School in 1892.

Abdul Hamid who, in the words of Arminius Vambéry, extended 'his attention to everything and everybody', also did much to strengthen the Ottoman army with the help of German advisers. By 1897, when it easily won a short war with Greece, there had been a great increase in its size, efficiency and speed of mobilisation and in the quality of its officers. The Sultan personally approved all promotions. In 1891 he formed the Hamidiye light cavalry and infantry from Kurdish tribesmen in an attempt to devide the Kurds and strengthen government authority in the region. He also had many Arabs in his service, such as Izzet Pasha, his influential and anti-European Second Secretary, and Nagib Pasha, head of the secret police. In 1887, of the 6,101 graduates of military colleges in the Ottoman army, 985 came from Arab-speaking areas. In 1898 the figures were 2,273 of 8,228. The Sultan also founded a special college in Constantinople for sons of tribal chiefs, many of whom he appointed as his ADCs. He even at one time wanted to make Arabic an official language with Turkish.[17]

However, all his good qualities did not save Abdul Hamid from what he feared most: deposition, and death as a prisoner in the palace of Beylerbey. His achievements were soon forgotten. His ruthless autocracy was increasingly resented, particularly by those people whose education he encouraged. For, like many Middle Eastern monarchs in this age of transition, he had two personalities. He was not only an intelligent moderniser, but also a tyrant devoured by fear. In 1878, when asking Layard for protection on a British warship, he stepped back with a look of terror when the ambassador approached him. 'Fear is the only motive which drives the Sultan,' wrote the French ambassador in 1892.

Too many people agreed with this view — including the Sultan's doctor Mavroyennis (like most Middle Eastern monarchs, Abdul Hamid preferred to employ a Christian doctor) — for it to be discounted as prejudiced. The Sultan kept loaded pistols on his person, maintained extraordinary security precautions in Yildiz and was so afraid of his own ruling class that 'no Turk [or rather very few] dare associate with foreigners or give a large dinner party to his own people'. Three Grand Vizirs were so frightened of the Sultan that, in 1881, 1905 and 1907, they took refuge in a foreign embassy or consulate. For the educated classes of the empire the reign of Abdul Hamid was a reign of fear.[18]

It was also, in some regions for some of the time, a reign of fear for Armenians. The traditionally good relations between the Ottoman government and the Armenians had begun to change in the 1870s. A minority of Armenians desired independence (although in the eastern provinces of Anatolia, where most Armenians lived, they did not form a majority) and turned to terrorism. The Sultan reacted by encouraging brutal attacks on Armenians — many of whom had no connection with the terrorists — by Kurdish bands in the east and even, in 1895, in the streets of Constantinople. For a time in eastern Anatolia one British consul found that 'Massacre was the one topic of conversation: people talked of massacre much as we in England discuss the weather.' Thousands died.[19] The reputation of Abdul Hamid, and even, to a certain extent, of the Ottoman Empire, has never recovered.

The Sultan's fear of his own army meant that it was not allowed to carry out large-scale manoeuvres, since they would cause too many troops to be together at the same time. The Sultan's fears even affected his attitude to modern technology. At first he was interested in every novelty from Europe, from Puccini to petroleum. He particularly loved photography and used it as a weapon. He kept files of photographs of government officials, and studied an individual's photograph before receiving him in audience. He despatched photographers round the empire to find out what it looked like and sent massive green and gold albums to the British, French, German and American governments, containing photographs of schools and other progressive subjects, to demonstrate its modernisation.

However, electricity filled him with alarm. His fear that it could be used for terrorism — perhaps aroused by a confusion between the words dynamo and dynamite — meant that he forbade the use of electricity in Constantinople (although not in Smyrna or Salonica), except in hospitals, embassies, Yildiz and the Pera Palace Hotel: a rare case of a monarch literally, rather

A park in Yildiz
*The harem and private quarters of Abdul Hamid's palace of
Yildiz were built as an Ottoman version of a Swiss chalet.
The private garden was open only to the Sultan and
his harem.*

than metaphorically, keeping his people in darkness.[20]

His fears for his throne − understandable considering the deposition of his two predecessors − led him to distrust all around him. He concentrated power in himself and his palace officials. *Irades* (orders) signed by a palace secretary assumed more authority than the *firmans* (decrees) of the Grand Vizir. But it was difficult to obtain an *irade* from the palace. The Sultan was determined not to delegate authority: decisions taken by his ministers would frequently be kept unsigned at his palace of Yildiz 'in limbo for months, years or even forever'.[21]

For thirty years Yildiz was the centre of the world for the Sultan and his subjects. Situated on the edge of Constantinople, it is the last great Islamic palace. Unlike Dolmabahçe or Beylerbey, it is a series of buildings in a park rather than a single block of architecture on the European model. Originally a kiosk or pleasure-house begun in the 1830s, under Abdul Hamid, who moved there from Dolmabahçe in 1877, Yildiz became a small city. It consisted of a palace for official business known as the great *Mabeyn*; the Chalet and Star pavilions for receptions; the little *Mabeyn*,

24

where the Sultan lived; a factory making the Yildiz porcelain which he sent as presents to fellow-monarchs; a café where he could pay for his own coffee; a theatre where French plays and Turkish wrestling matches were performed for his guests after dinner; an arsenal, a library, an observatory, a princes' school, a greenhouse, a *hammam* (bath-house), a museum, a picture gallery, two mosques, four stables for the Sultan's superb Arabian horses, workshops, barracks and the harem.

The decoration was in the distinctive style called Ottoman Italian. (The Sultan's official architect and painter, Raimondo d'Aronco and Fausto Zonoro, were both Italians.) Ottoman Italian is light and graceful compared to the decoration in European counterparts of Yildiz, such as Osborne or Miramar. The buildings were surrounded by 500,000 square metres of gardens full of rare plants, perfect green lawns and guards. Just as he employed a Christian doctor, Abdul Hamid had Arab and Albanian guards, known as the *zouaves à turban* and *zouaves à fez* respectively, whom he trusted more than Turks who had links with the local

A dining-room in the Chalet pavilion
Although Abdul Hamid liked European art, and founded a School of Fine Arts in 1883, some rooms in Yildiz were decorated in an Orientalist style and had doors inlaid with mother of pearl. There was silence at dinner except when the Sultan gave permission to speak.

The library in Yildiz
The Sultan's large, well-catalogued library contained books in Turkish, Persian, Arabic, French, German and English, as well as the albums from which these photographs are copied.

The Ceremonial Saloon in the Chalet pavilion
The Chalet pavilion was built for the Kaiser's first visit in 1889. The elaborate decor is a sign of the Sultan's determination to impress his guest. The carpet, made at the imperial factory at Hereke, is so big that part of the wall had to be knocked down to install it. The room has hardly changed since this photograph was taken.

population. In all, about 1,500 guards and 2,000 courtiers and servants lived behind the high walls of Yildiz.[22]

The most important part of the palace was the great *Mabeyn*, where the palace secretaries worked. As in most European palaces before the nineteenth century, almost anybody well-dressed could obtain access. The secretaries lived in rooms permeated by smells of food and coffee. One visitor found secretaries sitting curled up in armchairs with their inkpots poised perilously on the arms, the idea of having a writing table never having come into their heads. Some were squatting on the floor eating with their fingers off broad dishes placed on a low table. One was having a siesta in a corner.[23] It was here that the Sultan's enormous correspondence with governors, generals and ambassadors was composed, and where his innumerable spies sent their reports.

It was also from the terraces of the great *Mabeyn* that foreign guests and Ottoman officials watched the *Selamlik*. This ceremony, which had always been used to display the splendour of the Ottoman Empire, was now particularly impressive. Every Friday, usually later than the hour announced in order to forestall terrorist attacks (Armenians tried to blow him up in 1906), the Sultan went to the Hamidiye mosque outside the palace walls, some of whose woodwork he had carved himself (other pieces of his woodwork were sold for the benefit of the poor). The road between the palace and the mosque was soon packed with soldiers. The view from the palace terrace was unforgettable: the Bosphorus, the Golden Horn, the shimmering outline of Constantinople and, immediately in front, a sea of green turbans and scarlet fezzes — the Sultan's guards. The feeling of excitement at the prospect of seeing one of the most powerful monarchs in the world increased.

The first sign that the Sultan was coming was the appearance of water-carts and sand-sprinklers to prepare the road for his carriages. Then came his daughters and favourites — whose beautiful Circassian faces could occasionally be glimpsed through their veils — in closed carriages escorted by eunuchs. The procession was led by the Chief Eunuch, an important official with the title of Highness, whose 'unwieldy form wobbled rather than sat upon the gorgeously wrought saddle'. Next were Abdul Hamid's sons with their attendants, followed by all the pashas in the city, wearing magnificent uniforms. Then the music fell silent. Radiating power, dignity and anxiety, the Sultan appeared in a state landau, waving his white-gloved

hands. Beside him was his favourite son, Burhan ed-din Effendi; opposite him was the influential Marshal of the Palace, Ghazi Osman Pasha, the hero of the defence of Plevna. Behind the carriage came the bodyguard of Albanian *tufenkjis*, 'a magnificent collection of ferocious-looking men with black beards, wearing white tunics and red breast-plates', followed by chamberlains and ADCs. The soldiers roared 'Long live our Padishah!' (*Padişahmiz çok yaşa!*) As the Sultan reached the mosque, after a two-minute drive, the voice of the Imam sang out from the minaret to remind him that, for all his honour, glory, power and authority, there was one greater than him, the one and only God.

After half an hour in the mosque, the Sultan drove himself back in a small phaeton, drawn by two white horses given by the Emperor Francis Joseph. He was followed by a mass of splendidly uniformed courtiers, pashas and eunuchs, panting, pressing and hustling each other beside and behind his carriage. Then the Sultan disappeared into the palace, not to emerge until the following Friday.

The religious service was not the sole purpose of the *Selamlik*. It was also a display of the Sultan's power, authority and health. (Once, when he could not attend, the *tufenkjis* would not return to barracks until they had been reassured by his appearance at a window.) The presence of tributary princes such as the Khedive of Egypt or the Prince of Bulgaria — from the point of view of Ottoman etiquette, merely superior provincial governors — was a sign of the empire's power. The number and discipline of the troops showed that the empire had successfully modernised its army.[24]

After July 1908 a third group, in addition to the troops and the Sultan's guests, was permitted to watch the *Selamlik*. In 1908 the Sultan's acquiescence in the Young Turk revolution seemed to have opened a new era of liberty and happiness for his empire. The Sultan's subjects were now admitted and filled the air with enthusiastic cheers. His autocracy had alienated not the poor, who appreciated his charity and revered his authority, but the educated, whose pay, if they were officers or officials, was always in arrears. By 1906, according to one authority, sons of ministers and chamberlains at the Lycée Impérial de Galataseray would cry not *Padişahmiz çok yaşa!* but *Padişahmiz başağiya!* (Down with our Sultan!) The number of Young Turk exiles in western Europe, led by the Sultan's liberal nephew Sabaheddin Effendi, was

Regimental fête
The inscription reads 'Long live our Padishah!' Above it is the Sultan's tughra or sign. Despite such demonstrations of loyalty the Sultan was afraid of his army and in 1908 it turned against him.

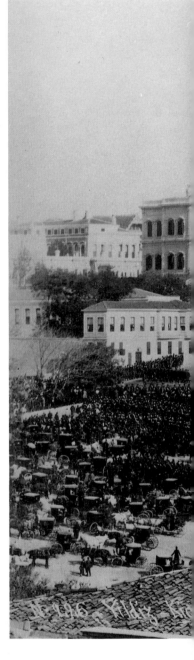

***Selamlik* at Yildiz during the Kaiser's visit in 1889**
On the right is the Hamidiye mosque; the large building on the left is the great Mabeyn. Troops cover the hill-side. A tourist who attended a Selamlik in 1893 wrote that they were 'a perfect marvel of discipline' and that 'the silence and the order were very remarkable'.

growing. The revolutions of 1905 in Russia and 1906 in Persia were signs of the times; and Abdul Hamid was determined to avoid a blunder such as Nicholas II's association with his subjects' deaths, when his own guards fired on a demonstration in front of the Winter Palace on 'Bloody Sunday' in 1905.

The blow came from some of the young officers who had been educated at the Sultan's military colleges. As so often in a Middle Eastern monarchy in this period, an internal crisis was provoked by the advance of European imperialism. The division of Persia into British, Russian and neutral spheres in 1907, followed by the meeting of Edward VII and Nicholas II at Reval in June 1908, convinced the Young Turks that something must be done to save the Ottoman Empire from a similar fate. At the end of June two handsome, forceful and idealistic young officers, Enver and Niazi, took to the hills outside Monastir in Macedonia, the empire's military headquarters in Europe. Acting for a well-organised revolutionary society, the Committee of Union and Progress, they called for a return to the constitution of 1876. They maintained momentum by shooting officers loyal to the Sultan, and were soon joined by other troops, alienated by years of trying to

keep law and order in Macedonia. In Constantinople the Sultan summoned troops from Anatolia and consulted the *ulema*. But the troops, whose pay was in arrears, were unreliable.

Moreover, just as in 1876 the *ulema* had pushed for the deposition of Abdul Aziz, so in 1908 they helped to end Abdul Hamid's autocracy. They told the Sultan that a constitution was not contrary to the *Sharia* (traditional Muslim law based on the Koran), and that a war between Muslims over this issue was illegal. The

ministers met at Yildiz as the 'constitutional' army advanced on Constantinople from Macedonia. They were convinced of the necessity of restoring the constitution of 1876, but dared not tell the Sultan. In the end the terrible task was given to Sheikh Abul Huda who, according to Sherif Ali Haidar (a member of the Hashemite dynasty of Mecca living in Constantinople), 'had great influence with his master, who regarded his utterances as inspired'. On 24 July the Sultan proclaimed the restoration of the constitution and the convocation of parliament. The empire went wild with joy. Aubrey Herbert, an Englishman who knew and loved the Ottoman Empire, was in Constantinople at the time and remembered that the city seemed to glow like a rose. Christians and Muslims embraced in the street. For the Sherif Ali Haidar the next few days were 'the sweetest moments of my life'.

The empire felt that it had come into daylight out of the night. Since it was going to be a constitutional monarchy like Britain, the British suddenly became

Abdul Hamid driving to a *Selamlik* in 1908
The Grand Vizir sits opposite the Sultan. A band plays an imperial anthem. The crowds, who would not have been admitted before the Young Turk revolution, cheer their beloved Sultan.

popular. The ambassador's carriage was unhorsed and dragged by cheering crowds up the hill of Galata to the embassy.[25] The Young Turks appeared moderate in their demands. The Sultan charmed the deputies (in 1908 there were 147 Turkish, 60 Arab, 27 Albanian, 26 Greek, 14 Armenian, 10 Slav and 4 Jewish deputies in the Ottoman parliament) when they came to dinner at Yildiz. They left full of admiration for his constitutional principles.

But the Young Turks began to alienate the old pashas – as well as the people of Constantinople, who still venerated the Sultan. Even Christians began to miss the security of the old regime. The troops in Constantinople, in particular the guards regiments, were alienated by reforms introduced by the Young Turks which increased their duties, diminished religious observances and replaced officers who had risen from the ranks by officers educated in military colleges. Moreover, the Young Turks were still afraid of the Sultan and were determined to be rid of him.[26]

On 9 April 1909 a mutiny, about whose instigators there is still a mystery, delivered Constantinople into the hands of soldiers devoted to the Sultan. The

deputies fled outside the city and there was a change of government. It is probable that Abdul Hamid was not directly involved, but his son Burhan ed-din was. The Sultan's powers were increased and, at what proved to be his last *Selamlik* on 23 April, Abdul Hamid received tremendous cheers from loyal troops and spectators. An English resident 'never on any former occasion saw the troops more enthusiastic in their demonstrations of loyalty nor the Sultan more smiling and gracious'. But at the same time a 'constitutional' army from Salonica, led by Mahmud Shevket Pasha (whose chief of staff was a brilliant young officer called Mustafa Kemal), was occupying Constantinople, the guards barracks and Yildiz itself. Many of the guards had already fled and on the Sultan's orders there was no resistance. On 27 April a deputation informed him of his deposition in accordance with a ruling from the Sheikh al-Islam accusing him of causing 'civil war and bloodshed among his own people'. But was not the Committee in reality responsible?

During the next few months the magic world of Yildiz disintegrated. An inventory was made of its contents, and many (including some splendid jewels) were sold in Paris. Many *tufenkjis* were killed, headed by their commander Marshal Tahir Pasha. The Chief Eunuch was hung from a lamp post on Galata Bridge. The women of the harem were taken to Topkapi; those lucky enough to have relations prepared to look after them then returned home. The Sultan himself, with two sons, three wives, four harem women and thirteen servants, was sent by train to Salonica on the day of his deposition. Well-mannered to the end, he helped the ladies into the railway carriage before boarding himself.

It was a sad end for a Sultan who had told Vambéry that he wanted to do his duty 'as a good Osmanli'. Many believed, like Woods Pasha, that he really had the welfare of his people at heart. Perhaps if Abdul Hamid had been less frightened of sharing power he would have been as popular with his educated subjects as he was with the uneducated. For, just as during his reign, he dominated conversation in the capital — Sir William Ramsay wrote: 'The conversation turned to the Sultan, as every conversation in Turkey always does sooner or later' — so after his fall he retained immense prestige among the poor of the Middle East. A fair judgement is that of Lord d'Abernon, who lived in Constantinople for many years as a commissioner of the Ottoman Imperial Debt. He called the Sultan 'a hunted animal pursued by the hounds of fate, snarling and biting at them like a fox at bay'.[27]

Abdul Hamid's brother, Mehmed Reshad, long known to be a liberal sympathetic to a constitution, became Sultan as Mehmed V in 1909. It was noticed that his first *Selamlik* and diplomatic reception had 'a character of great simplicity in contrast to the receptions of Abdul Hamid'. At the girding of the Sword of Othman, there was only one running footman dressed in blue and gold and very few guards.[28] The Sultan's powers were reduced by amendments to the Constitution of 1876. Mehmed V, unlike Abdul Hamid in 1876, even allowed the Young Turk government to affect the composition of his court. He gave 1,000 of Abdul Hamid's splendid horses to the army and kept only four secretaries, four chamberlains, four ADCs and a few personal servants. The Chief Eunuch lost the rank of Highness; the Sultan's guests

were served coffee in plain, rather than jewel-studded, gold cup-holders.

At first Mehmed V lived in Dolmabahçe but in 1912, to the joy of the court, he moved to Yildiz. He was a kind, simple, affable monarch. It is a temptation to agree with his friend, Sherif Ali Haidar, that he was 'much maligned and misunderstood...though his outward appearance was heavy and unintelligent, yet when one got to know him...he was well-read, courteous and to my mind fully worthy of the Throne he held'. Liman von Sanders, one of the many German officers in the Ottoman army, wrote that he had 'much greater independence of judgement than is generally assumed'.[29]

Whatever his personal merits, however, during his reign the empire suffered a series of catastrophes. The Sultan's adherence to the policies of the Young Turk Committee of Union and Progress appalled the princes of the dynasty who, after years of seclusion under Abdul Hamid, now enjoyed much greater freedom. Intelligent, well-educated princes high in the order of succession, such as the Sultan's brother Mehmed Vahdeddine, and his cousins Sabaheddin (as hostile to the tyranny of the Committee as to that of Abdul Hamid) and Abdul Medjid, spoke to the Sultan for hours on end 'in the name of the dynasty' about the consequences of the Committee's policies. For the hounds of fate were closing in on the empire of the Ottomans for the kill.[30]

The principal achievement of Abdul Hamid had been to maintain the political and financial independence of his empire. The Ottoman Imperial Debt was a vast European-run institution which by 1911 employed more people than the Ministry of Finance, and was to outlast the empire itself. But indebtedness never led to foreign control of the government, as it did in Egypt and Tunisia. Indeed, confidence in the Ottoman Imperial Debt allowed the Ottoman government to raise loans on more favourable terms than would otherwise have been possible.

Above all, Abdul Hamid had been able to play off the great powers and the Balkan states against each other and so to maintain an international situation favourable to his empire. The Committee lacked both his prestige and his skill. Only a few months after the Young Turk revolution, in October 1908, Austria annexed Bosnia-Herzegovina (still nominally Ottoman), and Bulgaria proclaimed its independence.

In November 1911 Italy invaded Tripolitania (modern Libya), although it was of no possible benefit

Mehmed V
Mehmed V, who had been kept in seclusion in Dolmabahçe
during his brother's reign, was delighted to replace him in 1909.
He was a weak, kind man who preferred poetry to politics.

to Italy. The celebrated writer Pierre Loti, the Ottoman Empire's greatest admirer in Europe and a friend of Abdul Medjid, wrote bitterly that Muslim countries seemed to have become fair game, to be hunted whatever the season. To demonstrate its commitment to the defence of an Arab province, the Ottoman government sent Enver, Mustafa Kemal and Aziz Ali al-Masri, brilliant young officers who had played important parts in the revolution of 1908, to Tripolitania. Nevertheless, the Italian navy was too strong, and by a treaty of October 1912 the government ceded Tripolitania, and Rhodes and its surrounding islands, to Italy.

The disastrous foreign policy and increasing tyranny of the Young Turks made them many enemies within the empire. In July 1912 Albania, hitherto loyal to the Sultan, rose in revolt against the Committee's insistence on extending the control of the central government and enforcing the use of Turkish in schools. The Sultan and experienced former ministers such as the aged and pro-British Kiamil Pasha, four times Grand Vizir, attempted to assert themselves. The Committee's agent in the palace, the Sultan's First Secretary, was dismissed. The Sultan issued a proclamation against the army's interference in politics. The imperial family and court were openly hostile to the Committee: in 1913 Damad Salih, husband of a princess, was involved in the murder of Shevket Pasha, the pro-Committee Grand Vizir. Abdul Medjid denounced the tyranny of the Young Turks, 'far worse than anything experienced under Abdul Hamid's reign', to the British embassy.

The number of the government's foreign enemies also increased. In accordance with its optimistic policy of encouraging Ottoman subjects to be proud of being Ottomans, the government had closed the Greek, Serb and Bulgarian clubs which Abdul Hamid had permitted in order to foster national rivalries. Hitherto irreconcilable nations united in a common hostility to the Young Turks. In the first Balkan War of October 1912 to March 1913 the Ottoman armies, weakened by political purges, performed unexpectedly badly against Bulgaria, Serbia, Greece and Montenegro. By the Treaty of London of 30 May 1913 the Ottoman Empire ceded all its territory in Europe, even Adrianople, except for a narrow belt along the Sea of Marmara. Over 400,000 Muslim refugees fled to the remainder of the Ottoman Empire.

Mehmed V in Salonica in 1911
Mehmed V, who is shaded by an umbrella, was the first Sultan to make regular visits to the provinces. The Ottoman Empire was still the greatest power in the Balkans and Salonica an Ottoman city in 1911. To the right of the Sultan are Talaat and Enver. Despite his deferential posture, Enver could be disrespectful and often kept the Sultan waiting.

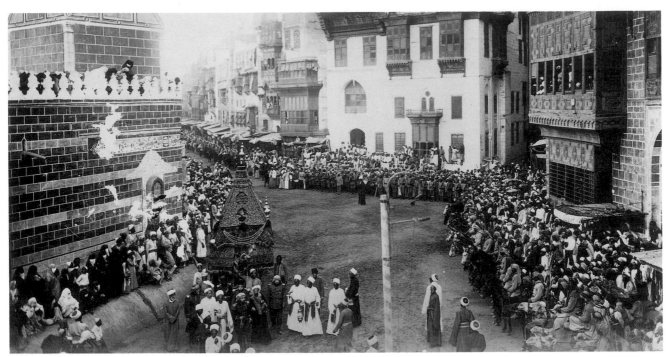

Procession of the *mahmal* in Mecca

Every year an ornamental covering or mahmal was sent to Mecca from both Constantinople and Cairo. Mecca and Medina were part of the Ottoman Empire and one of the Sultan's proudest titles was Servant of the Two Holy Places.

Sheikh Mubarak al-Sabah, ruler of Kuwait (1896–1915), with relations and guards

Although legally an Ottoman subject, Sheikh Mubarak, great-grandfather of the present ruler, signed agreements with Britain in 1899 and 1907 which made him practically independent. This photograph was taken in 1903, during the triumphant tour of the Gulf by Lord Curzon, Viceroy of India.

The empire appeared so weak that the young, ambitious Khedive Abbas Hilmi of Egypt remarked: 'It is terrible to have to say it, but Turkey is in its death throes.' Kiamil Pasha said that he wanted 'some adequate foreign control' of the administration. Although the government finally permitted the use of Arabic as the language of instruction in government schools, discontent began to reappear in the Arab provinces of the empire. In December 1912 and March 1913 an agent reported to Abbas Hilmi that leading personalities in Syria wanted him to replace the Ottoman Sultan as Caliph, and that '3,000 officers and NCOs [were] ready to unite with Egypt and serve your highness'.[31]

ABDULLAH FRÈRES   PHOTOGRAPHES DE S. M. I. LE SULTAN

Elèves de l'Ecole des Tribus nomades

Pupils from the School of Nomadic Tribes
In order to strengthen his control over the empire, Abdul Hamid founded a school for the sons of tribal chiefs in Constantinople, where they were taught to be good Ottomans. These pupils are Arabs; the one on the left wears the costume of Tripolitania.

An Ottoman prince
In the Ottoman dynasty succession went by age not by closeness of relation to the Sultan. All princes were equal and had the title Effendi *after their names. Kargopoulo was a firm of Greek photographers, founded in 1850, who became official photographers to the Sultan, like Abdullah Frères, in 1870.*

Sayyid Talib, a leading Arab politician, was intriguing with the British, the Sheikh of Kuwait and Abdul Aziz al-Sa'ud, the future founder of Sa'udi Arabia, perhaps in order to raise an anti-Ottoman insurrection in Mesopotamia. In late 1913 and early 1914 France, Germany, Russia and Britain signed agreements to divide the Ottoman Empire into spheres of economic influence, which many saw as steps towards partition. The empire's prestige had sunk so low that Albania chose as its new ruler an unknown German prince, Wilhelm of Wied (described by Edith Durham as 'a hopeless combine of pretentiousness and incapacity'),

rather than an Ottoman prince, despite its Muslim majority.

In January 1913 the Young Turks forced their liberal opponents out of office by bursting into the Sublime Porte and shooting the Minister of War. In September, thanks to divisions between the Balkan states, the empire recovered Adrianople and eastern Thrace. In 1914 Abdul Aziz al-Sa'ud signed a treaty with the empire acknowledging Ottoman suzerainty, in return for Ottoman recognition as hereditary *vali* of Nejd (central Arabia) and the coastal strip of al-Hassa; however, he had to keep the treaty secret from his own advisers.

Ahmed Nihad Effendi and his son Ali Vassib
Ahmed Nihad, a grandson of Murad V, had been brought up in the gilded prison of Çirağan. His son, lying on an especially decorated bed, is about to be circumcised, an important occasion which marks his entry into manhood. It will be celebrated lavishly and sons of the poor of the surrounding district will be circumcised at the same time.

Naciye Sultan and Enver Pasha
Enver Pasha, the hero of the Young Turk revolution, stands beside Naciye Sultan, Mehmed V's favourite niece, whom he has just married. The marriage between the princess and the revolutionary was a success.

The Ottoman government now had slightly more prestige. Its most important members included the Minister of the Interior Talaat, who had a fierce handshake, a hawk nose and what Aubrey Herbert called 'a light in his eyes rarely seen in men but sometimes in animals at dusk'. Jemal was an intelligent, modernising Minister of Marine; and Enver, the darling of the empire, was the youngest Minister of War in its history. In February 1914 his marriage to a niece of the Sultan was not only a great honour but also a sign that the Young Turks controlled the court and the imperial family as well as the government.[32]

More powerful than ever, the Young Turks turned to Turkish nationalism to save the Ottoman Empire. This was a new and potentially fatal factor in its destiny. It had survived the attacks of Balkan kingdoms and European empires, since all they wanted was territory. Turkish nationalism, however, wanted the cosmopolitan, dynastic empire to change its nature. Could it survive?

~2~
Khedives and Pashas

The Khedive Tewfik
Weak and well-meaning, Tewfik (1879–92) was reduced to powerlessness in his own country, first by Arabi Pasha then by the British.

THE Ottoman Empire was more than a state fighting for survival; it was also a great social and cultural commonwealth. For the manners, attitudes and laws of the Middle East, especially of its ruling classes, were dominated by Ottoman traditions. Ottoman influence was particularly strong in Egypt, which was still in theory a province of the empire.

Both the reigning dynasty and the ruling class of Egypt were Ottoman in origin. The founder of the dynasty, the great Mohammed Ali, was of either Kurdish or Albanian stock and had come to Egypt in the early nineteenth century from Kavalla, in the European part of the empire. The Egyptian ruling class consisted of about 20,000 'Turks'. Although they might be Albanian, Kurdish or Circassian in origin, they spoke Turkish or French among themselves (as some members of the Egyptian reigning family still do), and were often called *al atraq* — the Turks — by Egyptians. *Al atraq* led a separate life from the Egyptians. Until 1914 their social and cultural centre was not only Cairo but also Constantinople, where their great but recent wealth, sing-song accent and modern way of life often made them unpopular with the Ottoman dynasty and ruling class. One reason for the increasing extravagance of the Ottoman court in the 1860s and 1870s had been the need to compete with members of the Egyptian dynasty, when they came to spend the summer on the Bosphorus.

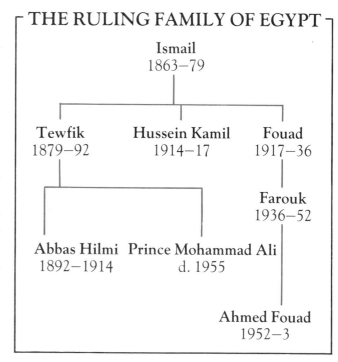

THE RULING FAMILY OF EGYPT

Ismail
1863–79

Tewfik   **Hussein Kamil**   **Fouad**
1879–92   1914–17   1917–36

Farouk
1936–52

Abbas Hilmi   **Prince Mohammad Ali**
1892–1914   d. 1955

Ahmed Fouad
1952–3

The Khedive Ismail, absolute ruler of Egypt under the suzerainty of the Ottoman Sultan, was himself an example of the continued influence of Ottoman traditions. He always wore the *stambouline* and, despite his love of Europe, spent most summers before 1873 in Constantinople. He even died there, an exile forbidden to return to Egypt, in 1895. When he was Khedive, however, such an end would have seemed inconceivable. After the celebrations of the inauguration of the Suez Canal, Egypt continued on its dazzling progress towards becoming part of Europe. In 1875 a new legal code went much further than the Ottoman code of 1857 in replacing Muslim religious mandates by modern secular laws. Between 1862 and 1879 the number of public schools increased from 185 to 4,817, railway mileage (at a time when the Ottoman Empire had almost none) from 275 to 1,185 and acres under cultivation from 4,052,000 to 5,425,000. Egypt was now, as it soon found out to its cost, economically and financially part of Europe.[1]

It was also becoming part of Europe socially. By 1880 there were about 100,000 Europeans working in Egypt, and more came for the winter. The opera in Cairo, playing in the opera-house erected for the celebrations of 1869 and heavily subsidised by the Khedive, was 'hardly to be surpassed in London or Paris', according to J. C. McCoan, an American journalist. The Duke of Sutherland founded a club in Cairo modelled on those in Pall Mall. The latest plays from Paris were performed in the palaces of the Khedive. Of the twenty-seven newspapers published in Cairo in 1878, nine were French, seven Arabic (which were to have an immense influence on modern Arab culture), five Italian, three Greek, one Turkish and Arabic, one Arabic and French, and one Arabic, French and Italian.[2] Cairo and Constantinople, under the Khedive and the Sultan, were truly cosmopolitan capitals, where different peoples were open to each other's cultures.

The court reflected the cosmopolitan character of the capital and the modernising tendencies of the Mohammed Ali dynasty. Since the reign of Said (1854–63) and even before, there had been European officials and servants in the palace. The Khedive Ismail had been educated in Paris and Vienna in the 1840s and spoke French like a Parisian (using it rather than Turkish with members of his family). He knew the courts of Europe at first hand, and his own court was European as well as Ottoman in style. The great Italianate palaces of Abdine in Cairo and Ras el-Tine in Alexandria were finished by 1874. They did contain neo-Islamic rooms decorated by local craftsmen, such as the splendid throne-room in Abdine. Indeed, the dynasty was sufficiently interested in Islamic art to found the first modern Islamic museum, in Cairo in 1880.

Abdine palace
Abdine palace has been at the centre of Egyptian politics since the reign of Ismail and is still the main residence of the President of Egypt. In this square a famous confrontation took place between Khedive Tewfik and Arabi Pasha in 1881, which ended in victory for the latter. Sixty years later British tanks surrounded Abdine to force King Farouk to change the government.

The Buffet, Abdine palace
Abdine was decorated in a mixture of oriental and European styles. This was one of the rooms used for state banquets.

Gezireh palace, Cairo
Gezireh palace was built to receive the Khedive's guests in 1869. It was sold to help pay the Khedive's debts and, after several changes of ownership, is now part of a hotel.

However, most rooms were decorated in the height of European luxury, with gilded French furniture (in the style soon known as Louis Cairo), Sèvres vases, silk and brocade on the walls, busts of Napoleon and Mohammed Ali and pictures of Egypt by French artists such as Gérôme and Frère. The effect was very grand. When the Prince and Princess of Wales proceeded to Egypt after their visit to Constantinople in 1869, the bedroom assigned to the Princess's lady-in-waiting contained a solid silver bed, and was so luxurious that it reminded her of a state drawing room at Windsor. The Khedive had a solid gold toilet set, Sèvres china and a mosquito net of crimson silk in his bedroom. Even his yacht, the *Mahroussa* (a doom-laden ship which was to take the Khedive, his grandson and his great-grandson in turn into exile) was 'one mass of silk hangings, gobelins, gildings, mirrors, tables of Italian marble, mosaic, mother of pearl, etc.'

Other members of the ruling dynasty lived in equally magnificent settings. The palace of Kasr-i Aali, residence of Ismail's mother, Hoshyar Kadineffendi (see Chapter VI), known as the Khedivah Mother, was so large that her granddaughter was rarely impressed by other palaces. Just before the First World War, when asked by the Kaiser to admire the Weisser Saal in the Schloss in Berlin, which he had restored, she

Ras el-Tine palace, Alexandria
Begun in 1834, finished by 1874, Ras el-Tine was the main summer residence of the rulers of Egypt. The Emperor Francis Joseph found that it had a 'curious mixture of beautiful and very common furniture some of which is in unbelievably bad taste'. In 1952 King Farouk left Egypt for ever from the quay at Ras el-Tine.

remembered that 'two of Kasr-i Aali's halls were at least three times as large and in far better taste. If adults stood at each end they were dwarfed by the distance and their features were indistinguishable.'[3]

Among the European staff at the palace were Commandant Haillot, the French governor of the Khedive's sons; Draneht, a Greek confidant of the Khedive who helped arrange the production of *Aida* in Cairo and made a fortune out of land; Tonino Bey, the Italian assistant Grand Master of Ceremonies; and innumerable English grooms and French chefs. The court of Egypt was also a haven for servants of less fortunate regimes. Former officials of the Emperor Maximilian of Mexico were happy to serve the Khedive of Egypt; the Master of the Horse, the Comte de Saint-Maurice, had been an equerry of Napoleon III; and the army was full of exiled Confederate officers. They found the Khedive a generous employer; but they were bewildered at serving in an army where so many fellow officers had dark skins.

The court of Egypt encased its rulers in the smooth and impressive, partly French, partly Ottoman 'Abdine protocol'. A British journalist who accompanied the Prince of Wales to Egypt in 1873 was overwhelmed by Abdine palace. Its banqueting hall, he noted with astonishment, was worthy of any court in Europe. 'To outward appearance the Khedive's court is at least royal. On his service, carriages, etc. there is the likeness of a kingly crown; his State is regal; the Consular corps accredited to him are ministers in all but name; and the *charges de la Cour* are on a scale worthy of a considerable power.'

The Khedive was so eager to impress Europeans that he was the first monarch in the region to give court balls. Every winter, at the height of the Cairo season, they brought together the official world of Cairo, the financial world of Alexandria and the Europeans wintering in Egypt. The Khedive greeted his guests in Abdine with his usual urbanity. After a concert given by the best singers from the opera there was supper, followed by dancing. The Khedive's sons danced, but his officials, in 'gorgeous uniforms, their breasts sparkling like diamonds, stood round the edge of the rooms, like men looking at monkeys'.[4]

The Khedive also invited important visitors, and his own ministers and senior officials, to lunch or dinner. In most courts of the Middle East food remained traditional. Cooks took days to prepare legendary dishes such as 'Sultan's pleasure', an aubergine puree with pieces of meat cooked in butter and tomato juice,

which had been given its name by a famished Sultan who lost his way hunting and was served it in a farmer's hut. Another famous Ottoman dish was *tavuk göğsü*, a pudding made of chicken breasts beaten to a smooth pulp, cooked with milk and sugar and served with cinnamon. Such traditional dishes could be found at the table of the Khedivah Mother. Guests ate with their fingers or a spoon.

The Khedive's meals, however — perhaps in order to impress his foreign visitors — were completely French. One guest wrote that they were 'in every respect worthy of the admiration of the most experienced gastronome, both as to the dishes and the service'. The Khedive drank Château Yquem, although he sometimes preferred champagne. The conversation was also in French. Whether traditional or European, meals at court ended with the elaborate ceremony of pouring coffee. The left shoulder and arm of the bearer of the coffee tray were covered by a velvet cloth, embroidered with gold thread and sewn with hundreds of pearls and diamonds. The coffee was poured into small china cups, in holders shaped like egg-cups called *zarfs*. The *zarf* was made of gold and encrusted with jewels.

Foreign visitors found Ismail charming: his 'power of fascination was in fact his most extraordinary gift, and I have never met a man who failed for the moment to succumb to it', according to *The Times* correspondent in the 1870s, Moberly Bell. His half-closed eyes (he had opthalmia) 'wandered all over you as if looking for your weak point', which, in the case of the Europeans descending on Egypt, was usually the same: money. But to his silent ministers and officials his eyes were more frightening than fascinating: 'his stealthy sea-green eyes terrified those around him', according to one of his most important ministers, Nubar Pasha, a supple and sophisticated Armenian who had served his father and grandfather. Another minister was Ismail Siddiq, a peasant's son with the face of a bird of prey. His mother had been the Khedive's wet-nurse and the Khedive had made him Minister of Finance and the most important man in the country. However, he was murdered on the Khedive's orders in 1876 — a warning of what might happen to other officials if they displeased their master.[5]

Ismail was more absolute than the Ottoman Sultan. He was his own chief minister and he used his power not only to modernise his country but also to pursue his personal ambitions. Nineteenth-century imperialism was not an exclusively European phenomenon, and he wanted to create an empire in Africa. His dominion in the Sudan was extended almost to the sources of the Nile by a series of vigorous governors, including General Gordon. In 1866 Egypt acquired control over two Red Sea ports, Massawa and Suakin, from the Ottoman government, and in 1873 it conquered part of Somalia. Thanks to Ismail it held its own in the struggle between Britain, France, Italy and the Ottoman Empire for control of East Africa and the Red Sea.

Ismail also used his supreme power to spend money. As a prince he had been economical and, in the words of the British consul in 1861, 'the only one of his family who appears to have anything like order in his private affairs and is not a spendthrift'. Like many other princes, however, he became a different person when he succeeded to the throne; his extravagance became as remarkable as his charm. He loved building, and construction, whether of palaces, schools or the smart new *boulevards* he drove through Cairo, has never been cheap.[6]

To a certain extent his expenditure can be justified as the inevitable cost, by the standards of the time, of setting up a modern state and dynasty. For example, the Khedive spent enormously on those presents to the Sultan, his courtiers and officials which secured greater autonomy for Egypt. His African empire was bound to be expensive: he fought a war with Abyssinia in 1876, which quarrels between ex-Confederate and Egyptian officers helped to lose. The Khedive Ismail also loved land and acquired an enormous proportion of the cultivable land of Egypt by purchase or confiscation (often from rival cousins). He then exploited it to raise the highest possible income, thereby causing incalculable suffering for the peasants or *fellaheen*.

In his dealings with European bankers, however, his good sense deserted him, and he often paid ludicrous rates of interest. In 1873, in order to finance his development schemes, he raised a loan of £32 million pounds and guaranteed to pay £77 million in return. In 1875, in one of the most celebrated financial deals of the century, he sold 176,000 Suez Canal shares to the British government, at only a quarter of their original cost. Disraeli wrote in triumph to Queen Victoria: 'You have it, Madam.' In 1877 the Khedive also had to finance an Egyptian contingent under his son Hassan to help the Ottoman Empire in its war with Russia. By 1879 the public debt, which had been £3.3 million in 1862, had reached the fatal figure of £98.54 million.[7]

In August 1878, in a desperate attempt to win popularity and prevent European intervention, the auto-cratic Khedive turned to constitutionalism. He installed a responsible ministry under Nubar Pasha, whose mission was to reform the administration 'on principles similar to those observed in the administration of the states of Europe': a legislature was also to be established. However, the possibility that Ismail might default on a loan raised with Rothschilds on the security of his family's estates (many of which had already been sold to pay the government's debts) led to his downfall. European governments, then as now, took such matters extremely seriously. In a move which shows that Ottoman suzerainty over Egypt was not entirely nominal, they combined to put pressure on Abdul Hamid. On 26 June 1879 a famous telegram arrived at Abdine from Yildiz, addressed to 'Ismail Pasha, ex-Khedive of Egypt', informing him that his son was now Khedive. Having lost the support of his ruling class, and having already tried to use popular agitation, Ismail knew that he had to go. After being the first to salute his son as Khedive, he steamed away from Alexandria on the *Mahroussa* to Naples, where his friend King Umberto of Italy lent him the villa of La Favorita.

However, true to his Ottoman background (and to please the women in his household who yearned to live in a Muslim country again), Ismail moved to Constantinople in 1888. He was occasionally seen at dinner at Yildiz, 'motionless and silent like the rest of the table, his eyes on the sovereign, only touching his food when the Sultan touched his'. He died in 1895. Opinions are still divided between admiration for his achievement in transforming Egypt into the first modern state in Africa, and anger at the cost of the transformation. Arabi Pasha, an officer in the Egyptian army who was one of his ADCs in 1879, called him 'the cause of the destruction of Egypt'.[8] The reason for such a harsh judgement is the fate of Egypt after 1879, in which Arabi Pasha played a prominent part. The new Khedive, Tewfik, was very different from his fascinating and extrovert father. He was a reserved, modest man, who at first, for example on a tour of upper Egypt in 1880, was received with 'overwhelming joy'. Unlike his father, he tried to lighten the burden of taxes and debts on the *fellaheen*.

Even his own dynasty, however, did not think highly of his abilities. His son wrote that he was *un homme honnête et doux*, in other words weak.[9] But Egypt in 1879 would have taxed the capacity of the most brilliant monarch. The Khedive was in an impossible situation, torn between the demands of the European

Sherif Pasha
Born in Constantinople in 1823, Sherif was a sophisticated, cosmopolitan politician who was three times Prime Minister of Egypt and tried to establish constitutional government.

Sayyid Jamal al-din 'al-Afghani'
'Al-Afghani' (who was in fact Persian) was an immensely influential Muslim thinker who taught that Islam and modernisation were compatible. He was an adviser, in turn, of rulers of Afghanistan, Egypt, Persia and the Ottoman Empire. This photograph still hangs in the study of one of his pupils, the Egyptian national hero Sa'ad Zaghloul.

Arabi Pasha
Arabi learnt his slogan 'Egypt for the Egyptians!' from Ismail's predecessor Said Pasha, and was an ADC of both Ismail and Tewfik. However, in 1881–2 he led a nationalist revolt against the Khedive and the Turkish ruling class, which provided a pretext for British intervention. After 1882 he was exiled to Ceylon but in 1901 returned to Egypt, where he died forgotten in 1911.

powers; a general desire in the educated elite for constitutional government; and Egyptians' growing resentment of the arrogance of some members of the Turkish ruling class.[10] The tension between Turks and native Egyptians had grown worse under Ismail. Arabi wrote in his memoirs that the Khedive gave Turks 'ranks, decorations, beautiful slaves, extensive and fertile lands, and spacious houses...gifts of money and precious stones sucked from the blood of the poor Egyptians'.[11]

In 1880 to 1882 the struggle for power between Arabi, other politicians such as Nubar Pasha and Sherif Pasha, and the Khedive Tewfik intensified. At first, Arabi was prepared to call Tewfik 'the only decent member of Mohammed Ali's family'. He was one of Tewfik's adjutants, and their wives had shared the same wet-nurse in the palace. However, on 9 September 1881, there was a dramatic scene in the great square outside Abdine palace when Arabi led an armed demonstration calling for a more nationalist ministry. Reflecting the autocratic instincts of his

family, Tewfik said, 'I am Khedive of the country and shall do as I please.' Arabi replied, 'We are not slaves and shall never from this day forth be inherited' — although his own career showed how high native Egyptians could rise. Tewfik had to yield, but began to consult his courtiers and the foreign consuls more than his ministers. Having no party on which he could rely, as he told the British consul in April 1882, he turned to Britain and France to free him from 'this nightmare'. He had been humiliated and wanted revenge.[12] Like many other Middle Eastern monarchs, he believed that the preservation of his dynasty justified foreign intervention.

The drama of the situation was heightened by Egyptians' awareness of the fate of other countries in the Middle East. The French occupied Tunis in April 1881. Arabi said, 'Tomorrow it would be Tripoli, next day Morocco, and the third day Egypt.' Like many Muslims in the late nineteenth century, he turned to the Ottoman Sultan. He believed that it was necessary 'to preserve the connection of Egypt with the head of the Moslem world ... We are all children of the Sultan.' Tewfik also asked the Sultan for troops to protect him from Arabi and the British. The Sultan kept in with both sides, but in the end repudiated Arabi who, he felt, favoured a republic in Egypt.[13] In fact Arabi, like many other Egyptians, wanted Tewfik's great-uncle Halim as Khedive. He felt Halim was more capable; moreover, according to traditional ideas, Halim had a better claim to the throne than Tewfik, since he was the oldest male in the dynasty.

The situation worsened and on 31 May 1882 Tewfik moved to Ras el-Tine: Arabi had made the error, funda-

Place des Consuls Alexandria, before the British bombardment in 1882
By 1882 Alexandria looked like a prosperous European city and the Place des Consuls was the centre of its economic life. The building at the end of the square is the bourse where so many non-Egyptian fortunes were made.

Alexandria after the bombardment
British ships bombarded Alexandria in July 1882 during Arabi's revolt, before British soldiers landed to 'restore order'. They did not leave until 1947.

mental in a country where the monarchy was so important, of not gaining physical control of the monarch. Order broke down in Alexandria, and even more Egyptians than Europeans died in the ensuing massacres. The massacres were the perfect pretext for intervention by Britain, which would not tolerate a hostile power straddling the route to India. France, hitherto a partner in the exploitation of Egypt, did not participate as the Chamber of Deputies and the French electorate were passing through an anti-imperialist phase. Arabi repudiated Tewfik's authority, and in Cairo the *ulema* quoted the Koran and the Hadith to prove that he should be deposed. British forces landed on 13 July and secured Ras el-Tine and the backing of the Khedive for their actions. Arabi and his army were easily defeated in the campaign which followed. Tewfik returned in triumph to Cairo, and on 30 October saluted 12,000 British troops at a historic review. An Egyptian chronicler wrote, 'Honour had vanished from the hearts of those who watched.'[14] Despite repeated

General Gordon
Gordon was devoted to the Khedives Ismail and Tewfik and served as Governor-General of the Sudan (then an Egyptian province) from 1877 to 1879 and from 1884 until his death at the hands of the Mahdi's forces in 1885. He is wearing Egyptian uniform and, as was obligatory for everyone in the service of the Khedive or the Sultan, the fez.

The Khedive Abbas Hilmi
Like most members of his dynasty, the Khedive Abbas Hilmi was equally at home in Europe and the Middle East. He kept a dog as a pet, although dogs were considered unclean by traditional Muslims.

Prince Hassan Toussoun and Mustafa Pasha Fahmy
Mustafa Pasha Fahmy was Prime Minister of Egypt from 1891 to 1893 and 1895 to 1908. He was so pro-British that Abbas Hilmi tried to replace him.

promises of the troops' imminent departure, they were to stay in Cairo until 1947, and in Egypt until 1956.

From 1882 until his death ten years later, Tewfik could observe from his splendid palaces the growth of British influence over the administration of Egypt. His authority over his subjects, and his power to appoint and dismiss ministers, were theoretically the same; but final decisions were taken by British officials. The most important was the Consul-General Sir Evelyn Baring, later Lord Cromer. By 1884 Baring felt that the ministers would 'on important matters do what they were told'. The Mahdi was a threat to British control. Claiming to be the descendant and successor of Mohammed and to be establishing true Islamic government, he was able to conquer the Sudan from the Khedive's dispirited troops and to take Khartoum and kill Gordon in 1885. However, he never advanced further, despite some Egyptians' prayers that he would

'deliver them from taxes, debts and Europeans'.[15]

Tewfik tried to limit the power of the British and renewed his links with the mosques and the religious fraternities. Like his father and many other members of his dynasty, he took an interest in education and founded schools, including one beside Abdine palace for his own and the pashas' sons. But in reality, as Baring wrote to Lord Salisbury, 'the Khedive . . . can always be squeezed without creating any upset'.[16]

On his death he was succeeded by his eldest son Abbas Hilmi, one of the most intelligent and resilient monarchs in the history of Egypt. Few people who met Abbas Hilmi, with the exception of Abdul Hamid and Lord Cromer, could resist his charm. One English writer in 1893 called him 'an extremely alert, charming and intelligent man with an unmistakable personal magnetism of his own'. From the moment of his accession,

**Inauguration of the Asyut-Girgeh line by the Khedive
Abbas Hilmi in February 1893**
*The Khedive's popularity at the beginning of his reign is shown
by the size of the waiting crowd; the chimney at the back is a
sign that industrialisation was coming to Egypt.*

although he was only eighteen, he was determined, as he later recalled, 'to do something for my country, to wake it up . . . to make it . . . realise that its salvation lay in independence and that independence could not be a present from foreigners'.[17]

At first his country responded with adulation. However, he was in a difficult position, which was symbolised by the ceremony of his inauguration as Khedive. The square in front of Abdine palace was lined with British as well as Egyptian troops, and after the Sultan's *firman* of investiture was read out, Donizetti's Ottoman was played before Verdi's Egyptian anthem. Hampered by British and Ottoman restrictions, Abbas Hilmi nevertheless tried to expand his power-base. He instituted the Private Cabinet as a means of intervention in politics: as the Royal Cabinet

it was to be an important instrument of royal power in the reigns of Fouad and Farouk.

He also tried to assert his control over the Egyptian army. In 1892 he favoured the appointment of Kitchener as Sirdar or Commander-in-Chief. However, on a tour of upper Egypt in 1894, he criticised the army's British officers and training: 'To tell you the truth, Kitchener Pasha, I consider that it is disgraceful for Egypt to be served by such an army.'[18] But Lord Cromer was a vigorous and determined enemy who frightened Egyptian ministers more than the Khedive did himself. Cromer grew to hate Abbas Hilmi, whom he called in December 1893 'an inexperienced, headstrong boy of no particular talent, who would probably not be able to maintain himself in power for six months without our assistance'. Abbas Hilmi was compelled to proclaim his confidence in Kitchener and to keep pro-British ministers in office. From 1893 decisions of the Council of Ministers taken in the absence of British advisers were deemed null and void. The number of British officials in the Egyptian administration rose from 286 in 1896 to 662 in 1906 — although Cromer knew that their salaries were even more resented than the British army of occupation by educated Egyptians.[19]

The British in Cairo and Alexandria were detested for their bad manners as well as their good jobs. The Aga Khan, the hereditary head of the Ismaili sect of Muslims, who had been made into an Indian prince and a Muslim spokesman in return for his services to the British Empire, could not believe the rigidity of the social divide between Egyptians and Europeans. Egyptians participated in what was called the Cairo season mainly as spectators or servants. Some of the most luxurious hotels of the day were built in Cairo, Luxor, Aswan and the fashionable spa of Helwan (known as Helwan-les-Bains), for the enjoyment of European visitors. For example Marie Vetsera (whose mother came from a rich Christian family of Constantinople, the Baltazzi) spent the winter of 1887–8 in Egypt flirting with a Portuguese prince and a Hungarian count, one year before her suicide pact at Mayerling with Crown Prince Rudolph of Austria. In 1907 the young Agatha Christie was taken to Egypt for the winter by her mother to find a husband; the search was unsuccessful, but she enjoyed herself enormously. She wrote: 'Cairo from the point of view of a girl was a dream of delight. We spent three months there and I went to five dances a week.'[20]

Except at the Khedive's balls and in the salon of his anglophile cousin Princess Nazli, there was no meeting-ground for Europeans and Egyptians: Kitchener made sure that Egyptians were no longer admitted to the Gezireh Club. Cromer never bothered to learn more Arabic than was necessary to shout *Walad! Koura!* (Boy! Balls!) to the staff on its tennis courts. The British brought the rigour of their class system to Egypt. British governesses and tutors who served at the court of Egypt could adapt to the food, the climate and the religion, but not to the weakness of class distinctions. The memoirs of a British tutor to Tewfik's sons, packed with sneers at the 'curious sort of democracy about an oriental court', and boasts of his refusal to eat with other courtiers, help explain why the British were so unpopular in Egypt.

Palace of the Khedive of Egypt at Beicos on the Bosphorus
The Egyptian ruling family enjoyed spending the summer on the Bosphorus. This palace, built in the 1830s, was one of the first made of stone and marble, rather than wood. The Khedive and his relations had many other palaces on the Bosphorus.

Running footmen or *sayces*
*Pashas in Cairo competed to have the smartest running
footmen. The footmen in each household wore a different
costume and had a special way of shouting to passers-by to get
out of the way of their master's carriage.*

The British victory in the power struggle with the Khedive left him with a restricted field of action: pressure from France and Russia, who were Britain's principal enemies until 1904, was unlikely to have concrete results. The Turkish ruling class, as Abbas Hilmi complained in his memoirs, was supine. The British occupation had deprived it of the vigour and confidence so marked before 1882. The princes of the reigning family, who once played a prominent part in public life as ministers and generals, now devoted themselves to good works, their estates and their pleasures. One of their principal pleasures was spending the summer on the Bosphorus.

Lined with the Sultan's palaces, which were followed at a respectful distance by those of the princes and princesses, and by the *yalis* or wooden houses of the pashas, the Bosphorus was at a particularly magical moment in its history, before the degradations of the twentieth century. It attracted people from all over the Ottoman world: the Princes of Samos and Montenegro and the Sherifs of the Hejaz, as well as the Khedive and his family. In the evening they took their caiques on the

The Opening of the Legislative Council, 1914
*The Legislative Council, established in 1883, had little power. On the
left of the Khedive is the diplomatic corps, including his enemy Kitchener;
on the right are court officials. Behind the Khedive are portraits of the
Khedive and the founder of the dynasty, Mohammed Ali.*

Bosphorus, and watched or talked to their friends. The blue and gold caique of the Khedivah Mother was the longest and smartest of all.

One of the most beautiful sights was the illumination by candlelight for the Sultan's birthday. The long façades of Dolmabahçe and Çirağan formed a ribbon of light glittering in the water. The owners of the *yalis* competed to have the most attractive decorations. Emine Foat Tugay, a granddaughter of the Khedive Ismail who spent many summers on the Bosphorus as a child, remembered: 'as the deepening darkness effaced the outlines, the palaces of the Sultanas, the great *yalis* and the rolling hillside of the parks assumed an unearthly beauty, forming luminous designs reflected in the sea and throwing a network of lights over the hills which melted into the infinity of the firmament above.'

Abbas Hilmi spent most summers on the Bosphorus after 1893. Although he disliked being spied upon by the Sultan's agents, he frequently went to dine at Yildiz. He had already built a hideous new palace at Montazah near Alexandria, and in 1905 he started building an art nouveau house of his own at Çubuklu on the

Meeting of the Khedive Abbas Hilmi and King George V, Port Said, 1911.

Standing, left to right: Sir Reginald Wingate, Sirdar or Commander-in-Chief of the Egyptian army and Governor-General of the Sudan; an unknown British officer; Dia el-din Effendi, eldest son of Sultan Mehmed V; the Khedive; George V; Lord Kitchener, British Consul-General in Cairo. Sitting: Queen Mary and Kiamil Pasha, four times Grand Vizir of the Ottoman Empire. The King was on his way to the Delhi Durbar for his inauguration as Emperor of India. His gesture in offering his chair to the aged former Grand Vizir evoked admiration throughout the Middle East. In Ottoman etiquette both the Grand Vizir and imperial princes took precedence over the Khedive of Egypt.

Bosphorus. He remained popular in Egypt and was greeted with cheers, and curses on the British, as he drove through the streets of Cairo in a carriage with coachmen in smart chocolate-coloured liveries, escorted by bare-footed *sayces* or running footmen. He also had immense wealth, and he used all his ability and his position as Khedive to increase it. A brilliant young nationalist politician like Mustafa Kamil (a good Ottoman who called Constantinople 'the citadel of the Muslims and seat of the Caliph of the Believers') now worked with funds supplied by the Khedive. Abbas

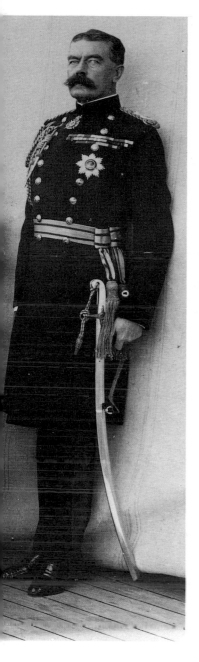

Queen Mary and the Grand Vizir
George V and Queen Mary receive the homage of Prince Mohammed Ali (left) and the former Grand Vizir Kiamil Pasha (right). Kiamil Pasha came from English-occupied Cyprus and was so pro-English that he was called English Kiamil.

Hilmi was Egypt's last defence against the British; if he was alienated, like his father before him, he might turn to the foreigners. [21]

However, the Khedive's position was weakened by the Anglo-French entente of 1904: one of its principal causes had been Britain's need for French approval for strengthening its grip on Egypt. That year, to Mustafa Kamil's fury, the Khedive accepted a British ADC and took the salute at the King's Birthday Parade of the British army, as he did in subsequent years. He knew there was no hope of a British withdrawal. In 1907 there

was a break in the conflict between the palace and the residency with the arrival as Consul-General of Sir Eldon Gorst. He soon established excellent relations with the Khedive — one of the few cases of a British official working with, rather than bullying, a Middle Eastern monarch in this period.

But Gorst was replaced by Kitchener in 1911 and the Khedive's position deteriorated again. Kitchener had new weapons against the Khedive in the hostility of the Young Turk government to his designs on Syria (see page 35) and the unpopularity of his business speculations in Egypt. Kitchener called him 'this wicked little Khedive' and dreamt of being Viceroy of a British Empire in the Middle East. In 1914 the Khedive's power over the *waqfs*, the Muslim pious foundations, and over the award of lesser titles and decorations (the Sultan awarded the others), was diminished. [22] That summer, which the Khedive spent on the Bosphorus as usual, his future seemed bleak. Even his life was in danger: there was an attempt to assassinate him, possibly instigated by the Young Turks, when he paid a visit to the Grand Vizir.

~3~

Beys and Sultans

The Bardo palace
The Bardo, outside Tunis, was the official residence of the Bey of Tunis. Successive Beys had added to it since it was begun in the eighteenth century and it contained a museum, shops and offices as well as magnificent reception rooms. It is still a museum today.

IN North Africa, France and Italy took the place of Russia and Britain as the principal threat to the monarchs of the Middle East. Although still in theory part of the Ottoman Empire, Tunisia had been ruled by Beys of the Husseinite dynasty since the early eighteenth century. Mohammed al-Sadiq (1859–82) lost his financial independence to a French–controlled commission in 1869. In 1875–8 the great reforming minister Khaireddin, a Circassian bought for the Bey in the Constantinople slave-market, succeeded in putting order into Tunisian finances. He also founded the first modern secular schools. However, as in many other courts, the personal extravagance of the monarch hindered the reforming efforts of his ministers. According to Khaireddin, 'The Bey, while showing himself satisfied in appearance with my administration, secretly regretted the former state of affairs which allowed him as well as his entourage to dispose freely of public and private wealth and to waste millions.' Khaireddin resigned and left for Constantinople in 1878.

The Bey's extravagance, together with his suspicion of his subjects' desire to participate in the government, destroyed Tunisia's chances of an independent future. By one of those calculated divisions of spoils so common in the golden age of European imperialism, France had acquiesced in Britain's occupation of Cyprus in 1878 in return for a free hand in Tunisia.[1] In April 1881, alleging outrages committed by Tunisian tribes in Algeria, and the need to offer assistance to the Bey, France invaded Tunisia. By treaties in 1881 and 1883 the Bey handed over control of the country to a French Resident-General and army of occupation.

Although he retained the right to appoint the Prime Minister and the Minister of the Pen, all the Bey's decrees now had to be approved by the French Resident-General. The commander of the French army of occupation acted as the Bey's Minister of Defence. Surrounded by a deferential half-Ottoman, half-French and Italian court, maintained by a generous civil list, the Bey moved from one splendid palace to another, increasingly ignored by his subjects and the French authorities. An English traveller in the 1890s compared him to an extinct volcano. The Bey was so far from embodying national aspirations that some educated Tunisians supported the reforms introduced by France, although they were at the expense of national independence.[2]

Like Arabi Pasha in Egypt, the Beys of Tunis had hoped to prevent a French or Italian invasion by emphasising their links with the Ottoman Empire, which were confirmed by the *firman* of investiture sent to the Bey by the Sultan in 1871. Coins were issued, and prayers recited, in the name of the Ottoman Sultan in Tunis. Many Tunisians still regarded Constantinople as the centre of their world: after his fall from power in Tunis, Khaireddin became Grand Vizir of the Ottoman Empire from December 1878 to July 1879. However, when the Bey appealed for help to the Sultan in 1881, all he obtained was advice to be prudent. During the

Ali, Bey of Tunis (1882–1902)
The Bey is wearing the special Tunisian version of the fez called the chachiya.

The Bey al-Mahalla (left) with a prince
The Bey al-Mahalla (Bey of the Camp), was the title given to the heir apparent of the Bey of Tunis.

Visit of President Loubet to Mohammed al-Hadi, Bey of Tunis (1902–6), 1903
The Bey appears to be the equal of the President of the French Republic; in reality he was a French puppet. The Minister of the Pen, distinguished by the white plumes in his bicorne, is on the right.

Mohammed an-Nasir, Bey of Tunis (1906–22), and his ministers, 1911
These splendidly uniformed men had less power in Tunisia than many minor French officials.

French protectorate his secretaries corresponded with those of the Sultan, but there were no concrete results.

The principal interest of the Ottoman Empire in North Africa was not Tunisia but Tripolitania, which was directly ruled from Constantinople. The great religious order of the Senussi, led by the family of the Senussi, was the real ruler of the province beyond the coastal strip. Like many other Middle Eastern dynasties, such as the Hashemites in the Hejaz or the Shehab in Mount Lebanon, the Senussi regarded the Ottoman Empire as their best protector against local rivals and imperialist powers. The Sultan often sent ADCs to confer with the head of the order, and the empire and the order fought together against the Italian invader after 1911.[3]

Visit of Sidi Mohammed el-Habib to President Millerand in Paris
Sidi Mohammed el-Habib succeeded a distant cousin as Bey of Tunis in 1922 and reigned until 1929

Ahmad Pasha, Bey of Tunis (1929–42)
Despite some nationalist agitation, the French retained complete control during his reign.

The impact of the Ottoman Empire is shown by the difference between Tunisia and Morocco. Tunisia, still in theory part of the Ottoman Empire, was open to the outside world and had been the first Middle Eastern country to have a constitution and a legislative assembly, from 1860 to 1864. In contrast Morocco, inhabited by Arabs and Berbers who were proud that they had never been conquered by the Turks, was a world of its own. Unlike the Ottoman Empire, in Morocco non-Muslims were (and still are) forbidden to enter mosques.

There was an ancient antipathy between the Sultan of Morocco and the Ottoman Sultan. In 1887, in response to German endeavours to encourage an alliance between them which might check French expansion, the Sultan of Morocco said: 'Any alliance between us and Turkey is impossible.' In his eyes 'the Sultan on the Bosphorus is no Sherif'. In other words, he was not descended from the Prophet and was not therefore, in theory, eligible to be Caliph. The Sultan of Morocco, on the other hand, was proud of his descent from the Prophet, which was an essential element in his authority. More than any other monarch of the Middle East, he was a religious figure as well as a political ruler, and his religious authority was acknowledged even by tribes who refused to pay their taxes.[4]

The Sultan who displayed such indifference to the Ottoman Empire was Moulay Hassan (1873–94). Intelligent, industrious, over six feet tall and 'in complexion very dark', he was one of the ablest sultans of modern Morocco. A French diplomat wrote in 1887 that 'he wants to see and direct everything himself'. He used his army as an instrument of civil administration, and after 1877 a French military mission and an English instructor known as Kaid (Chief) Maclean gave some units modern military training. Moulay Hassan travelled throughout his empire to suppress tribal disturbances in person. There were over six hundred tribes in the country, whose territory, known as the *bilad al-siba* in contrast to the government-controlled *bilad al-makhzen*, was only nominally subject to the Sultan. Fear of tribal uprisings was so great that the Sultan's death in 1894 was concealed until the court had reached Fez in safety, and the new Sultan had received the allegiance of its notables.[5]

In the Sherifian dynasty the Sultan was usually succeeded by his eldest son, who was held to inherit his *baraka* or religious prestige. However, the new Sultan was Moulay Hassan's second son, Moulay Abdul Aziz (1894-1908). The change in the order of succession was arranged by the all-powerful Grand Chamberlain, the former slave Si Mousa bou Ahmed, a huge black man over six feet tall 'and broad in proportion'. His father had been a cleaner in the royal household; he himself became a very rich man and ruled Morocco as Regent and Grand Vizir until his death in 1900.[6]

His power was a sign that the court was the principal instrument of government in Morocco. The inner court, which was controlled by the Grand Chamberlain, consisted of four departments responsible for the Sultan's ablutions, tea, bedding and prayer-mat. The first two departments were composed of black slaves, the third of representatives of *makhzen* tribes and the fourth of cousins of the Sultan. The outer court, under the Kaid el-Mechouar, consisted of the stables, staffed by black slaves, 500 messengers and 3,000 guards. One guard unit was recruited from *makhzen* tribes, but since the Sultans distrusted their own subjects the most reliable of all, the Abeed al-Bukhari, were black slaves:

they owed their name to the fact that they were slaves (*abeed*) who swore an oath of loyalty to the Sultan on the works of the great Muslim scholar al-Bukhari.

The court of Morocco was known as 'the people of the sword'. 'The people of the bag' formed the government which, as in most other Middle Eastern monarchies except the Ottoman Empire, still accompanied the monarch wherever he went, and had its offices in his palace or tents. The Sultan's palaces in Rabat, Fez and Marrakesh were cool white buildings with roofs of green tiles, built around gardens and courtyards. They were entirely traditional and were decorated with Moroccan tiles and contained few pieces of furniture. The ministers and the Grand Vizir worked in simple rooms around one of the courtyards; crowded with scribes and petitioners, they were furnished with nothing but carpets.[7]

The court and guard of the Sultan helped make his public appearances almost as impressive as those of his despised rival on the Bosphorus. An embassy from Britain was overwhelmed by its reception in Fez in 1880. To Philip Trotter, one of its officials, the guards, wearing every colour of the rainbow, 'seemed all to blend into one harmonious whole, which was quite indescribable but upon which the eye never grew wearied of gazing'. They formed a brilliant contrast to the court officials, who wore robes of white muslin. 'Of mounted men or even officers there were none, for on State occasions like this all must appear on foot before the Sultan of Morocco "whose throne is his saddle, whose pavilion is the sky"'. The Sultan appeared on horseback, preceded by the Grand Chamberlain, followed by black guards and escorted by attendants who slowly and rhythmically shot forth long white cloths towards his head to drive away the flies. Above his head was a red state umbrella. The troops fell on their knees while the entire crowd simultaneously roared 'Our lord and master! Our lord and master!' The great annual ceremonies for the two feasts after Ramadan and the Prophet's birthday were celebrated with even greater splendour. A French traveller wrote: 'No monarchical or religious ceremonial was ever better organised to impress the masses.'

At the time he wrote, however, there were fewer public ceremonies and less public enthusiasm than in the past, for the young Sultan of Morocco was unpopular.[8] Abdul Aziz was not stupid and he had 'a pleasant smile and by no means an unintelligent face'. But he was more interested in pleasure than in power. He had a passion for photography and a Frenchman, M. Veyre,

was hired to give him lessons. The Sultan was soon able to take colour as well as black and white photographs. His harem was a favourite subject and he taught some of the inmates to take photographs themselves.

Some of his pleasures could be defended as popularising the wonders of modern technology among his subjects, but they were also a sign of his indifference to government business. In the year of the Sultan's accession Kaid Maclean, who became the principal supplier of phonographs, cameras, motorbicycles and tennis equipment to the Sultan as well as Commander-in-Chief of his troops, said, 'It is curious to see the way business is transacted at court, the Sultan amusing himself with his picture books and mechanical toys, while the Grand Vizir sits on the floor in front of him working with his secretaries outside.' The Sultan's desire to break with the traditions of his dynasty alienated his subjects even more than his government's attempts to raise taxes and control the tribes.[9] His personal extravagance contributed to his government's decision to raise foreign loans after 1902.

Although slaves such as Si Mousa bou Ahmed could rise to the highest positions, there was more of an aristocracy in Morocco than in the other monarchies of the Middle East. The most important families inhabited the ancient religious city of Fez, and it was said that the Sultan was only really secure when he 'has been proclaimed as such at Fez by a council of the priests and principal personages of that city'.[10] There was also an aristocracy of tribal chiefs, of whom the most powerful in the first half of the twentieth century was el-Glaoui, a savage voluptuary whose power-base was around the southern capital of Marrakesh.

The forces of el-Glaoui and of the religious aristocracy combined with the Sultan's brother Moulay Hafid, governor of Marrakesh, to attack Moulay Abdul Aziz in 1908. Morocco was in chaos. The rival brothers' troops consisted largely of deserters from the other side. In addition a pretender in the north called Bou Himara, who claimed to be their elder brother, was fighting for the throne. France had established a debt commission with control over 60% of customs revenue in 1904, and was waiting for a pretext to intervene. A 'massacre' of European merchants in Casablanca in 1907 (nine died) was as convenient an occasion as the 'massacre' in Alexandria in 1882 had been for Britain.

Hostility to Britain, France and Russia, and the Kaiser's personal sympathies, made Germany the only European power with any desire to help the monarchs of the Middle East. However, neither the Kaiser's visit to Tangier in 1905, nor the despatch of a German battleship to Agadir in 1911, could delay Morocco's fate. French troops gradually spread across the country, which they controlled by 1912. A visitor to Casablanca in August 1912 found the Café du Commerce in the Place du Commerce full of French officers at white-topped iron tables drinking *apéritifs*. They could have been in France.

As in other Middle Eastern monarchies, such as Bokhara and Egypt, the intervention of an imperialist power could help the monarchy it decided to 'protect'. By the treaty of Fez of 30 March 1912, France promised to protect 'His Sherifian Majesty against all dangers which may threaten his person and his throne' in return for the right to introduce the 'administrative, judiciary, scholastic, economic, financial and military reforms which the French government will judge

Moulay Abdul Aziz (1894–1908)
Such photographs, showing the Sultan wearing European-style uniform and orders, helped to alienate the people of Morocco, who believed that he had become a Christian. During the reign of Moulay Abdul Aziz, the monarchy suffered a rapid decline in power and prestige.

Moulay Hafid (1908–12)
After reigning for four years, Moulay Hafid, who had seized the throne from his brother Moulay Abdul Aziz, was compelled to sign the treaty of Fez in March 1912, which turned Morocco into a French protectorate. Four months later, unable to endure the role of a puppet monarch, he abdicated.

Moulay Youssef (1912–27)
Moulay Youssef's irreproachable morals and piety helped to restore the prestige of the monarchy in Morocco.

Moulay Youssef on a journey

The Sultan's journeys between his capitals of Rabat, Fez and Marrakesh were splendid occasions marked by an absence of French troops. Here Moroccan troops escort the Sultan, who is shaded by a gold and crimson parasol.

Mohammed V (1927–61) and his son Crown Prince Hassan visit the Paris mosque, 1931

At first Mohammed V gave the French authorities no trouble. On this visit he praised la France protectrice for having saved the Moroccan monarchy from ruin.

useful'. French officials under a Resident-General gradually took over most of the government: the Sultan was reduced to signing the decrees placed before him by the Resident-General, although he retained some influence over the choice of Moroccan officials.[11]

However, his authority over the religious life of the country was maintained, and the French government encouraged him to restore the traditional court ceremonial. In the words of a report written in 1916, 'the first measure was to revive the personal prestige of the Sultan by recreating around him the ancient traditions and the old court ceremonial'. Lyautey, the first, most tactful and most successful Resident-General, praised the new Sultan Moulay Youssef for celebrating Friday prayers and the Eid festivals 'with a degree of pomp and veneration for tradition unknown since Moulay Hassan'. Lyautey himself was a convinced monarchist who had revered the French pretender, the Comte de Chambord, and shared the Moroccans' cult of hierarchy and tradition. He was convinced that French control was maintained, above all, by the support of a sultan who was regarded as 'the only legitimate Caliph of the Prophet'.

An important element in France's control of the Moroccan monarchy was its ability to manipulate the

Mohammed V and Crown Prince Hassan going to Friday prayers
Only the Sultan and his heir are on horseback. All officials, including French officers, have dismounted. The escorting soldiers cry 'Long life to Our Lord the Sultan!' as he proceeds to the mosque.

Mohammed V, Crown Prince Hassan and Moulay Abdullah at a Circumcision Feast, 13 July 1942
The Sultan has seated two sons beside him on the throne. Crown Prince Hassan ascended the throne in 1961 and reigns today as Hassan II.

Mohammed V
Mohammed V was so popular that Moroccans claimed to see his face in the moon when he was exiled by the French government in 1953 for supporting the struggle for independence. He returned in triumph three years later.

succession. In 1912 France had arranged for Moulay Hafid to be replaced by a younger brother, Moulay Youssef, who was more respectable than his predecessors. Like Moulay Abdul Aziz, Moulay Hafid retired to lead a comfortable existence in Tangier, where the two brothers survived, without speaking to each other, until the 1930s. On the death of Moulay Youssef in 1927, his third son was chosen to succeed him because he was thought to be *le plus effacé*.[12]

However, Sultan Mohammed V was a subtle, patient politician. It was he who, with fervent popular support, led the long struggle against France, el-Glaoui and rivals within his own family, which finally succeeded in winning Morocco's independence in 1956.

~4~
Shahs and Mullahs

**Nasser al-din Shah (1848–96) in front of the Peacock
Throne in Gulestan Palace**
*It is towards the end of the Shah's reign. He has become
unpopular and looks uneasy. The throne was probably not the
legendary Peacock Throne of the Mohgul Emperors captured
by an earlier Shah, but an early nineteenth-century imitation.*

THE Shah of Persia was the principal rival of the Ottoman Sultan among the monarchs of the Middle East. Both were called *zill-ullah* (shadow of god), and the Shah had an even grander title than the Sultan: *shahanshah* (king of kings) as opposed to *padishah* (great king). They also had more concrete causes for rivalry: territorial disputes in the Caucasus and Mesopotamia, and the ancient religious antagonism between Sunni and Shia Muslims. Like most Muslims the Ottoman Sultans were Sunni, adherents of the first four Caliphs after the Prophet Mohammed, with a different philosophy, legal code and view of history from the Shia. Like most Persians and most inhabitants of Ottoman-ruled Mesopotamia, the Shahs of Persia were Shia, followers of the Prophet's son-in-law Ali. In 1890 Arminius Vambéry, who knew them both well, wrote: 'There is a strong undercurrent of hostility between the Sultan and the Shah.'[1] Their monarchies had contrasting characters as well as ambitions.

Unlike the Ottoman Sultans, the Qajar Shahs, who had ruled Persia since 1770, represented a particular section of their country, namely the Qajars, a tribe of Turkish origin settled in the north-east of Persia. Tehran had been chosen as the capital of Persia since it was near the Qajar tribal heartland. The Shah was proud of being a Qajar and of his alleged descent from Gengis Khan. He was a tribal chief as well as Shah of Persia and signed official documents 'al-Soltan Nasser al-din Shah, Qajar'.

The Qajars were treated as a privileged race, almost as an alternative government, under the Ilkhan, or chief, descended from a brother of the second Qajar Shah. Persia contained other tribes and races besides the Qajars — Kurds in the west, Arabs in the south and the great tribal confederations of the Qashgais, the Luris and the Bakhtiaris in the centre. A large proportion of the population, including the Qajars themselves, spoke Turkish. These tribes and races could be used as power-bases by rebellious princes or foreign powers opposed to the Shah such as Britain, Russia and the Ottoman Empire.

Nasser al-din Shah on a shoot
A courtier reads to the Shah. The Shah, who was passionately fond of hunting and shooting, waits for sport to begin.

Muzafar al-din, heir of Nasser al-din and Governor of Azerbaijan, with advisers, Tabriz, 1862
Whatever his age, the heir to a Qajar Shah was usually appointed Governor of Azerbaijan in order to assert government authority in this important frontier province next to Russia. Second from left is Muzafar al-din's tutor Rezaqoli Xan Lhedayat, first director of the first modern school in Persia, the Dar al-Funoon.

The Shah's camp
The Shah and his court are on a hunting expedition in the mountains. The tent wall on the right separates the Shah's quarters from those of his courtiers.

However, Nasser al-din Shah (1848–96) had one of the strongest personalities and longest reigns in Persian history. Like other powerful Middle Eastern monarchs, such as Abdul Hamid or the Khedive Ismail, he gave 'minute attention to affairs of state, directing even the details, more than do many sovereigns'. He spent much of the morning giving audiences to his ministers, some of whom were committed to modernisation. Mirza Hussein Khan, for example, inspired by the Ottoman Empire where he had been ambassador for ten years, was a reforming Grand Vizir in 1871 and reorganised the Persian ministries on the model of those of other nations.

The Shah also took an interest in education. In 1851 he founded the Dar al-Funoon, which provided a modern education, including instruction in science, foreign languages and mathematics, and sent many students to Europe. Like many of his dynasty he was economical and contracted only one foreign loan. Tehran, still an entirely traditional city in the early 1860s, began to be modernised on his orders after 1867.[2] He knew French, read the foreign press and published diaries of his trips to Europe in 1873 and 1878. They display greater interest in the outward appearance than in the inner mechanism of European palaces, cities and people. By the force of his personality, the strength of his army and his ability to manipulate ministers and courtiers, the Shah maintained his authority in Persia for most of his reign (otherwise he would not have been able to travel to

Courtyard in Gulestan palace
The Gulestan palace in Tehran was a collection of buildings in both traditional Persian and modern European styles.

The *khabga* or palace of sleep in the *anderoun* (women's quarters)
The Shah slept with his favourite wife in the khabga, which he built in the 1880s. It was one of the first buildings in a European style in Persia.

Salaam in Gulestan palace
Nasser al-din Shah sits on the eighteenth-century 'marble throne' (in fact made of translucent green alabaster) and receives the homage of his leading subjects. The pomp and formality of such occasions was a sign of the strength of Persian monarchical traditions.

Europe). On 10 January 1890, for example, he was able to write in his diary: 'In this year, praise be upon Him, in all of the provinces of Iran there is an abundance of provisions, low prices and security. God willing, may it always be thus!'[3]

When not travelling abroad, the Shah spent much of his time in the Gulestan palace in the middle of Tehran. Like Yildiz, Gulestan was a city within a city (it was larger than it is now, since much of it has been replaced by modern ministries). It contained an arsenal, a picture gallery, a museum, a treasury, a telegraph office, the Ministries of War and Foreign Affairs, the Dar al-Funoon, a barracks, gardens, stables for the Shah's innumerable splendid horses (their tails dyed pink to show that they belonged to the Shah) and a *takie*, or theatre for Shia religious spectacles. Nasser al-din Shah added many buildings in a 'Euro-Persian' style, including an orangery and the Shams al-Imaret or sun building, which he used as his private residence. It was decorated in flamboyant polychrome tiles, depict-

ing garlands of roses and the Lion and Sun emblem of the Qajars.

The Gulestan palace also contained the legendary crown jewels of Persia, and workshops for jewellers cutting and polishing new acquisitions. Nasser al-din Shah loved jewels and, in keeping with Persian traditions of royal splendour, wore emeralds, pearls, rubies and diamonds on state occasions (the Ottoman Sultan Abdul Aziz made fun of his love of jewels by giving him diamond-encrusted wooden shoes to wear in the bath-house). In 1873 he acquired one of the most remarkable objects of royal luxury ever created, a globe made of 51,000 gems and 75 pounds of pure gold. The sea consists of emeralds, the land is a mass of rubies or red spinels (although Persia, England, France and part of south-east Asia are outlined in diamonds, and Africa

69

south of the Sahara and part of Egypt in sapphires). The globe was not the Shah's only acquisition. In 1894 one of his most venal and unpopular ministers, Amin as-Sultan, son of a steward in the royal household, gave him a sword made of pearls, rubies, diamonds and emeralds. Even under the Islamic Republic the crown jewels remain a vital part of Iran's currency reserves.[4]

The court receptions or *salaams*, held in Gulestan palace for Nowruz (the pre-Islamic Persian New Year), Bairam and the Shah's birthday (and on a lesser scale on other occasions), revealed the theoretical basis of the Persian monarchy. The Hon. George Nathaniel Curzon, a future Viceroy of India and Foreign Secretary, was one of the many ambitious Englishmen who travelled in the Middle East in this period, in order to study an area which might one day pass under

The Museum in Gulestan palace
The Museum was built between 1873 and 1882 to contain the legendary crown jewels of Persia, and the Shah's purchases and presents from Europe. Until 1926 it was the scene of the coronation of the Shah of Persia.

embroidered cushions on the marble throne, with the Crown of the Qajars (made of diamonds, pearls, rubies and emeralds) beside him. In Persia monarchical traditions were so strong that, like Persian monarchs before the Muslim conquest and unlike other Muslim monarchs, the Shah had a crown and a coronation. He was received by the assembled officials and officers with three bows almost to the ground. Bands played the national anthem. The Prime Minister made a speech; a *sayyid* (as descendants of the Prophet were called) recited prayers; the court poet read an ode. The Ilkhan of the Qajars threw specially minted gold coins called *shahis* to the assembled courtiers. The ceremonies ended with a march past by the troops.[5]

The Qajar court was not a world of its own, cut off from the people of the capital by its traditions and language, as were, to a certain extent, the courts of Constantinople and Cairo. After showing himself to his officials in the palace, the Shah gave an audience to his people from a balcony overlooking a public square. There were performances by swordsmen, jugglers, dancers, wrestlers, performing animals and 'the Shah's giant', seven feet eight inches tall. Then, when the Shah appeared, the entire crowd bowed to the ground three times, and at the end there was a mad rush for gold *shahis*.

Except at the formal *salaams*, the etiquette surrounding the Shah was less strict than that around his rival the Sultan. When the Shah visited Abdul Hamid in Constantinople in 1900, the Serbian minister was struck by the contrast between the Persian and Ottoman courtiers: 'While the latter stood quietly and humbly in the presence of the Sovereign, bowing deeply and salaaming whenever the Sultan addressed a word to them, the members of the Shah's suite were quite at their ease.'[6] This was natural, since the Shah often spent the evening talking with favourite courtiers. He was accessible to other subjects as well. When the Shah left his palace and drove around the capital or the countryside, he did not allow 'for any redundant zeal on the part of the *ferrasshes* [footmen] and [was] accessible to any one of his subjects who may press forward to offer him a petition'.[7]

The Shah's accessibility, and his habit of roaming Tehran at night in disguise, meant that he could not ignore the increasing discontent of his subjects. Although less extravagant than the Khedive Ismail, the Shah also found his court and monarchy expensive to maintain, and European financiers extremely persuasive. The Reuter Concession of 1872 in theory

English control. He knew Persia well and wrote: 'The theory of the Court Levées in Persia is not that the subjects attend upon or are introduced to the sovereign [as in the Ottoman Empire or Egypt] but that the sovereign displays himself to his awe-struck and admiring subjects.'

In an open pavilion in one of the palace courtyards the Shah, blazing with jewels, knelt on pearl-

handed over almost all potential sources of wealth in Persia (including the right to build railways) to a British company headed by Baron Julius de Reuter, in return for a substantial annual income. It aroused so much opposition that it could not be put into practice.

The economic and political life of Persia, like that of other monarchies of the Middle East, was increasingly dominated by European powers, in Persia's case by Russia and Britain. Russia was a neighbour in the Caucasus and Turkestan; Britain was a neighbour in India and the Gulf; and they both maintained enormous legations in Tehran. The Shah himself turned to them for support, despite the obvious danger of relying on imperialist powers. From 1885 he was guarded by the Cossack Brigade, Turkish-speaking soldiers from the north-west of Persia, trained and commanded by Russian officers, who were responsible not only to the Shah but also to the Russian Viceroy of the Caucasus. It was soon the most reliable armed force in the capital.

His sons Zill as-Sultan (Shadow of the Sultan) and Naib as-Sultaneh (Lieutenant of the Kingdom) were so pro-British that the former helped grant Britain a concession in south-west Persia in return for the Grand Cross of the Order of the Star of India (seen as protection in case of danger to its holder), while the latter in 1896 wanted to become a British subject.[8] In 1890 the Shah granted a group of British businessmen a concession to manage the tobacco crop which threatened to put even more of Persian economic life into the hands of foreigners: already many traditional crafts, with the exception of carpet-weaving, had withered away in the face of foreign competition.

Shia traditions of resistance to the state, strengthened by the fact that the great Shia centres of Najaf and Kerbela were in Mesopotamia beyond the reach of the Shah, fortified Persians' determination to resist. Moreover, the Shah himself was becoming unpopular. As a recent historian has written: 'His reasonable and reformist decisions in state matters were frequently undermined by his own capricious and arbitrary acts.' Among these acts was his appointment of a spoiled young favourite, Aziz as-Sultan (beloved of the Sultan) as a brigadier-general at the age of eight. According to Curzon, 'If the lad is not well the Shah is at once in a bad temper and is incapable of attending to affairs of state...the smallest detail is submitted to him.' Since a decision was often reached in Persia, even by the Shah, according to the amount of money paid by those who wanted it (his French doctor, M. Feuvrier, particularly admired the way the expression on the Shah's face varied according to the weight of the bag of coins presented by a petitioner), Aziz as-Sultan was soon very rich. Since he was an unpleasant, bad-tempered child, he was also extremely unpopular.[9]

The Shah's obsession with Aziz as-Sultan (who was sometimes given precedence over the Prime Minister) was a sign that pleasure occupied as much of his time as government business. Photography was one of his

Zill as-Sultan
Zill as-Sultan, the Shah's elder son, was Governor of Isfahan. He wears around his neck the Grand Cross of the Order of the Star of India, a symbol of his pro-British leanings.

Mirza Mohammed Reza, the assassin of the Shah
This photograph was taken between the assassination, on 1 May 1896, and the execution of the assassin, a religious fanatic, on 12 August.

Muzafar al-din Shah, Portsmouth, August 1902
In the Shah's cap is one of the largest diamonds in the world, the Darya-i Nur or sea of light, sister diamond to the Koh-i Nur in the British crown jewels. The Shah's discontented look may be due to his bad health or to Edward VII's refusal to give him the Garter. Since the entire Cabinet threatened to resign unless the Shah received it, the King was later forced to change his mind.

favourite pastimes, as it was of Sultan Abdul Aziz of Morocco. The Shah took and developed photographs himself, usually of his mother or his harem. A special building in the Gulestan palace was called the 'abode of photography'. In the words of a court chronicler: 'At times when His Majesty sought relief from matters of state he would honour that place with His Presence and observe its operation and progress.' He also liked hunting. Five or ten thousand people followed the red royal tents into the mountains on expeditions to hunt ibex, gazelles and tigers. The Shah also spent hours in the *anderoun* or women's quarters. An uncle complained: 'the King is busy day and night living in pleasure... Hunting is his utmost desire...he is exceedingly infatuated with women.'[10]

The result was an explosion of unrest, led by the mullahs, then as now the natural political leaders of the people. The Shah was forced to withdraw the tobacco concession in 1892. He had to promise to consult the mullahs in future, and to thank them for 'strengthening the foundation of the state'. The humiliation was worse than the loss of income: one of the Shah's brothers compared Persia to 'a lump of sugar in a glass of water which is gradually melting away'.

In 1896, while visiting a mosque outside Tehran, the Shah was shot at point-blank range by a fanatical follower of the celebrated Muslim thinker, Sayyid Jamal al-din 'al-Afghani', now a pensioner of Abdul Hamid. The assassin, Mirza Mohammed Reza, who had also lived in Constantinople, was outraged by the state of Persia and hoped to regenerate Islam by drawing all Muslims 'towards the Caliphate and making the Sultan the Commander of the Faithful over all Muslims'. Thus in the 1890s the influence of Yildiz and the Ottoman Empire was so powerful that it could kill the Shah of Persia.[11]

The reaction of the Shah's chief minister, Amin as-Sultan, was similar to that of the Sultan of Morocco's chief minister on his master's death two years before. He propped up the Shah's body on cushions in the carriage, as if he were still alive, and raced back to the capital. The location of power in the Qajar monarchy was revealed by his instructions to the colonel commanding the Cossack Brigade 'to collect all the Cossacks and appoint them in groups to patrol the city to prevent disorders'. In fact, contrary to British and Russian expectations, the Shah's heir, Muzafar al-din, succeeded without disorder or opposition from his brothers.

Muzafar al-din was described by Vambéry in 1900 as 'a very weak man, bodily and mentally weak'; he had a bad bladder, heart and kidneys. In addition, he lacked his father's ability to control his officials, and was easily manipulated. Within a year people in the bazaars were talking of dethroning him. He was 'groaned', or cursed to his face, when the price of bread was high. In 1899 a British diplomat wrote: 'The Shah is a most excellent, kind-hearted and well-meaning man, but the people aren't afraid of him, and the rich men grind the faces of the poor without having their own ground.' (However, he admitted, in a rare flash of European honesty about the Middle East, that the Persian poor were 'not quite as miserable as ours'.) He concluded that 'the only stable element in the country is the regiment of Persian Cossacks'.[12]

Indeed, from then on the Qajars became more pro-Russian. The Shah contracted two Russian loans in 1900 and 1902 (in return for a guarantee that no railways would be built). They were used to pay government expenses and to finance two tours to Europe, which were partly necessary for the Shah's health but were also pleasure trips. Mullahs accused the Shah of selling 'the government and faith of Persia to the Christians by your own whim and caprice'. Although there had been reforms in the administration of customs and taxation, Persia had not been modernised like Egypt and the Ottoman Empire. Like the Shah himself it was visibly wasting away. In 1901 a pamphlet complained that 'the two-headed eagle of the Russians has laid its eggs in the Gulestan Palace of the Ruler of the East'.

The Qajars had become so pro-Russian that Britain turned to the mullahs (which is one reason why some Iranians believe that Britain is behind Khomeini today). On 5 February 1902 an official of the British legation gave Sayyid Abdollah Behbehani, one of the most popular mullahs in Tehran, money 'to cover working expenses'. He added, presumably with a diplomatic smile, the qualification that any action taken 'must be consistent with loyalty to the Shah and government'. The alliance between Britain and the mullahs was crucial in strengthening resistance to the Shah.[13]

The Shah and Edward VII, Portsmouth, August 1902
Front row, left to right: the Prince of Wales, the Shah, Queen Alexandra, Edward VII, Princess Victoria. Standing between the Shah and Queen Alexandra is one of his least popular ministers, Amin as-Sultan.

Deputies to the first Majlis

This extraordinary montage shows not only the number of mullahs (recognisable by their beards and turbans) among the deputies but also the popularity of photography as a means of record in the Middle East.

Organised by men such as Sayyid Abdollah Behbehani, and expressed through the closure of the Tehran bazaars, and a mass *bast* or taking of sanctuary in the grounds of the British legation, popular discontent finally led the Shah to promise a constitution on 5 August 1906. Unlike his father, he was prepared to reign as a constitutional monarch rather than a traditional autocrat, as is shown by his resigned remark: 'The Kings of Europe all govern with the help of a parliament and they are a great deal stronger than the Shah of Iran.' But for many Persians the constitution was popular because it was felt to be an expression of Islamic ideas about the rightful distribution of power among believers.

The constitution transformed the monarchy. Hitherto Persia had been a traditional autocracy, where there was no clear division between the court and the government. Under Nasser al-din Shah the head of the royal footmen became Minister of Justice, and the superintendent of the royal kitchens was Governor of Mazanderan. Now the power of the Shah and the size of his court and civil list were drastically reduced: the Shah was allowed only two palaces.[14] Muzafar al-din might have accepted the situation; however, he died in January 1907 and was succeeded by his son, Mohammed Ali Shah.

Mohammed Ali Shah (1907–09)
The Shah is wearing the jewel-studded crown of the Qajars. His attempts to rule as an autocrat led to his expulsion in 1909.

Russian and Persian officers in the Cossack Brigade
The Russian-trained Cossack Brigade was the best disciplined force in Persia. It was used by Mohammed Ali Shah to bomb the Majlis in 1908 and by Reza Khan to carry out his coup d'état in 1921.

The new Shah was capable, ruthless and economical. Unlike his father and grandfather, he was more interested in power than in pleasure. Encouraged by the Russian minister, he was determined to restore the power and prestige of his dynasty. On 9 January 1907 he had the most elaborate coronation of any Qajar. Eight Qajar princes carried the Shah's insignia. The Ilkhan of the Qajars and representatives of the numerous divisions of the tribe attended with the Shah's special Qajar guard. The Grand Vizir crowned the Shah with the Qajar crown on the throne of Fath Ali Shah in the Museum. A *sayyid* recited verses from the Koran in honour of King David and concluded with praise for 'the Sultan, son of the Sultan, son of the Sultan, the Sultan Mohammed Ali Shah, Qajar... May the pulpits of Islam eternally resound with the sound of the *khutbas* [the ruler's name invoked before Friday prayers] pronounced for his reign!' The ceremony showed that some Islamic traditions, and some *ulema*, supported autocratic hereditary monarchy. Three hundred of the highest dignitaries of the monarchy attended. The deputies to the Majlis (parliament) were not invited.[15]

The conflict between the Majlis and the Shah grew more bitter. Amin as-Sultan was assassinated in 1907 and there was an attempt to assassinate the Shah in February 1908. The Shah wanted a confrontation. The Anglo-Russian agreement of 1907, dividing Persia into Russian, British and neutral spheres, which had convinced the Young Turks that they must save the Ottoman Empire, convinced the Shah that the constitutionalists had been abandoned by their British allies and he should save his throne.

On 3 June 1908 the Shah left Tehran and demanded an end to the attacks of the Majlis. The Cossack Brigade, larger and better trained than before, under the dynamic and ruthless Colonel Liakhoff, took control of Tehran and shelled the Majlis building. Three of the most prominent constitutionalists and hundreds of ordinary people were killed. However, a combination of Caucasian soldiers from the north and a Bakhtiari army from the south was able to take Tehran on 12 July 1909. The next day the Shah, with five hundred loyal troops, his servants, family and many of the crown jewels, fled to the Russian summer legation outside Tehran. Later that year he left Persia with the guarantee of a pension of £16,000.[16]

Some pro-British Bakhtiari Khans may have been thinking of proclaiming a Bakhtiari Shah instead of a Qajar. The popularity, or at least acceptance, of the Qajar dynasty, despite recent bloodshed, was shown by the proclamation of the Shah's eldest son Sultan Ahmad as the new Shah. The first Regent, the Qajar Ilkhan, was succeeded on his death by Abu'l Qaim Khan, who was elected Regent by the Majlis in 1911. He was little help. In the words of Morgan Shuster, an American hired by the Majlis to modernise the administration: 'His Highness was decidedly more fond of describing obstacles and difficulties than of making any practical attempt to overcome them.'[17]

It is true that the difficulties were almost overwhelming. The authority of the central government was withering away in face of the power of the tribes. The Sheikh of Mohammerah, who had become chief of the Arab tribes of south-west Persia in 1897 by killing his brother, was now almost independent, although he continued to pay tribute to the Shah. Thus the British government relied on his forces, rather than those of the Persian government, to protect the districts where, in 1912, the Anglo-Persian Oil Company (ancestor of BP) began to extract petroleum. Until the start of the Iraq-Iran war in 1979 they were among the richest oilfields in the world.

Persia and its constitutional government were also under threat from Russia. In 1897 Nicholas II, known in the Middle East as the Ak-Khan or White Tsar, had said (according to a British diplomat) that, although 'Russia had already quite as much territory as she could manage...he personally thought that our relations would be more friendly and satisfying if there were no Persia between us.' There was increasing Russian economic penetration of Persia; and Russia seemed so powerful and attractive that many Persians, including Qajar princes, went to Saint Petersburg, rather than Paris or London, for their education.

After the Anglo-Russian entente, Britain no longer opposed Russian encroachments in Persia, outside the British zone of influence in the south. In July 1911 the former Shah landed from Russia at Asterabad, in the Qajar heartland east of the Caspian, in an attempt to recover his throne with Russian help. His principal power-base was the Turcoman tribes of the north. In the west there was a rising by Kurdish tribes led by his brother Salar-u'd-Dowleh (highest of the state), who had a Kurdish mother and wanted to establish an independent Kurdish principality. The ex-Shah also had support among ordinary Persians longing for strong government. In Tehran confidence was so low that many rich Persians leased their property to Russians in order to have Russian legal protection.

Heads of Turcoman chiefs stuffed with straw and brought to Tehran
Chiefs of Turcoman tribes in northern Persia had supported the unsuccessful attempt of the ex-Shah, Mohammed Ali, to recover the throne with Russian help in 1911.

Sultan Ahmad Shah with the Regent at a window in Gulestan palace
Torn from his parents at the age of eleven, Sultan Ahmad Shah had a miserable childhood. The Regent had been the first Persian undergraduate at Oxford and encouraged the Shah to be a constitutional monarch.

However, Shuster helped to organise resistance. Although Russian troops remained throughout northern Persia, the ex-Shah was persuaded to leave in March, and Salar-u'd-Dowleh in October 1912.[18] Somehow a Persian government continued to exist. In 1914 the Majlis was allowed to sit again, and Sultan Ahmad was crowned Shah. But under a boy Shah, threatened by hostile neighbours and rebellious tribes, the prospects of the Qajar monarchy could hardly have been worse.

Salaam in a provincial court
In the absence of the Shah, mullahs pay homage to his photograph.

~5~
Khans and Emirs

Abd al-Ahad, Emir of Bokhara (1885–1910)
The Emir's turban was green, indicating descent from the Prophet, and he wore make-up. He was such an impressive sight that according to a Russian diplomat 'it seemed as if all the might of his state was moving with him' when he walked.

LIKE the Ottoman Empire, Persia had immense social and cultural influence outside its frontiers. In the independent monarchies of central Asia, of which the most important were the Khanate of Khiva, and the Emirates of Bokhara and Afghanistan, Persian was the language of the court and of literature — as well as of part of the population. These monarchies shared Persia's problems as well as her cultural heritage: they had to face, in an even more aggressive form, the expansionist drive of the Russian Empire, and they had to decide how to modernise.

Between 1865 and 1870 Russia conquered Tashkent, Samarkand and the surrounding region. In 1873, in accordance with the Tsar's famous request 'Konstantin Petrovich, take Khiva for me', General Kauffmann and

Mohammed Rahim, Khan of Khiva (1864—1910)
The Khan of Khiva was over five foot ten, strongly built, and usually had a twinkle in his eye. He wore a black sheep-skin cap and thick silk coat even in summer. His Russian orders and medals were signs that he was a vassal of the 'Great White Tsar'.

A notable of Samarkand
Although Samarkand had been a Russian city since 1868, its inhabitants maintained local traditions of dress and behaviour, as many still do.

a Russian army stormed the palace of the Khan of Khiva. By a treaty that August, the Khan, Sayyid Mohammed Rahim (1864—1910), head of a dynasty which had reigned since 1767, thanked the 'Great White Tsar and the illustrious *Yarim Padishah* [General Kauffmann, the 'half-Padishah'] for their great kindness and forbearance to me' and said that he would 'always be their friend'. Thereafter he reigned with the advice of a council of seven, four of whom were appointed by the Russian Governor-General of Turkestan.

However, as other monarchs of the Middle East discovered, European imperialism did not necessarily work to their disadvantage. Just as the authority of the Khedive of Egypt was restored in 1882, thanks to British troops, so Russian troops helped the Khan of Khiva defeat the attacks of Turcoman tribesmen, and ensured that there was no serious threat to him from his own subjects.[1] However, he did lose the right to organise the slaving raids into Persia which had been a source of great wealth.

The Khan of Khiva lived relatively simply. His palace which, like the Gulestan in Tehran, also housed his ministers, guard and treasury, was far from impressive. Although some rooms had pillars and domes covered with brightly coloured tiles, the building where he slept, according to Vambéry, 'resembles a poor mud-hut, like all the other houses in town, and is of course without windows'. Vambéry, who was familiar with the courts of Constantinople and Tehran, found that 'Nowhere are any signs of splendour perceptible: the large train of...lackeys are the sole insignia of the ruler.' The palace courtyards were filled with 'good-looking boys of an effeminate appearance, with long hair streaming down their shoulders, and dressed a little like the women, [who] lounged about and seemed to have nothing in particular to do'.

The Khan's system of government was as simple as his palace. According to the Danish traveller Olufsen, the Khan 'governs in person. He is the supreme judge of the country and all lawsuits are settled by him. In the forenoon and afternoon he passes some hours in the harem, which is said to consist of sixty women. The rest of his time is spent in government affairs.'

This included giving audiences to any of his subjects with a grievance. Most travellers found the Khan intelligent and affable, interested in European civilisation, which he had discovered when staying as a guest of the Tsar in Saint Petersburg. Characteristically, 'what really excited his curiosity was the state of European politics, the relationship between the different states, their military strength compared to that of Russia'.[2]

Throne of the Emir of Bokhara
Whereas most furniture in the Emir's palaces remained traditional, this throne, a present from his suzerain, the Tsar of Russia, was European.

Entrance to the *erg* or citadel, Bokhara
The erg, *the ancient residence of the Emirs of Bokhara, contained a palace, mosques, barracks and a prison from which few of the Emir's enemies emerged alive.*

Unlike the court of Khiva, the neighbouring court of Bokhara was a haven of luxury and etiquette. Bokhara was a city of 100,000 at the centre of a fertile plain, and was famous throughout the Muslim world for the number of its mosques and the piety of its population. A thousand years earlier it had produced the famous scholar al-Bukhari, on whose works the Sultan of Morocco's guards swore their oath of loyalty. Although no longer a centre of learning, it still had one of the largest bazaars in central Asia. The Emir of Bokhara was a member of a dynasty which was descended from Genghis Khan like the Qajars, and had ruled Bokhara since 1785. In contrast to the 800,000 subjects of the Khan of Khiva, he had three million, mainly Uzbeks speaking a form of Turkish. Like the Khan of Khiva, he had obtained a relatively favourable treaty with Russia in 1868. The Emir's absolute authority over his subjects was confirmed and his territory slightly extended. All he lost was control of foreign relations.

The Emir Muzafar al-din (1860–85) was a debauchee who wore make-up on his cheeks and round his eyes. After his death in 1885, his fourth son, Abd al-Ahad (1885–1910), seized the throne, having obtained the permission of Tsar Alexander III to supplant his elder brothers while attending the Tsar's coronation in Moscow. He was able to maintain his autonomy since the Russian Foreign Office (unlike certain Russian generals) wanted to keep Bokhara as, in the words of one Russian diplomat, 'a safety-valve against Muslim discontent with Russian innovations'.[3] The discontented could always migrate from Turkestan to Bokhara, where they could enjoy a traditional way of life under the absolute Emir.

The Emir of Bokhara, known as *Hazreti Padishah* (Exalted Padishah), lived in palaces built in traditional Bokharan style. He was served by a splendid and ceremonious court, whose officials wore some of the finest costumes in the world. Dressed in robes of cotton, satin, silk or gold brocade according to their rank, they looked like animated rainbows when they walked. The *parvanatshi* or peacock man, the title given to the Master of Ceremonies, wore peacock feathers on his robe. The chamberlains carried golden or multicoloured wands, the ADCs gold axes. The guard were 'superb men with mink capes of the greatest beauty'.

The future Viceroy of India and Foreign Secretary, Curzon, who travelled to Bokhara and Afghanistan as well as Persia, found that the Emir was 'treated as a sort of demi-god whom inferior beings may admire from a distance'. After eating an enormous meal in the presence of a large number of courtiers, visitors were ushered through a series of rooms, the number of attendant courtiers diminishing as they approached *Hazreti Padishah* himself. They were received in a room 'fitted up with magnificent painted and gilt stucco on the walls and otherwise only decorated with fine woven carpets on which silk quilts and bolsters were placed . . . and a row of gilt armchairs for the Europeans'. If the visitor was lucky, he received a magnificent *khalat* or robe of honour from the Emir at the end of the audience. The Emir's power was so great that his subjects turned pale with fear in his presence (or was this partly 'impression management', designed for gullible foreigners?).[4]

The Emir's government was as traditional as his court. In Olufsen's words, 'the principal object of the Emir's government is regular and abundant payment of the taxes', which was achieved by means of his 15,000 strong army. Although they could not defeat the Emir's foreign enemies, they found it easier to overawe his subjects (however, as in Khiva, Russian troops had to intervene to crush discontent in 1870 and 1910).

The emirate was administered by provincial governors called *begs*. As in other Middle Eastern monarchies, there was no ruling class based on heredity: 'Everybody can rise both to *beg* and to other high offices, and several of the highest Bokhara officials are sons of Persian slaves or have even been slaves themselves.' The *begs*, who had titles giving them rank and office at the Emir's court and who maintained their own courts in the provinces, were bywords for corruption.

The Emir Abd al-Ahad enjoyed excellent relations with Nicholas II. He founded an Order named the Sun of Alexander in memory of Tsar Alexander III, presented a destroyer called *The Emir of Bokhara* to the Russian navy and made a very successful visit to Tsarkoe Seloe in 1906. The reasons for its success were his lavish presents to the Tsar and the courtiers and his familiarity with the Russian court: 'He knew all the recent promotions, the rank of the important people and their actual influence.'[5]

The Emir's friendship with the Tsar enabled him to rule as he pleased, despite being attacked as 'a libertine, a tyrant, a glutton and a hypocrite' by discontented subjects. For the younger generations in Khiva and Bokhara wanted modernisation so much that they were prepared to accept greater Russian control. Tsarist

The Emir Sher Ali of Afghanistan (1863–6, 1868–79) with British officers on a visit to the Viceroy of India, Ambala, March 1869
The Emir's relations with Britain later deteriorated and Britain invaded Afghanistan in 1879.

Russia seemed the embodiment of progress compared to the Emirate of Bokhara. A writer called Fitrat, who had been educated at Constantinople, published pamphlets against the Emir and the *ulema*, in which he wrote that 'the decline of Muslim greatness is the work of your hands'. Even in the heart of Asia the influence of Constantinople was so great that in August 1909 a delegation of secret political societies, inspired by the Young Turk revolution, asked the Emir to sack his unpopular Shia Prime Minister. After repeated demonstrations he was finally dismissed in February 1910.[6] Said Mir Alim Khan, who succeeded his father as Emir the same year, was another traditional autocrat who not only failed to grant a constitution but in 1914 abolished the few modern schools which had been opened.

The ease with which Khiva and Bokhara were attached to the Russian Empire, despite decades of warfare before 1873, was a tribute to the tact of Russian officials. The Muslims of the Russian Empire were no more oppressed than its Christians, nor were they isolated from fellow-Muslims in the Middle East, as they are today. Members of the Muslim ruling classes, including a brother of the Khan of Khiva, were happy to serve in the Russian army. In Curzon's words, 'Russia unquestionably possesses a remarkable gift for enlisting the allegiance and attracting the friendship of those whom she has subdued by force of arms. The Russian fraternises in the true sense of the word.'

Since it could command affection as well as respect, the Russian Empire before 1917 had greater influence in the Middle East than the Soviet Union after 1945; and perhaps its moderation in Khiva and Bokhara was intended as a signal to its friends in Afghanistan and Persia that they too could profit from alliance with the Great White Tsar.[7]

Whereas the population of Khiva and Bokhara consisted mainly of Uzbeks speaking a form of Turkish, Afghanistan was composed of a variety of tribes: Turcomans, Uzbeks and Tajiks, as well as the Pushtuns who formed the core of the state. It had been ruled by Emirs of the Barakzay clan of Pushtuns since 1819. Afghanistan was an independent kingdom with greater power and prestige than Bokhara or Khiva. Nevertheless, it faced similar problems: the lure of modernisation and the menace of imperialist neighbours.

The Emir Sher Ali, the first modernising ruler of Afghanistan, established definite ministries, and founded government workshops to make weapons for his army.[8] Although blocked from direct contact with central Asia by Persia and Russia, the Ottoman Empire exercised considerable influence there, due to its reputation for modernisation, as well as its prestige as

The Emir Abdul Rahman of Afghanistan (1880–1901) on a visit to the Viceroy of India, Rawalpindi, March 1885
Left to right: Captain Balfour, Mr Mackenzie Wallace, Mr Durand (author of the Durand Line which is still the frontier of Pakistan), the Duke of Connaught, General Biddulph, the Emir, Captain Talbot, the Viceroy of India, Lord Dufferin, the Sepah Salar Ghulam Haydar Charkhi. The Emir was gratified by what he called his 'very cordial and very grand' reception and had no trouble with Britain during Lord Dufferin's viceroyalty. He left the conduct of foreign relations in the hands of the government of India.

the seat of the Caliphate. The rulers of Bokhara and of Kashgar, in western Sinkiang, on the slopes of the Karakorum mountains, appealed to Constantinople for teachers, officers and officials experienced in 'the new Ottoman administration' in the 1870s. From 1873 to 1877 the Ottoman flag flew in Kashgar. In 1877 an Ottoman mission, with British encouragement, was sent to the Emir Sher Ali urging him to attack Russia during the Russo-Turkish war.[9]

However, the Emir had established good relations with Russia, and was more interested in fighting Britain. In the second Afghan War of 1878 to 1880, Britain's attempt to take control of Afghanistan ended in chaos. The Emir Yaqub, who reigned from April to October 1879, was deported by the British and died in Bombay forty-five years later. Order was finally restored under the brutal but effective rule of Sher Ali's rival and cousin, the Emir Abdul Rahman (1880–1901). Afghanistan's mountains and the quality of its soldiers and Emir had saved it from absorption by a European empire.

The Emir Abdul Rahman, whose personality can be

studied in his remarkable autobiography, was one of the most capable monarchs of the Middle East in this period. In his own words, 'I dream of nothing but the backward condition of my country — a goat torn by a lion on one side and a bear on the other.'[10] By the time of his death, largely through his own exertions, his country resembled a very tough goat indeed.

To rule Afghanistan it was necessary to be a good judge, a good host and a successful commander in the field. Having fought in many wars himself, Abdul Rahman knew how to maintain the Afghan army as an effective fighting force — certainly more effective than the Persian army. Like the Shah of Persia or the Khan of Khiva, he conducted much of the business of government in person. He tried to impose order on the tribes, and was particularly harsh towards non-Pushtuns: he made a minaret of skulls from the thousands of Hazaras (Afghan Mongols) whom he had killed. He inspired such awe that petitioners went pale with fear in his presence. In view of some of his judgements, their fear was undoubtedly sincere: for example, in the middle of winter he condemned a rapist to be put in a hole in the

The Emir Habibullah (1901–19) at a review
The Emir was pro-British and wears a British-style uniform.
He held two reviews a year.

ground into which water was poured 'until he was converted into an icicle and frozen alive. As the Emir sardonically remarked: "He would never be too hot again."'

Like the Shah of Persia he found mullahs a problem. His favourite saying was that 'more wars and murders have been caused in this world by ignorant priests than by any other class of people', and he stopped the allowances paid to mullahs and *sayyids*. The subsequent revolt in 1886 was ruthlessly suppressed. Having learnt from the wars and quarrels of his youth, he kept the princes of his family in the capital under the orders of his eldest son.[11]

The Emir was a moderniser. Partly in order to encourage a modern outlook in their wearers, European-style uniforms had been introduced at the courts of Constantinople, Cairo and Tehran by 1850. After his visit to India in 1885, the Emir of Afghanistan employed an English tailor, Mr Walter, to create modern uniforms for his officers and officials. The result was that, in the Emir's words, 'All the civil and military officials of my court can be easily distin-

guished.' Abdul Rahman also expanded Sher Ali's workshops, which now made leather, brass and silver goods as well as munitions and uniforms, and gave prizes for their best products.[12]

The court was the centre of power as well as the source of new ideas. It was housed in the *erg*, a twenty-acre compound in Kabul which contained living and reception quarters for the royal family; a conservatory full of flowers and singing birds; store-houses; the treasury; the archives; and barracks for the special *hazabash* guard, which was always ready to escort the ruler out of Kabul to quell rebellion.[13] The Emir wrote that the most important people at court were the *hakims* or doctors; the secretaries; the ushers; the Lord of the Seal; the head of the royal kitchens, who had 'the duty of bringing all petitions before me'; the officers of the guard, who acted as executioners while they were at court; musicians; storytellers; professional chess and backgammon players; and 'a reader of books to me at night'.

One of the most important posts at the court of Afghanistan was that of page, or *ghulam batchi*. In the

The Emir Habibullah on a hunting expedition
The Emir stands to the left of the tripod; his son Sardar Enayatullah, an enthusiastic photographer whose photographs are reproduced in this book, to the right. Like other dynasties in Europe and the Middle East, the Afghan royal family found that photography was an ideal way to fulfill its traditional desire for visual commemoration of its activities.

**The wedding of Sardar Enayatullah, eldest son of the
Emir Habibullah, Kabul, 1909**
*Because Afghanistan was never conquered by a European
power, European dress did not acquire the stigma it had in
India. The costume of both princes and princesses of the
Afghan ruling family is now completely European.*

**Mahmoud Beg Tarzi with his daughter Khayriya and her
son Khalilullah Enayat Seraj (collector of many of the
photographs of Afghanistan reproduced in this book)**
*As editor of the newspaper Seraj-al-akbar (1911—18) and
later as Foreign Minister, Mahmoud Beg Tarzi was the most
important advocate of modernisation in Afghanistan. His
daughter Khayriya, wife of the eldest son of the Emir
Habibullah, can also be seen in the previous photograph.*

An Afghan prince in Scottish dress
*The Afghan royal family liked European clothes so much that
one prince dressed up in a tartan kilt.*

words of the Emir, 'My page-boys consist of the sons of
members of the royal family, sons of the nobility and
chiefs, sons of the officials of my court; in addition to
these are my slave-boys... They are dressed like
princes in velvets and most valuable uniforms...
When they grow up, owing to their having been
trained by me, they are appointed to the highest posts
in the kingdom.'

The Emir arranged good marriages for them and gave
them 'houses and furniture and all requirements of life,
better than those possessed by princes of the royal
family'. One reason for their success was their looks,
for, according to the Emir's doctor John Gray,
'Personal beauty is a fairly certain cause of rapid
promotion at the Amir's Court.'[14]

Abdul Rahman had an overpowering personality.
Even after resigning in disapproval of the traditional
doctors and remedies employed at court, John Gray
admitted: 'Such is the fascination of the Man that, had
one to consider none but oneself, the temptation for
his sake to re-enter the life [the Court] would be almost
irresistible.'

Abdul Rahman's son and successor, Habibullah
Khan (1901–19), who is alleged to have had his father
poisoned, was also an able and strong-willed ruler, even
more intent on modernising his court and kingdom. He
made a speech promising to introduce reforms at his
own inauguration. Whereas his father preferred traditional styles of architecture and decoration, Habibullah had his palaces (some of which he designed
himself) furnished in the richest European style:
chandeliers were carried to Kabul from India on the
backs of elephants. He was so modern that he played
golf and wore tweeds. In 1904 he founded the Habibiya
College, where instruction was in Urdu and English:
for he believed, as he said on a visit to India in 1907,
that 'unless you acquire Western knowledge you will
remain without bread'. His zeal for modernisation, like
that of his cousin and adviser Mahmoud Beg Tarzi, was
due to the influence of the Ottoman Empire as well as
that of Europe. He introduced the fez, contributed to
the cost of the Hejaz railway and imported Ottoman
doctors and engineers.[15]

Although Afghanistan was an absolute monarchy, it
did contain elements of government by consent, as was
shown by the ceremonial at Habibullah's inauguration;
after being presented with a Koran, relics of the
Prophet and a holy flag, he was, in theory, elected
Emir. The Emir Abdul Rahman himself had occasionally assembled the *sirdars* (the provincial aristocracy),
elected representatives (called the *khawanin mulki*) and
mullahs to consult them about matters of policy. In
November 1893 he explained his latest agreement with
the government of India to an assembly of four hundred
sirdars: at each pause in his speech there were shouts of
'Approved! Approved!' The Emir Habibullah continued this practice: in 1916, for example, he sought
the approval of a *durbar* or assembly for his policy of
neutrality in the First World War.[16] Thus even in the
remote and autocratic monarchies of central Asia,
people were attracted by the idea of government by
consent, or at least explanation.

~6~

Harems

Corridor leading to the harem in the palace of Çirağan.

WITHIN the courts of the Middle East there also existed parallel female courts called harems, from the Arabic root meaning sacred or forbidden. Little first-hand information about them is available, for they were shrouded in secrecy. Adults entering the service of the harem of the Ottoman Sultan had 'to renounce all regular contact with the city and to live in the greatest reserve'.

Such a renunciation was usually unnecessary, however, for most inmates had entered the harem as children, and had little knowledge of the world outside the palace walls. Like footmen entering a large European household, once inside the palace they were given new names, such as Duzudil or Nergizeda, to suit their character and appearance. In the 1890s an elderly official of the Ottoman harem, living in Yildiz, knew so little about Constantinople that she asked a visiting Egyptian princess: 'People often talk about a place called Beyoglu [Pera, the European quarter of Constantinople]; where is it and what does it look like?' So strong were the harem's traditions of seclusion that the princess felt compelled to answer: 'You are fortunate never to have visited such a vulgar, ugly place, Ustam. I am sure that, being accustomed to the palace, you would not have liked it.'[1]

One reason why royal harems were isolated from the surrounding capital was that their inmates were often foreign slaves without local roots. The slave supply, even more than the social and political life, of the monarchies of the Middle East reflected the overwhelming importance of Constantinople. For it was there that the best-looking white Circassians from the Caucasus, often bred for slavery by their parents or landlords, were available for purchase. For example, on a journey to Russia, Nasser al-din, Shah of Persia, found the female company provided by his hosts unsatisfactory. He ordered his ambassador in Constantinople to buy two Circassians and send them to him at once (rather as a European monarch ordered ladies from the *corps de ballet* to be sent round after the performance).

Dr Comanos, the Greek doctor of the Khedive Abbas Hilmi, bought Circassian slaves for his master in Constantinople in the 1890s. After the usual medical examination, they were intended to wait on the Khedive's future wife; in the end, to the horror of his mother, the Khedive married one himself. Even the Sultan of Morocco, normally so disdainful of the Ottomans, was happy to marry beautiful slaves from Constantinople. That slaves continued to be sold in Constantinople until the Young Turk revolution, despite the proximity of inquisitive and 'humanitarian' Europe, is a sign of the persistence and independence of Ottoman traditions.[2]

In 1900, according to the official registers, there were between 400 and 500 slaves, most of them Circassian, in Yildiz palace or attached to the households of the imperial family. Living in the enclosed world of the harem, they had a special, partly Circassian, partly old-Turkish, vocabulary. Such words as *payzan* for barefooted, for example, were unknown outside the palace. They also had a distinctive style of cooking, which has almost disappeared under the Turkish Republic. The *sherbetjis*, or sherbet-distillers, were so skilled that 'the palace *lemonata* was indeed a nectar for the gods, as different from the insipid, tasteless liquid the world. . . calls lemonade as water is from champagne'.[3]

A harem was a mixture of escort agency, finishing school and domestic science course; it served as a musical academy as well. In the Ottoman (and the Egyptian) harem there was a special female orchestra which wore a hussar uniform of dark red velvet. It was as good as the Sultan's male orchestra, and could play tunes from *Guillaume Tell* and *La Traviata* as well as traditional Turkish music. In the reign of Abdul Hamid, who appreciated European music as much as European technology, Ottoman princes and princesses were raised to the sound of Verdi. They were such good musicians that they formed a special orchestra, composed only of princes and princesses.[4]

Harems were a separate female world. Inmates never saw men, apart from the Sultan or their closest relations, except through veils or lattices (a latticed gallery above the throne-room in Dolmabahçe enabled the harem to watch ceremonies at the Ottoman court). In the Ottoman harem there was a special hierarchy of female court officials which included the *saray usta*, the mistress of ceremonies, and the seven *haznedar ustas* or treasurers, who supervised the other servants. One *haznedar usta* looked after the Sultan's private apartments and was the intermediary through whom he gave orders to the harem. But the head of the harem was the Chief Eunuch, one of the most important officials in the empire.

The composition of a court usually reflects a monarch's quest for servants whom he can trust. Middle Eastern monarchs' use of eunuchs and slaves is merely an extreme expression of that quest. Since eunuchs and slaves were physically or legally incapable of forming ties outside the court, with people who were not dependent on the monarch, they were considered more trustworthy than the whole and the free. As children of former owners invariably insist, slaves were part of the family. They were so proud of their masters' confidence that they felt superior to mere servants.

The Chief Eunuch was so trusted that in the reign of Abdul Hamid, according to the Sultan's daughter Princess Ayesha, his duties were 'to lock and unlock the doors of the Imperial Harem every evening and morning, to take shifts guarding the doors, to watch those entering and leaving and not to allow anybody in from the outside'. There were 194 serving or retired black eunuchs at the Ottoman court in 1903. They had

Princes, pages and eunuchs at the court of Persia, 1862
The eunuchs are in the back row. Through the trust placed in them by their master or mistress, eunuchs could become extremely powerful in the courts of the Middle East.

Princesses with a eunuch, upper Egypt, 1891
Eunuchs acted as the escorts and representatives of their mistress. They began to disappear from the court of Egypt in the 1920s, but there were still a few in Abdine palace at the time of the fall of the monarchy in 1952.

usually been seized in the Sudan and castrated before sale and many had been sent as presents to the Sultan from the Khedive, the Sherif of Mecca or provincial governors. After the disappearance of the Ottoman court in 1924 some eunuchs were recruited by the court of Tunis; others formed a club and lived together off their savings in Constantinople.[5]

Some slaves and eunuchs of the imperial household were attached to the Sultan and the princes of the dynasty. Most, however, served the female hierarchy of the dynasty, which was headed by the Valide Sultan or mother of the Sultan, the most important woman in the empire. After her came the daughters of sultans, or of sons of sultans, whose rank in the dynasty, like their brothers', was determined by age. The Sultan's consorts or *kadines*, and his favourites, called *iqbals*, were not considered royal and came much lower in the hierarchy.[6] The Ottoman dynastic structure exalted the Sultan and, after him, all members of the dynasty equally. In contrast to European monarchies, it did not give special status to the monarch's consort, heir and immediate relations, and succession went by age. The Ottoman dynasty thereby avoided the innumerable conflicts between monarchs and their heirs, the accession of minors, and the dynasties of discontented cousins with hardly a hope of the throne, which caused such havoc in European monarchies.

The ladies of the harem were famous for the 'correction and distinction of their manners', as well as for the luxury of their surroundings. The harem quarters in Dolmabahçe are only slightly less grand than the Sultan's. The Empress Eugénie, who stayed with the Valide Sultan in Constantinople in 1869, wrote to Napoleon III of a 'luxury of which we in the West have no idea'. Since she herself presided over the most luxurious court in Europe, the Ottoman court must have been extraordinary. The fact that it had only

Princess Nimet Moukhtar and her eunuch
The princess, a daughter of the Khedive Ismail, is leaving Egypt to spend the summer of 1938 at Marienbad. She is preceded by her eunuch Becheragh, the most important person in her household.

acquired modern palaces, furniture and tableware in the last thirty years, so that everything in the Ottoman court was new, even by the standards of the Second Empire, may account for the Empress's amazement.

The Empress noticed that Turkish ladies seemed 'to want to throw away their yashmaks'.[7] However, their lives remained restricted until the revolution of 1908 or beyond. Princess Ayesha, daughter of Abdul Hamid, selected her husband from a photograph: she never met him before their wedding day. When a lady of the harem in Yildiz fell in love with an Italian painting frescoes in the palace, her *khalfa* or maid was shocked and told her that it was a sin for a Muslim to love an infidel. The odalisque was so dismayed that she committed suicide by throwing herself into the furnace heating the harem baths.[8]

A lady of the Ottoman harem, c. 1867
In the Ottoman harem women were divided into kadines *(consorts),* iqbals *(favourites) and* guezdes *(those 'noticed' for a moment). It is not known to which category this inmate belonged.*

Mehmed Nazim Effendi and his sisters (grandchildren of Mehmed V), c. 1910
Ottoman princes and princesses were now almost indistinguishable in clothes and bearing from their European counterparts.

Nevzut, the last wife of the last Ottoman Sultan, c. 1960
Mehmed Vahdeddine married Nevzut, the daughter of a palace gardener, in 1919, at a time when he was losing control of his country.

The wives of Suleiman Effendi
After the death of their husband, a nephew of Mehmed V, two of his wives were such close friends that they continued to live together.

**Inge Hanoum, first wife of
Said Pasha (1854–63)**
*The bead cap on her head is a
sign that, like most harem
inmates, she is Circassian; the
long, jewel-encrusted pipe
shows her wealth and rank.
In 1882 she supported Arabi
Pasha and gave him her
husband's state tent.*

The most emancipated harem was that of Egypt —
always a little ahead of the Ottoman Empire. Since the
seclusion of women was a sign of rank, pride was one
reason for the existence of harems; and pride was also
behind their disappearance. In 1872 the Khedive
Ismail arranged for four princes, including his heir
Tewfik, to marry four of their cousins. Unlike the usual
beautiful Circassians from the harem, the princes'
wives were their husbands' equals in rank. Polygamy
was more difficult to practise when it meant showing
disrespect to princesses of your own dynasty.

The celebrations for the weddings outshone even
those held for the inauguration of the Suez Canal. Each
bride's trousseau — including tiaras, bracelets and
necklaces of gold and diamonds, and gold and silver
plate — was paraded through the streets of Cairo, under

Princess Chafak Nour
*Known as the Fourth
Princess, Princess Chafak
Nour was the only wife
whom the Khedive Ismail did
not take into exile in 1879,
when her son Tewfik became
Khedive.*

military escort, for Egyptians to admire. Hoshyar Kadineffendi, the Khediva Mother, who was the most important woman at court, gave most of the entertainments. In the opinion of Emmeline Lott, one of the many English nannies and governesses who helped to modernise the dynasties of the Middle East (she looked after one of the Khedive's sons), Hoshyar Kadineffendi was 'a perfect lady in the fullest acceptation of the term, with grey hair and large piercing black eyes but commanding in her manner, often too imperious and stately in her carriage'. In Cairo she held court receptions for ladies, at which those of high rank kissed her hand and pressed it to their foreheads, while the others kissed the hem of her robe. For each wedding she gave three grand dinners *à la franque* (that is to say, European food eaten with knives and forks), in a room

Princess Nazli Fazil
Princess Nazli Fazil was independent and emancipated and received men as well as women in her salon in Cairo. She supported Arabi Pasha out of hatred for her cousin Tewfik but later became pro-British and a friend of Kitchener.

Sultane Melek
Daughter of an Ottoman officer, Sultane Melek had been adopted by the third wife of the Khedive Ismail before marrying Sultan Hussein Kamil (1914–17). Her chair shows the Egyptian ruling family's taste for Pharaonic, as well as Islamic, decoration.

with a glass palm-tree at both ends. After dinner dancing girls performed the polka and the mazurka as well as Egyptian dances. The Khedive's daughter, Princess Zeyneb, who was marrying her cousin Ibrahim Fehmi, wore a dress from Paris in the latest fashion, with a train six feet long. A double line of eunuchs holding six- and seven-branch candlesticks escorted her when she left the room.

Another English woman, the princess's governess, Miss Ellen Chennells (author of an ecstatic royal governess's memoir, *Recollections of an Egyptian Princess*), wrote that 'She wore as many of her jewels as could possibly be arranged on her person, or as she was able to carry. She was supported by two eunuchs and she needed support, for I had felt the weight of the dress, ornaments and jewels, and they were no trifle to carry. Visitors mounted on chairs and sofas to get a view of her as she passed but the lights were so dazzling it was not easy to do so.'

Sitting on her throne, the bride received the guests' congratulations, while slaves scattered gold coins in the throne-room and silver in the large saloon. There were fireworks in the streets of Cairo, and bread and meat were distributed to the poor, for four days at each wedding.[9]

Royal wives were now well-educated figures who wanted to play a part in public life. Wives who were also the monarch's cousin, such as the Khediva Emina, wife and cousin of the Khedive Tewfik in Egypt in 1879, and Malekeh Jehan, wife and cousin of Mohammed Ali Shah in Persia in 1907, were the first to assume the rank of royal consorts.

Information about other royal harems is hard to obtain, beyond estimates of their size. The Emir of

The family of the Khedive Ismail
Front, sitting, left to right: Baheya Hanem and Saneya Hanem, daughters of Princess Tevhide (back right). Behind, left to right: Princesses Djananiar second, Shahreette first and Tchachme Affet third, wife of the Khedive Ismail. All are in European dress. The Khedive had a total of fourteen wives.

Bokhara had 130 female slaves in his harem in the 1890s, and he had a male harem as well. It was estimated that there were 1,600 inmates, including eunuchs, in the harem of Nasser al-din, Shah of Persia, in the 1890s: he was survived by eighty-five former wives. The Shah's senior wife, not his mother, ruled the harem of the Qajars, and received the homage of other ladies at female *salaams*. There were 1,500 inmates in the harem of the Sultan of Morocco in the 1880s.[10] The present King of Morocco still maintains a traditional harem, served by slaves and eunuchs and replenished with daughters offered by grateful or ambitious subjects.

Most accounts agree about the boredom of life in a royal harem. Since there were so many slaves and servants, there was little to do but play dominoes or smoke hashish. Not every inmate could expect to be 'noticed'. Some consoled themselves with a eunuch or each other, or with conversation. Emmeline Lott wrote: 'Their conversation, which becomes abolutely tiresome, continuing from hour to hour, invariably touched upon things which in Europe are regarded as criminal, abominably indecent, filthy and disgusting.'

Not all the women, however, were preoccupied by sex. Monotony and seclusion could produce exceptional characters, with a deep interest in power or religion. A Turkish writer was impressed by one of Abdul Hamid's wives, who survived into the 1950s: 'such simplicity, such purity, I never saw in my life!' A British officer legendary for his knowledge and love of the Middle East, Gerald de Gaury, visited another survivor of a late Ottoman harem in 1946, and wrote: 'She spoke intelligently of many things and places, and even now in her old age had a brightness in her look and a vivacity of mind that would outdo that of many of her contemporaries of equal standing in the surrounding countries.'[11]

Proud, intelligent, with time on their hands, some ladies acquired greater political influence than their European counterparts. In the Ottoman Empire it was said that 'one of the surest methods of preferment for individual Turks is to have some connection through their wives with the imperial harem.' Sultan Abdul Aziz was so susceptible to feminine influence that the Grand Vizir Fouad Pasha refused to allow him to marry Tevhide, the beautiful daughter of the Khedive Ismail, for fear of the power the Khedive might acquire. Through her influence over her son, Abdul Aziz's mother, the Valide Sultan Pertevriyal, was a political

figure in her own right. She was a fierce woman, who slapped the Empress Eugénie on the face when she thought the Empress was becoming too friendly with her son. She also gave orders to the Minister of Police — a privilege few mothers of adult monarchs have enjoyed in Europe. However, in 1876 the intrigues of her rival, Sherketza Kadineffendi, helped prepare the deposition of Abdul Aziz in favour of Sherketzya Kadineffendi's son, Murad V.[12]

Malekeh Jehan
Cousin and wife of Mohammed Ali, Shah of Persia (1907–09), Malekeh Jehan was described as 'an extremely capable woman who exercises a considerable influence over her husband'.

Another influential political mother was Hoshyar Kadineffendi, mother of the Khedive Ismail. She and the Valide Sultan Pertevriyal were sisters from the Caucasus, who had been separated when one was bought for the Constantinople, and the other for the Cairo, harem. It was a major event when she came to spend the summer in Constantinople. She made frequent visits to the Ottoman harem, laden with presents and covered in diamonds, sapphires and rubies, whose colours matched the embroidery of her dress. She wore a diamond tiara fashioned with the Sultan's crest and, as a sign of his rank, her chief eunuch wore an ermine-trimmed red velvet cloak over his European costume.[13] Her visits and her presents helped her son to win further autonomy for Egypt from the Ottoman Empire and to fix the succession on his eldest son rather than the eldest male in the family.

In Persia, Nasser al-din Shah (1848–96) knew that during his reign 'the women's quarters' were more powerful than they should be. In 1873 they helped

Khedive Tewfik, his wife and children
Tewfik led a more European life than his father. He is sitting with his only wife, the Khediva Emina (left), and their children, Nimetullah, Abbas Hilmi and Hadidja.

engineer the dismissal of his reforming minister Amir-Kabir, who had prevented them accompanying the Shah on his first journey to Europe. Some Qajar princesses were sufficiently important, or demanding, to be appointed governors of provinces, to enable them to draw the salary. The wife of the last Qajar Crown Prince hoped to save her dynasty by offering her husband's rival Reza Khan 'a special cup of coffee', when he visited her husband in the women's quarters. Fortunately for the future Reza Shah, however, he never entered the *anderoun* of the Qajars.[14]

Since Muslim inheritance laws allowed women to own property, some princesses were rich as well as influential. In 1880 in Egypt, for example, Hoshyar Kadineffendi owned 144,927 of her dynasty's total of 425,729 *feddans*. Another formidable political operator was the wife of the Khedive Tewfik, the Khediva Emina, who was descended from the Ottoman Sultans as well as the great Mohammed Ali. 'A woman of great tact and charm, [she] was well informed about current and world events, and a varied and interesting conversationalist, who also encouraged others to state their views', in the words of her cousin Emine Foat Tugay. The quality of her food was as remarkable as the splendour of her entertainments: her dancers changed their costumes to suit the different European and Turkish tunes and dances played by her private orchestra.[15]

Her return to Egypt in 1923 was a major political event and infuriated King Fouad, whom she regarded as an usurper who had taken the place of her son the ex-Khedive Abbas Hilmi. Secret agents' reports, intercepted for the ex-Khedive, stated that 2,000 people signed her visitors' book: 'The *omdeh* [village headmen] and the notables have not forgotten the visits the ex-Khedive paid to them in their houses in 1913.'

Princesses were not the only inmates of harems interested in politics. An old Turkish *khalfa* or maid was one of the few people whom King Fouad saw when he was ill. She had enough influence over the King to be mentioned in diplomatic despatches, and to inspire the jealousy of his wife Queen Nazli, the last woman from the ruling class to be kept in a harem in Egypt (from which she occasionally wrote letters to the Prime Minister, imploring his intervention in her quarrels with her husband).[16] Time in the harem was spent in the pursuit of power as well as pleasure. Making the most of their seclusion, and the opportunities it provided to see the ruler alone, some inmates were able to acquire as much influence as the most powerful consorts in Europe.

Emir Habibullah of Afghanistan with fourteen *surati*, Kabul, c.1915

Surati or consorts of the Emir were higher in rank than concubines but lower than wives. The Emir Habibullah had more than twenty-five; since some were taken for political rather than personal reasons, he did not sleep with them all.

~7~

The End of the Ottomans

The last Caliph, Abdul Medjid II (1922-4)

I N 1877 in *The Amir's Soliloquy*, Sir Alfred Lyall had put in the ruler of Afghanistan's mouth the words:
But the kingdoms of Islam are crumbling
And round me a voice ever sings
Of death and the doom of my country.
Shall I be the last of its kings?

By 1914 it seemed as if his prophecy had been fulfilled. Tunisia, Egypt, Morocco and Tripoli had been occupied by European powers. European traders had penetrated everywhere, from Kabul to Casablanca. European technology had built railways even as far as Medina. European ideas had led to the establishment of parliaments in the Ottoman Empire, Egypt and Persia. The modern age, so alluring and impressive at the opening of the Suez Canal forty-five years earlier, had arrived in the heart of the monarchies of the Middle East.

However, contrary to Lyall's prophecy, not all the kingdoms of Islam had crumbled. Persia survived as, in theory, an independent monarchy. Afghanistan remained genuinely independent. Even in monarchies occupied by imperialist powers, such as Egypt and Morocco, the dynasty had been maintained. Above all, the most important monarchy of the region, the Ottoman Empire, had made a determined effort to modernise itself, and its success is shown by its influence on countries as different as Afghanistan, Bokhara, Persia, and Egypt.

Whereas Abdul Hamid had been proud that he was 'still a virgin' and had no allies, the Young Turks felt that the empire was in such a desperate position, and the European empires were so ravenous, that it needed a strong ally. Approaches by Talaat to Russia, and Jemal to France, in early 1914 had been unsuccessful.[1] In August, after the outbreak of the First World War, Britain infuriated the Ottoman government and people by seizing two warships for which they had already paid. In contrast two German warships, the *Goeben* and the *Breslau*, which had taken refuge from the Royal Navy in the Bosphorus, were immediately loaned to the Ottoman navy. They were renamed the *Yavuz* and the *Medelli*, their German crews donned the fez and they were the main attraction at a ceremonial naval review by the Sultan a few days later.

The First World War could also be called the War of the Ottoman Succession. It was, in part, a struggle between Austria and Russia for domination in the areas in the Balkans once ruled by the Ottoman Empire. Its first shots were fired in the former Ottoman city of Sarajevo, some of whose officials can be seen, still wearing the Ottoman fez, in the last photograph of the Archduke Franz Ferdinand before his assassination. However, the Ottoman Empire had lost interest in the Balkans and could have remained neutral. Throughout the summer and autumn of 1914, as the European empires were locked in battle, the Ottoman government hesitated. Finally, at the end of October, against the wishes of most of his colleagues, Enver Pasha, the most pro-German minister in the government, decided to attack Russian targets with the new warships in the Black Sea. His decision led to war on the side of Germany and Austria, the collapse of the Ottoman Empire and the end of stability in the Middle East.

The alliance between the Ottoman Empire and the Central Powers worked well. In the Middle East in the first half of the twentieth century, Germany was not the source of horror that it was in Europe. For most

THE MONARCHIES OF THE MIDDLE EAST 1914

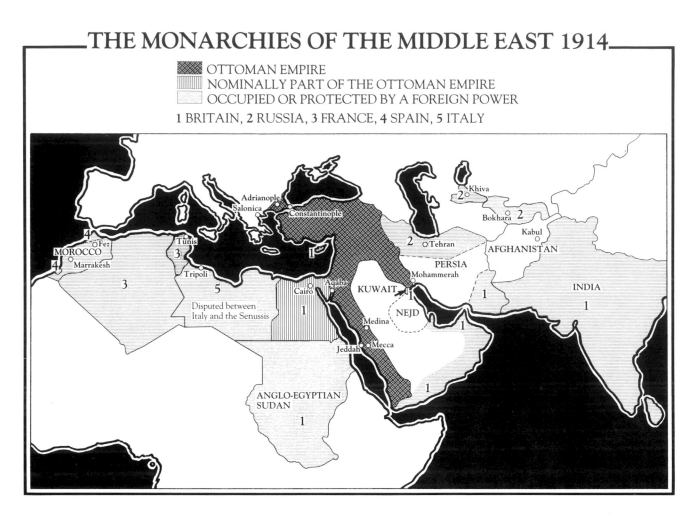

OTTOMAN EMPIRE
NOMINALLY PART OF THE OTTOMAN EMPIRE
OCCUPIED OR PROTECTED BY A FOREIGN POWER

1 BRITAIN, 2 RUSSIA, 3 FRANCE, 4 SPAIN, 5 ITALY

monarchs and peoples of the Middle East, Britain, France and Russia were the enemies, or the feared and resented 'protectors'. By comparison, Germany appeared friendly. The Kaiser had a well-deserved reputation for being, as a group of Persian liberals declared, 'the only European monarch animated by friendly feelings towards Islam'.[2] The Ottoman government calculated that its alliance with the Central Powers would restore the glory of the empire, help it to recover some of the islands lost to Greece in 1913, and perhaps lead to an extension of territory in Turkish-speaking central Asia.

When it entered the war in 1914, the Ottoman government proclaimed a *jihad* or holy war in the name of the 'Servant of the two holy cities, the Caliph of the Muslims and Commander of the Faithful' and summoned all Muslims to rally around the imperial throne.[3] Despite the eloquence and accuracy of its denunciation of France, Britain and Russia for their oppression of Muslims, this proclamation had little practical effect. Although there was mass resistance to

Group photograph in front of the Kasino
Germany and the Ottoman Empire are allies: German officers in sun-helmets and Ottoman officers in wool kalpaks surround Jemal Pasha, Governor of Syria and Minister of the Marine. Syrians still remember him as 'the butcher' for his execution of Arab nationalists.

The Niedermayer Expedition in Kabul, 1915
An expedition of thirty-seven Germans, led by Oberleutnant Niedermayer (centre), reached Afghanistan in August 1915 in the hope of persuading the Emir to invade India. However, he remained neutral. Von Hentig, on Niedermayer's left, was later in charge of Germany's Middle East policy under Hitler.

The Kaiser greeting the Sheikh al-Islam, Constantinople, October 1917
Between them is the exiled Khedive Abbas Hilmi of Egypt. Behind the Kaiser is the
Grand Vizir Talaat; Sultan Mehmed V is on the Kaiser's left and behind the Sultan
is Enver Pasha. Enver was so popular with Germans that they called the empire
Enverland. The alliance with Germany was the most important single cause of the
fall of the Ottoman Empire.

The Emperor Charles of Austria and the Sultan leaving the station, May 1918
This visit was intended to strengthen ties between the Allies. In May 1918 Russia
had made peace and the German offensive in the west was rolling back the French
and British armies: the Central Powers seemed bound to win.

Habsburg, Bourbon and Ottoman, May 1918
The visit of the Emperor Charles of Austria and of his wife Zita, born a Bourbon, to the Ottoman Sultan was the only meeting of a Habsburg, a Bourbon and an Ottoman in history. It represented a unique concentration of sovereignty, since no other dynasties have reigned for so long over so many subjects.

conscription in 1916, most Russian Muslims served the Tsar faithfully. When the Ottoman army drew near the Suez Canal in 1915, the expected uprising of Egyptians against the British did not materialise. Feelings of Muslim solidarity were less strong than a desire to see which was the winning side. Nevertheless the Allies, especially Britain, were alarmed by the possibility of Muslim uprisings in response to the Sultan Caliph's proclamation. Therefore Britain decided to play a card held in reserve since the early nineteenth century,

Sayyid Mohammed Idris al-Senussi
He is wearing Ottoman uniform, since he fought with the Ottoman Empire in Tripolitania against Britain and Italy. He went into exile in 1922 but returned to reign as King Idris of Libya from 1951 until the revolution which put Ghaddafi in power in 1969. He died in Cairo in 1983.

Osman Fouad Effendi
Osman Fouad, a grandson of Murad V, was sent to Tripolitania by submarine in 1917 to help the Senussis. His presence there and the fact that he wears an Arab head-dress (probably the only Ottoman prince to do so in the history of the empire) symbolised the empire's commitment to a specifically Arab cause. He left in 1918 and died in exile in France in 1973.

Proclamation of Sherif Hussein as Sherif and Emir of Mecca, 1908
Sherif Hussein, to the left of the official reading a speech, was at first a loyal servant of the Sultan. He only began the Arab Revolt after months of hesitation.

namely the Hashemite Sherifs and Emirs of Mecca.

The Hashemites were, in Albert Hourani's telling words, 'a family whose claim to descent from the Prophet was at least as good as any other'. They were the most powerful family in Mecca and since 1517 had acknowledged the authority of the Ottoman Sultans, although there were recurrent periods of tension. In 1700, for example, the Sherif of Mecca was said to have called the Sultan 'the son of a Christian whore', and to have threatened to transfer his allegiance to the Sultan of Morocco.[4] In the last quarter of the nineteenth century, rumours of Hashemite ambitions for the Caliphate and allegations of Hashemite friendship with Britain were circulating in Constantinople.[5]

However, these were only rumours. There had in fact been a reassertion of Ottoman authority in the Hejaz, as in other Arab provinces, under Abdul Hamid. A leading Hashemite, Sherif Hussein, and his sons Ali, Abdullah and Faisal had been 'invited' to live in Constantinople by the Sultan in 1894. Thereafter they always spoke Turkish as well as, if not better than, Arabic and retained great veneration for Abdul Hamid.

In 1908, to the fury of an elder branch of the Hashemites, Abdul Hamid made Sherif Hussein Sherif and Emir of Mecca. Thereafter there was a rise in tension between the Arab subjects of the Ottoman Empire and its increasingly 'Turkish' government.

Nevertheless, Sherif Hussein remained loyal to the Ottoman Empire. His quarrels with the Ottoman *vali* or governor of the Hejaz were partly due to jealousy over who was the Sultan's senior representative. He helped an Ottoman expedition sent to crush Arab rebels in Asir in 1911. The principal historian of Ottoman-Hashemite relations, Professor Dawn, has written: 'The Sherif was obsessed with the need to acquire strong support against his Arab neighbours [such as his hated rivals the Al-Sa'ud] . . . In the face of such formidable opponents in Arabia, Ottomanism was an advantageous policy for the Amir of Mecca.'[6]

However, other Arabs had different ideas. The secret society Al-Ahad, founded in Constantinople in 1914, although not completely anti-Ottoman, advocated a dual Turkish-Arab monarchy like Austria-Hungary. Among its members were 315 of the 490 Arab officers in Constantinople and Aziz Ali 'al-Masri' (the Egyptian — in fact he was of Circassian stock from Basra), 'an idol of the Arab officers', and a personal enemy of Enver Pasha. Another Arab sympathetic to nationalist ideas, at that time deputy for Mecca in the Ottoman parliament, was Sherif Hussein's second son Abdullah.

The Ottoman plan to extend the Hejaz railway from Medina to Mecca threatened the Sherif's authority in his own power-base. The Khedive Abbas Hilmi had gone on pilgrimage to Mecca with his mother in 1909;

Group at Jeddah, October 1916

Left to right: Said Bey Ali, commander of an Egyptian battery; Colonel Wilson, British Resident in the Hejaz; the Emir Abdullah, second son of King Hussein of the Hejaz (sitting); Aziz Ali al-Masri; Ronald Storrs. The Arab Revolt received British and Egyptian help from the start. Aziz Ali al-Masri was an inspiring, eccentric officer who participated, in turn, in the Young Turk revolution, the defence of Tripolitania, the Arab Revolt, the training of the Iraqi army, the education of King Farouk, pro-German plots in the Second World War and the Egyptian Free Officers Coup in 1952.

Emir Faisal with French officers, Aqaba, 1917

Aqaba had been captured with the help of T.E. Lawrence. The French officers beside him symbolised Faisal's principal problem in 1918 to 1920: France's determination to control Syria. To Faisal's right is Nessib Bey al-Bakri, from a prominent family in Damascus which acted as a link between the Hashemites and Syrian nationalists.

Nuri al-Said
Nuri al-Said, an Ottoman officer born in Baghdad, joined the Arab Revolt in 1916. The ablest minister of the Hashemites of Iraq, he was murdered while trying to flee, disguised as a woman, in the revolution of 1958.

Abdullah stayed with him in turn in Abdine palace on his way to a session of the Ottoman parliament in 1914. During this visit Abdullah had several conversations with Lord Kitchener, which despite their innocuous content represented the first official contact between the British government and the Hashemite dynasty.[7]

The Ottoman declaration of war horrified Sherif Hussein, who wrote to the Sultan that to enter the war on the side of Germany 'would be either ignorance or high treason'. The demands of war added a new strain to the relationship between the Hashemites and the Ottoman government, and encouraged the former to turn to the British, and vice-versa. As early as November 1914 Kitchener was in favour of a 'new *khalif* at Mecca or Medina of the proper race', as was Izzet Pasha, an Arab former Second Secretary of Abdul Hamid. By the summer of 1915 Sherif Hussein was in correspondence with the British High Commissioner in Cairo.

In 1915, at Gallipoli and in Mesopotamia, Ottoman troops showed that they could defeat British armies. Gradually, however, the fortunes of war turned against the Ottoman Empire. Economic hardship in the Hejaz, Ottoman repression in Syria and refusal to send money to Sherif Hussein, joined to a conviction that the Allies were winning and that the Young Turk government was anti-Arab, made Sherif Hussein decide to cut loose from the Ottoman Empire.[8] On 10 June 1916, a decisive date in the history of the modern Middle East, he launched the Arab Revolt and declared himself King of the Arab Lands (Britain and France recognised him simply as King of the Hejaz). However, his justificatory proclamation was written in the language of an old-fashioned Ottoman subject. He praised 'the Sultans of the House of Osman (may the dust of their tombs be blessed and may they dwell in Paradise!)', and attacked the Committee of Union and Progress as bad Muslims and bad Ottomans: 'They have extinguished the power of the most mighty Sultan and robbed him even of the authority to choose the chief secretary of the *Mabeyn* of the noble Sultanate or the chief of his honoured, exalted Privy Chamber, let alone to attend to the affairs of the Muslims.'

Hashemite belief in their superiority to the Ottomans, never entirely extinct even when they were Ottoman subjects (it is said that when there was a proposal for a marriage between the two families a Sherif remarked: 'Arabs do not mate thoroughbreds with cart-horses'), convinced them of their right to revolt. *Al-Qibla*, a newspaper edited under the supervision of King Hussein, announced on 2 November 1916 that the Arabs had restored 'their ancient fame and the oldest reigning house in the entire world'.[9]

Led by King Hussein's sons, Hashemite forces, with help from Britain — organised, in part, by T.E. Lawrence — and Egypt, tied down large numbers of Ottoman troops in Medina and Syria. However, Ottoman troops lost Baghdad in March and Jerusalem in December 1917 to British armies. There was no Arab rising in Syria or Iraq against the Ottoman Empire, nor were there massive Arab desertions from the Ottoman army. Many Arab nationalists remained loyal to the Ottoman Empire, such as Azzam Pasha, later the first Secretary-General of the Arab League, and Shakib Arslan, later the most celebrated Arab nationalist writer. However, on 1 October 1918, Arab and Australian forces occupied Damascus. The Ottoman government signed an armistice, and withdrew its troops to Anatolia.

After the First World War the fate of the Middle East still seemed to depend on its monarchs. The first Muslim republic of modern times had been proclaimed in Azerbaijan on 28 May 1918. But its leaders had praised 'the centuries-old ideal of all Turkish peoples — unification under the banner of the Sultan'.

The strength of the bond connecting the Turks and their Sultan was confirmed by the survival of the Ottoman Empire at the end of the war, whereas in 1917 the Russian, and in 1918 the German and Austrian, empires disappeared. The Ottoman dynasty was, in the words of a proclamation of the Sultan of May 1919, 'a six and a half centuries old dynasty sprung from the bosom of the nation'.[10] Whereas there had always been Persians in Persia or Arabs in Arabia, it was only thanks to the Ottoman Sultans that Turks lived in Constantinople and western Anatolia. The dynasty's survival was helped by the fact that it was not blamed for the country's entry into the war. Like the death of over a million Armenians in 1915–16, it was attributed to the Committee of Union and Progress, whose leaders escaped into exile on a German battleship in November 1918.

The ruler who had replaced Sultan Reshad, his younger brother Vahdeddine (1918–22), had long been known for his sympathies with Britain and France. He was, according to a British diplomat, 'a man of considerable dignity, amiable disposition and un-affected manners'. Yet he was clearly the wrong Sultan for the empire in 1918. His photographs show a sceptical, unimpressive old man, who looks what the last of a dynasty might be expected to look like. His relations' children called him 'the owl', because he always appeared as if he was about to announce a disaster.

After the armistice he pursued an openly pro-Allied policy in the belief, shared by many of his subjects and most Constantinople newspapers, that it was the only way to salvage something from the wreckage. From November 1918 British, French, Italian and Greek

Inauguration ceremony of Sultan Mehmed VI in Topkapi palace, July 1918
The Sultan is sitting on the gold ceremonial throne of the empire, receiving the homage of his senior officials. A general is pressing a gold-embroidered ribbon held by a chamberlain to his forehead — the particular gesture of respect performed on these occasions. Abdul Medjid, heir to the throne, is on the left of the throne, the Grand Vizir Talaat second from right. The Sultan sits in one corner as if uncertain of his authority.

Allied battleships in the Bosphorus
The presence of Allied battleships in the Bosphorus in 1919 symbolised the defeat of the Ottoman Empire. Three years later the last Sultan left Constantinople for ever on a British battleship.

troops controlled Constantinople. From March 1919 relations between the Allied High Commissioners and the Ottoman government, headed by the Sultan's brother-in-law Damad Ferid, were much more intimate. One British diplomat, Sir Andrew Ryan, wrote of his 'constant visits to the Grand Vizir'. The Grand Vizir asked for Britain to receive a mandate over the empire, with the right to appoint 'advisers' throughout its territory: the Arab provinces were to be given autonomy but not independence.[11]

The Ottoman government's slavish attitude only convinced the Allies that they could behave as they pleased. Italian troops landed in Antalya and Greeks in Smyrna. Soon the Greek army controlled western Anatolia, where it practised, in the words of an Inter-Allied Commission of Enquiry of 1921, 'a systematic plan of destruction of the Turkish villages and extermination of the Muslim population'. The Sultan's policy of subservience to the Allies was leading to disaster.

Constantinople in 1919 was at a particularly dramatic moment in its history. Thousands of Arabs who had remained loyal to the Ottoman Empire were leaving the city which had been the centre of their lives for the new states of Syria, Iraq and Palestine; the city would never see so many Arabs again until the oil boom of the 1970s restored their tradition of summering on the Bosphorus. At the same time White Russian refugees were pouring in, thereby finally realising — although not exactly in the way they had planned — the old Tsarist dream of reaching Constantinople. They opened race-courses, restaurants and clinics for venereal disease; but some were so destitute that they were allowed to sleep in the stables of Dolmabahçe.

Greeks who had spent a lifetime proclaiming their loyalty to the Ottoman Empire abandoned the symbol of their allegiance, the fez, and forced Turks to salute the Greek flag in the streets of Constantinople. The Turks were defeated and demoralised, and many were

Mustafa Kemal Pasha, c. 1919
Mustafa Kemal, the founder of the Turkish Republic, is covered in Ottoman orders and medals: by 1919 he had risen high (but not as high as he wanted) in the Sultan's service.

close to starvation. When Abdul Hamid had been buried in March 1918, people lined the route of the procession crying to their 'father' not to abandon them. Glass was so rare that photographers sold their glass plates for use as windows. Aubrey Herbert wrote: 'There is robbery and no morals anywhere.'[12]

In this nightmare some members of the Ottoman ruling class decided to act. The most famous was Mustafa Kemal Pasha. Born in Salonica, educated at the military schools founded by the Sultans, he had had a brilliant military career despite his rivalry with Enver and dislike of the German alliance. Although many Turks believe that he always wanted to abolish the monarchy, he showed no signs of republicanism in the summer of 1918: he did not finally break with the Ottoman dynasty until six years later. He had been an ADC of Vahdeddine since 1917 and they got to know each other well during a visit to Germany that year.

Indeed, it is said that Mustafa Kemal felt close enough to the Sultan to ask for his daughter's hand in marriage in the summer of 1918. If Kemal, like his enemy Enver, had married an Ottoman princess, his subsequent career might have been different. However, out of concern for his daughter, knowledge of Kemal's history of venereal disease or distrust of his ambition, the Sultan refused. He also rejected Kemal as Minister of War in October 1918: Kemal already had a plan for the government to take refuge in Anatolia which did not appeal to Vahdeddine. Therefore in early 1919 Kemal was one of the thousands of unemployed (and unpaid) Ottoman officers in Constantinople.[13]

He was appointed Inspector-General of armed forces in northern Anatolia and on 16 May left Constantinople to take up his post. The exact motives for his appointment are still a matter of controversy. It seems likely that he was sent 'because his superiors in the Ministry of War, and probably the Grand Vizir and the Sultan, fully expected him to organise resistance'. Thus he was originally a very senior Ottoman officer following an Ottoman plan of resistance — like many others at the time. When he arrived in Anatolia, Mustafa Kemal at first wore the uniform of an ADC of the Sultan and claimed to be acting on his orders.

However, a rift rapidly developed between the general and his superiors. In early June Mustafa Kemal resigned, at the same time as he was dismissed, from the army and thenceforth no longer wore the Sultan's uniform.[14] He soon won the support of the leading Ottoman generals, officials and landowners in eastern Anatolia, including Kazim Karabekir, commander of 18,000 of the best remaining Ottoman troops. On 11 September 1919, while affirming loyalty to the Sultan, he published a savage attack on the Sultan's government, in which he stated: 'You are conspiring with the foreigners against the nation.'[15] As more and more Turks rallied to his cause, the general, not the Sultan, began to seem the best representative of the nation.

In late 1919 and early 1920 there was a reconciliation between the Sultan and the nationalists. The last Ottoman parliament, dominated by the nationalists, met at Constantinople rather than at Kemal's base at Ankara. Kemal was restored to his army rank and the

Ministry of War resumed its supplies of men and munitions to his forces. A British intelligence report complained that it was providing 'every assistance to the national forces'. However, perhaps due to Allied pressure, the understanding did not last. In March 1920 British troops occupied the Ministry of War. In April Damad Ferid returned to power. The Sheikh al-Islam denounced Kemal and his supporters as heretics and rebels. While the Greeks were extending their control of western Anatolia, the Sultan sent forces known as the Armies of the Caliphate against the nationalist armies. After a bitter struggle, the Armies of the Caliphate were defeated by the end of June.[16] Thereafter the authority of the last Ottoman Sultan, like that of the last Byzantine Emperors five hundred years before, was restricted to Constantinople and its surrounding district.

The Sultan's encouragement of civil war, at a time

Visit of Abdul Medjid Effendi and his son Omar Farouk to a Turkish Hearth, 1920
Omar Farouk always regretted staying in Constantinople instead of joining the national forces in Anatolia in 1920. Turkish Hearths could be attended by both men and women. Women had occasionally appeared unveiled in Constantinople since 1908.

when Turks were under attack from Greeks, Armenians and Kurds, seemed unforgivable to many Ottoman princes. In the crisis of their dynasty, although some Ottoman princes danced on board a British battleship (this was thought particularly shocking since traditionally Ottoman princes did not dance themselves, but watched professional dancers perform), others displayed more character. The Sultan's heir was his forty-five-year-old cousin Abdul Medjid Effendi, an impressive, cultivated prince who fasted once a week to show his sympathy for the sufferings of the Turkish people. He displayed better judgement than his cousin. On 12 June 1919 he wrote to the Sultan urging him to form a ministry which inspired general confidence. The Damad Ferid ministry 'reduces the whole Ottoman people to utter despair'. Privately he was saying that the Sultan was proving 'the ruin of the country, the Caliphate and the Sultanate'. He had to act.

In August 1920 it was said that Abdul Medjid wanted to go to Ankara, and it is probable that Kemal was still so Ottoman, or so vulnerable, that he would have welcomed Abdul Medjid with open arms. In September

Princes at the Lycée Impérial de Galataseray, 1920
Standing, second from right: Mehmed Abid, youngest son of Abdul Hamid; fourth from right, Ali Vassib, great-grandson of Murad V; second from left (in white), Abdul Kerim, great-grandson of Abdul Medjid and future Japanese protégé in central Asia. Sitting, left: Nazim, a grandson of Mehmed V; right, Orhan, a grandson of Abdul Hamid. The education of princes at the Ottoman Eton, rather than in the palace, symbolised the modernisation of the dynasty at the end of the empire.

the Sultan was so afraid that his cousin would leave that he held Abdul Medjid prisoner in Dolmabahçe. He was released by October but had already authorised his twenty-two-year-old son Omar Farouk to communicate with Mustafa Kemal. Omar Farouk wrote to Mustafa Kemal on 19 September, requesting information and advice. The logical conclusion would be, as Kemal requested, for him to join the 'national forces'.

However, Omar Farouk hesitated. He had recently married his beautiful cousin Sabiha Sultan — the same princess who had been refused to Mustafa Kemal — and wanted to be with her for the birth of their first child. In April 1921, after she was born, Omar Farouk crossed into Anatolia driven, as he wrote to the Sultan, by an 'irresistible feeling of patriotism'. It was too late. The Ankara press had already started to attack the Sultan in person: Ottoman princes were no longer welcome. Omar Farouk was forced to return to Constantinople.[17]

The national forces were now sufficiently strong not to need outside help. By December the Armenians had been crushed with the help of the Soviet Union, Mustafa Kemal's sole ally and best source of munitions. The Kurds, who had hoped to establish an independent state under the powerful Bedr Khan family, were defeated. In June 1921 the Italians left Antalya. By September 1922 the Greek army, which had almost seized Ankara, had been driven out of Anatolia. The Greek attempt to revive the Byzantine Empire had failed, and led to the expulsion of 1,200,000 Greeks from Anatolia and 400,000 Muslims from Greece. Ancient communities and traditions were destroyed, and thousands of lives were lost, as a result of the folly of some Greek politicians, encouraged by Lloyd George.

When Mustafa Kemal's troops came into contact with British troops at Chanak on the Dardanelles in November 1922, there was the possibility of war. However, Britain had no desire to fight, and this mood sealed the fate of the Sultan (and of Lloyd George, who was blamed for the 'Chanak Affair' and lost Conservative support for his government as a result). Like many other Middle Eastern monarchs, he had relied on a foreign power to maintain his authority. But, in part due to its Ottoman heritage, Turkey was able to decide the fate of its monarchy itself. In March 1921 the Sultan had begged the British to take measures against the nationalists, 'men without any real status in the country', led by 'a Macedonian of unknown origin' (but he had been sufficiently 'known' to be the Sultan's own ADC). As late as November 1922 he believed, or said he believed, that if only the Allies would take 'a firm grip of the situation here', there would be 'a reaction in his favour': he was indeed, as Mustafa Kemal had alleged, conspiring with foreigners against the nation.

Although they abandoned his cause, the British did arrange his escape. Most of his courtiers had left. At the last audience he gave the British High Commissioner on 6 November, there was only 'one old chamberlain instead of the usual rows. The Sultan was very dignified. He is awaiting events and is guarded by the Grenadiers.'[18] At his last *Selamlik* on 10 November, the imperial anthem could not be played, as the band had deserted. On 16 November 1922 he wrote to General Harington, commanding the Allied forces in Constantinople: 'Considering my life in danger in Constantinople, I take refuge with the British Government.' At 6 a.m. on the morning of 17 November, in pouring rain, he was driven away in a British ambulance from a side entrance to Yildiz to a battleship waiting in the Bosphorus.

He was more composed than his entourage and, in thanking the diplomat who arranged his departure, said that 'since they were both monarchs, he expected sympathy from His Majesty King George'. All he received was a pencilled royal addition to a telegram drafted by the Foreign Office: 'I trust Your Majesty is in good health, George RI.'[19] British officials complained about the cost of his stay in Malta and refused to let him live in British-controlled territory. He died in San Remo in 1926.

Although the Sultan, who had never been popular, was easily deposed, the dynasty was still so deeply rooted in the life of the nation that Mustafa Kemal dared not propose its immediate expulsion. One of his most powerful lieutenants, Refet, told him in late 1922: 'I am still bound by conscience and sentiment to the Sultanate and Caliphate.' Most Turks agreed: the father of the writer Aziz Nezim, for example, although he fought for Mustafa Kemal, was devoted to the Sultanate.

Moreover, after 1918 there had been an upsurge of non-Turkish concern for the Ottoman Caliphate. In the shipwreck of their traditional world, Muslims clung to it as, in the words of the Aga Khan, 'a spiritual link of the utmost significance'. Caliphate Conferences in India in 1919 and 1921, as well as bringing Muslims and Hindus together in an anti-British cause, reaffirmed support

Arrival of Mehmed VI in Malta, 1922
Accompanied by his doctor, his bandmaster, a secretary and his only son Ertoghrul, the last Ottoman Sultan walks out of history into exile. He died four years later in San Remo.

for 'His Majesty the Sultan of Turkey, Commander of the Faithful'.[20]

In these circumstances it was difficult for Mustafa Kemal to abolish the Caliphate. Abdul Medjid was persuaded to accept the Caliphate by Kemal and the Grand Assembly in Ankara, which declared him to be 'that member of the Ottoman house who was in learning and character most worthy'. On 24 November he drove to his first *Selamlik* in the same carriage as Refet.

However, Abdul Medjid was in an impossible situation. He believed that the Caliphate should be attributed to 'the most powerful monarch in Islam', not to a powerless figurehead. As Mustafa Kemal complained, he liked pomp and ceremony and made his weekly *Selamlik*, held in the different mosques of the capital, as splendid as possible. He became a focus for discontented politicians and for those religious traditions which Mustafa Kemal was trying to sweep away. Relations between the Caliph and the govern-ment deteriorated during 1923: the Caliph complained that 'death might be better than this continual humiliation'.

Finally Mustafa Kemal, determined to launch a campaign of laicisation, and annoyed by continued foreign interest in the Caliphate, decided to abolish it. At ten o'clock on the night of 3 March 1924 the governor of Constantinople arrived at Dolmabahçe with orders for the Caliph to leave. The Caliph was reading Montaigne's *Essays*; at first he refused to go, but in the end his wife convinced him that resistance was useless. Next day he and his family were put on the Orient Express at Chatalja, outside Constantinople, for fear of demonstrations if they left from Constantinople itself. During the next month the entire dynasty, except for wives and widows, had to leave.[21]

Members of the dynasty scattered to Nice, Beirut and Alexandria, and, after a few years, lost hope of returning to Turkey. Some led miserable lives. Abdur Rahim, a son of Abdul Hamid who had fought bravely in the First World War, had to sell his gold teeth to pay

Jemal Pasha and King Amanullah of Afghanistan, *c.* 1920
From 1920 to 1921 Jemal Pasha was Inspector-General of the Afghan army. He then helped to arrange the treaty which ensured a supply of Soviet munitions for Mustafa Kemal and was shot dead by an Armenian, in revenge for the Armenian massacres, in 1922.

his debts and finally committed suicide. However, the Ottoman dynasty retained considerable prestige. A son-in-law of Abdul Hamid, Ahmed Nami, was Head of State in Syria from 1926 to 1928. Mehmed Abid, a son of Abdul Hamid, married a sister of King Zog of Albania and became Albanian ambassador in Paris. When Japan was trying to establish an empire in Asia in the 1930s, Abdul Kerim, a grandson of Abdul Hamid, was briefly Japanese candidate for the throne of Bokhara. In 1931 the Caliph, who had settled in France, was able to marry his daughter and her cousin to sons of the Nizam of Hyderabad, one of the richest men in the world and a great admirer of the Ottoman dynasty. Other Ottoman princesses married into the Egyptian and Jordanian royal families. Almost until his death in 1944, the Caliph may have hoped to resume a

The end of the Ottoman Empire liberated the people of Turkey from imperial responsibilities which, since the Arab Revolt and the defeat of 1918, had lost all appeal. However, it also deprived them of part of their heritage. With the Ottoman dynasty, Turkey lost an institution of international prestige, a sense of tradition, a code of manners and an ability to live with religions and races other than Islam and the Turks. Non-Turkish inhabitants of the Turkish Republic gradually left; in contrast to Constantinople before 1924, Istanbul today is an almost completely Turkish city. The very identity of the Kurds is denied. Few breaks with the past have been as total as that by which the Turkish Republic replaced the Ottoman Empire.

The end of the Ottoman Empire was also seen as the liberation of the Arabs. However the new Arab regimes owed more to it than they cared to admit. As a British diplomat wrote, in an unconscious tribute to the empire: 'educated men who had grown up under the Turkish regime could make themselves at home in any of the newly-created Arab states.' There had been greater Arab unity under the Turks than under the Arabs themselves. Almost all the early ministers of Iraq and Transjordan were former Ottoman officials. An Arab officer who had remained loyal to the empire until 1918, Fawzi al-Kaoukgi, helped modernise the Sa'udi army, taught in an Iraqi military college, led Palestinian guerillas against the British and, after spending the Second World War in Berlin, led the Lebanese army against Israel in 1948.

Even in the Yemen, which became independent under its Imam in 1919, 200 Ottoman officials remained behind to run the country, although many of them yearned for Constantinople. [23] The role of former Ottoman officials in the new Arab regimes is evidence of the empire's success as a modernising monarchy. Perhaps if leaders and circumstances had been different, the dream of an Arab-Turkish dual monarchy under the Ottoman Sultan could have succeeded.

Mahmud Nedim Bey, former Ottoman *vali* of the Yemen, with an envoy from the Imam of Yemen
Like other Ottoman officials, the former vali stayed behind to serve the new Arab ruler of the Yemen.

political role. For in July 1942, in a last display of Ottoman grandeur, he wrote to congratulate the Emperor of Japan on Japanese victories, and to applaud 'the re-establishment of the sovereign rights of my disciples, the Sultans of Johore and Malacca'. [22]

~8~
Kings of the Arabs

Emir Abdullah of Transjordan

THE fall of the Ottomans could have led to the emergence of the Hashemites as the leading dynasty of the Middle East. Much of the Arab world looked to King Hussein of the Hejaz and his sons for leadership. From October 1918 Faisal, the magnetic hero of the Arab Revolt, ruled Syria as the representative of his father, 'Our Lord the Sultan, the Commander of the Faithful, the Sherif Hussein'. He was pulled through the streets of Beirut by people shouting the old Ottoman cry, now applied to the Hashemites, 'We will not have anyone [as ruler] except the Sultan!'

In reality, the French were in Beirut and wanted the interior of Syria as well. Faisal was in an impossible situation, torn in different directions by French and British imperialism, Zionism and his own extremist supporters. However, he never alienated national feeling by relying on a foreign power, as did Mehmed VI. On 8 March 1920, in an attempt to forestall a French takeover, he was proclaimed King of the United Kingdom of Syria. The French invaded from the coast and, with the help of Moroccan and Algerian troops, defeated the Hashemite forces on 24 July.[1] It was the end of the Hashemite Kingdom of Syria. Faisal left on 1 August with his brother the Emir Zeid, seventeen guards, seventy-two followers and twenty-five women.

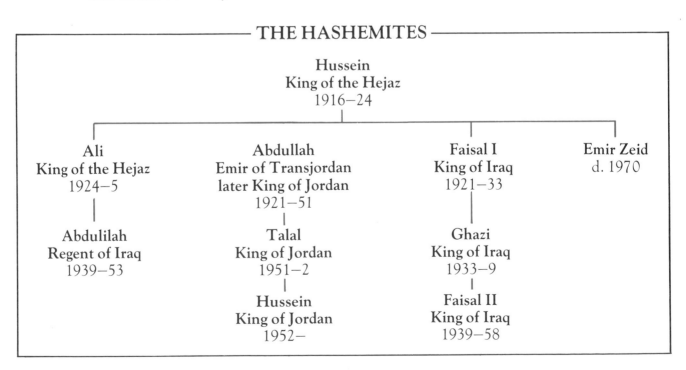

THE HASHEMITES

Hussein
King of the Hejaz
1916–24

Ali	**Abdullah**	**Faisal I**	**Emir Zeid**
King of the Hejaz	**Emir of Transjordan**	**King of Iraq**	**d. 1970**
1924–5	**later King of Jordan**	**1921–33**	
	1921–51		
Abdulilah	**Talal**	**Ghazi**	
Regent of Iraq	**King of Jordan**	**King of Iraq**	
1939–53	**1951–2**	**1933–9**	
	Hussein	**Faisal II**	
	King of Jordan	**King of Iraq**	
	1952–	**1939–58**	

Emir Abdullah with Mr and Mrs Churchill, Jerusalem, April 1921

Abdullah looks cheerful because his assumption of power in Transjordan has been accepted, and a subsidy promised, by the Colonial Secretary Winston Churchill. Abdullah reigned there until his assassination in 1951. King Hussein of Jordan is his grandson.

Meeting in Amman, April 1921

Left to right: Gertrude Bell, Major Walsh, Colonel T.E. Lawrence, Sir Herbert Samuel, the Emir Abdullah, Major al-Adwan. After 1918 Britain dominated the Middle East. Abdullah and Faisal acquired thrones in Baghdad and Amman with the help of Lawrence and Gertude Bell respectively.

As a riposte, King Hussein sent Faisal's elder brother Abdullah to Ma'an in southern Syria in November, in the hope that Syria would rise against the foreign invader. The response was, in Abdullah's words, 'discouraging': the Syrians realised that the French had come to stay. On 2 March 1921 Abdullah moved to Amman.[2] It appealed to him because it was on the Hejaz railway, the inhabitants had requested his presence and Circassians had been settled there by the Ottoman government. They were a military race whom, like many monarchs of the Middle East, he trusted more than Arabs.

Abdullah's presence in Amman, and proclamations against the French, were in open defiance of Britain, which held the mandate for both banks of the Jordan, and had promised self-government to Transjordan.

Nevertheless, at meetings with Winston Churchill in Jerusalem in March and April 1921, an agreement was reached that, in return for Abdullah's temporary abandonment of his ambitions in Syria, he would be Emir of Transjordan with a British annual grant. Thus a new country was created, and Amman became a capital, not as a result of nationalism or British imperialism, but by chance and the will of one prince.

At first, Abdullah was far from popular in Transjordan. He himself admitted that 'I owe the greatest share of my success to this army' — the (in part) British-officered and financed Arab Legion — and he rapidly formed a Circassian Guard.[3] He had so little money that he lived in an encampment of tents, while one of his early Prime Ministers, Hassan Khaled Abul Huda, son of Abdul Hamid's religious adviser, lived in a mud-hut.

However, Abdullah liked pomp and splendour. When teased by a British diplomat, Sir Alec Kirkbride, over his fondness for ceremonies and reviews, he replied: 'There is no point in becoming a king if one does not treat oneself as such.' He soon built a palace called the Basman palace and a small pavilion in the oriental style, furnished with emerald-coloured cushions covered in pink roses. After taking photographs of Abdullah, Cecil Beaton wrote with distaste: 'It is difficult to be impressed by these modern palaces with their geometric furniture by the acre, their meals served on modern crockery stamped with gold crowns, dubious drawing-room wall-paper.'

Abdullah usually wore Arab dress and maintained the traditional division between *haremlik* and *seramlik*. He divided his leisure between his two wives, a favourite black slave and writing Arabic poetry. He was a charmer with laughing eyes. Englishmen who left Amman missed his smile. However, he ruled Transjordan as an autocrat and until his assassination in 1951 never abandoned hope of becoming King of Syria. In fact, despite the ambition of Faisal, Abdullah, their brother Ali, their cousin the Sherif Ali Haidar and the ex-Khedive Abbas Hilmi to become King of Syria, or perhaps because of the sheer number of candidates for its throne, Syria became the first independent Arab republic in 1946.

At home with Gertrude Bell, Baghdad, April 1920
Left to right: Sayyid Talib, Sheikh Khaz'al of Mohammerah, Sir Hugh Bell. Standing: the sons of the Sheikh of Mohammerah. Both Sayyid Talib and Sheikh Khaz'al had ambitions to be King of Iraq. However, although they were friends of Gertrude Bell, they did not have British backing. The former died in exile in Munich, and the latter while under house arrest in Tehran.

Antechamber in the royal palace, Amman
Abdullah's palace looked modern, but his way of life and form of goverment were traditional.

Abdullah also had ambitions in Palestine, which were partially realised when the West Bank became part of his kingdom of Jordan after the war of 1948. Nevertheless, cursed with a divided leadership, the Palestinians were destined to suffer more than any other people of the region. Like many other Arabs, they soon began to regret the end of the Ottoman Empire. Abdul Hamid looked after the Palestinians better than they did themselves. In 1896 he had refused an offer by the founder of political Zionism, Theodore Herzl, to buy land in Palestine with the words: 'I cannot sell even a foot of land for it does not belong to me but to my people . . . Let the Jews save their billions. When my Empire is partitioned, they may get Palestine for nothing.'[4]

While Abdullah was establishing himself in Transjordan, his brother Faisal was an exile in Europe. However, many British officials felt guilty about his fate. Moreover, Iraq, which had been occupied by British troops since 1918, had in 1920 risen in a bloody and expensive revolt. Now that Faisal had lost Syria, might he not be, in Churchill's revealing words, 'the best and cheapest solution' to Britain's problems in Iraq?

At first there were other candidates for the throne of

129

The installation of Emir Faisal as King of Iraq, Baghdad, 23 August 1921

Left to right: Sir Percy Cox, British High Commissioner; Kinahan Cornwallis; Tahsin Qadri, the King's ADC; King Faisal; Sir Aylmer Haldane, British commanding officer; and Sayyid Hussein Afnan, secretary of the Council of Ministers. The ceremony took place at 6 a.m. because of the heat. Hussein Afnan read Sir Percy Cox's proclamation, which stated that 99% of the country wanted Faisal. Faisal declared 'the whole nation is my party'. In reality, as the looming British generals and diplomats make clear, it was Britain not the Iraqis who had selected Faisal.

Iraq. In January 1921 Sir Percy Cox, one of the most influential British officials in the Middle East in the early twentieth century, reported from Baghdad, where he was High Commissioner, that an Ottoman prince (probably Burhan ed-din, whose father Abdul Hamid was still venerated in Iraq) was the most popular candidate for the throne. Another candidate, the Naqib of Baghdad, said that he preferred the Turks 'a thousand times' to the Hashemites: 'He could not agree that the Sherif and his family had the slightest claim to concern themselves with Iraq.'[5]

Nevertheless British officials were determined to

The opening ceremony at the Alwand oil refinery, 2 May 1927

The reign of petrol in the Middle East is beginning. King Faisal I is accompanied by four ministers and the Resident Director of the oil company. He praised oil for achieving a social revolution, but most Iraqis felt they were not receiving a fair share of the profits. He is wearing the faisuliyya, the hat he had introduced to replace the Ottoman fez.

install Faisal. Sayyid Talib of Basra, probably the most dangerous Iraqi candidate, was seized on 16 April after a tea-party with Lady Cox at the British residency in Baghdad, and sent to Ceylon. Faisal arrived in Basra on a British battleship on 24 June. The platforms were almost empty at the stations through which his train passed on the way to Baghdad.[6] Whereas Faisal had been an independent monarch in Syria, in Iraq he described himself, with resignation, as 'an instrument of British policy'. This was, indeed, one reason for his acceptance by the Iraqis, who knew they were in British power. An American consul reported in

January 1922: 'Faisal has never been popular. He was forced upon the country and almost all the Arabs are said to harbour a resentment.' The Shias of southern Iraq were as hostile as they are to their Sunni leaders today. The Royal Air Force had to intervene to support Faisal's government against rebellious tribes 130 times between 1921 and 1932.[7] Faisal spoke Arabic with a Hejazi accent and was accompanied by Hejazis, who were far from popular with Iraqis.

However, in the next twelve years Faisal managed to overcome some of these disadvantages and to create a relatively strong and popular Hashemite monarchy in Iraq. He distanced himself from the British and dominated Iraqi politics more than contemporaries realised. As Ja'afar Pasha, one of his Ministers of War, wrote: 'He was a born leader, one whom it was not easy to lead. He could always persuade one, even against one's will, to adopt his point of view.'[8]

Everyone who met King Faisal, Arabs and Europeans alike, was impressed. Lawrence of Arabia, to the Hashemites an embarrassing and rather pathetic family friend, described him as 'full of dreams and the capacity to realise them'. Gerald de Gaury, who knew Iraq and the Hashemites better than most Englishmen, wrote: 'He was very slim with small bones, narrow shoulders, thin fingers and hands and a rather long face of great beauty in which large liquid eyes could appeal almost irresistibly.'

They certainly appealed to his British supporters. In daytime his office in Baghdad was frequented by

King Faisal I on the SS *Esperia*, Alexandria, 1933
King Faisal I passed through Egypt every year on his way to spend the summer in Europe, away from the heat of Iraq. He is shown here with his friend Princess Lody Lutfullah, a celebrated Alexandrian hostess, and the captain of the ship in which he is about to sail. He died a few weeks later.

politicians striving to obtain his support; sometimes it took them more than a day to reach the King's presence. In the evening he often played bridge with Iraqi notables and British officials. The great archaeologist Gertrude Bell, one of the founders of the Kingdom of Iraq, was always there. Due to his education in Constantinople, King Faisal knew French better than English and spoke in Arabic, using French bridge terms. His ADCs usually made sure that the King won the game.[9]

Because of the harsh Iraqi climate, King Faisal liked to spend the summer in Europe, often with his Egyptian mistress Victorine Sadiq, a clever, ambitious woman who had arranged a meeting with him on a boat going from Alexandria to Europe. He was with her when he died suddenly in a Swiss hotel in 1933.

He was succeeded by his son Ghazi, a dashing young man whose charm, nationalism and tragic early death made him an object of adoration for many Iraqis. Ghazi had been sent to Harrow on the advice of the royal

King Ghazi (1933–9)
King Ghazi is wearing the uniform created for his father by a London tailor. Until his death in a car crash, King Ghazi was an idol of Arab nationalists.

family's friend Dr Sinderson, known as 'Sinbad'. He hated it, and said he would only return with his army at his back. He retained a dislike of the British from his school-days and broadcast anti-British speeches from his private radio in the royal palace, Qasr al-Zuhoor, which replaced the simple house of King Faisal after 1933. He urged Syria to rise against the French, Kuwait against its Emir and both to join Iraq. Iraq was not only a focus of Arab nationalism under King Ghazi: in 1936 it experienced its first military coup, led by the Kurdish general Baqr Sidqi.

King Ghazi did not protest. He was immature and enjoyed running an electric current through objects in the palace, so that visitors received an electric shock picking them up. He liked drink, fast cars and American films and built an octagonal villa, surmounted by a large gilt crown, where he could entertain unsuitable friends in private. In 1939 he died in a car crash when driving to fetch a film to show his friends, after several drinks. Suspicion of British

133

**King Faisal II (1939–58)
on his throne, 1942**
*Charming, intelligent and
asthmatic, King Faisal II left
power in the hands of his
uncle Abdulilah, even after he
reached his majority in 1953.*

King Faisal II in front of Qasr al-Zuhoor, 1942
Qasr al-Zuhoor ('castle of flowers') was the main palace of the Iraqi Hashemites. After his mother's death in 1950, however, the young King Faisal II went to live with his unpopular uncle Abdulilah in another palace, Qasr al-Rihab. They were murdered there with their family and servants in the revolution of 1958.

King Faisal II with the Regent Abdulilah, 1942
The English atmosphere and decoration in the residence of the Iraqi royal family helps to explain why it became so unpopular.

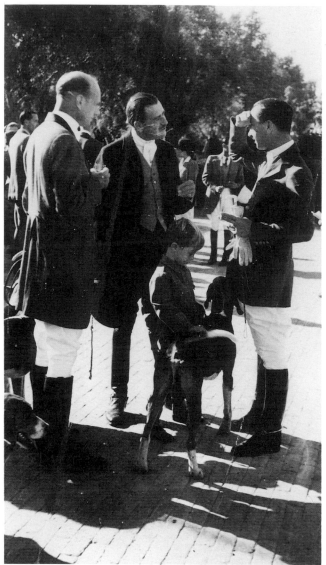

The First Meeting of the Royal Harithiyah Hunt
Left to right: Stewart Perowne, Oriental Counsellor at the British Embassy; Lieutenant-Colonel Gerald de Gaury; James B. Moose jr, son of the U.S. Chargé d'Affaires; the Regent of Iraq. The Regent of Iraq liked British people, customs and politics and later, to the horror of Arab nationalists, signed a military alliance, the Baghdad Pact, with Britain, Turkey, Iran and Pakistan.

intentions and ruthlessness was so strong that many Iraqis blamed Britain for his death.

Ghazi was succeeded by his young son Faisal, whom his tutor remembers as 'a wonderful little boy...the perfect monarch'.[10] King Ghazi's widow Queen Aliya, with whom he had had difficult relations, ensured that the Regent was her brother Abdulilah, son of ex-King Ali of the Hejaz, rather than the senior male of the family, Faisal I's younger brother the Emir Zeid. Under Abdulilah, Baghdad became the most English court in the Middle East.

Hitherto France had been the main foreign influence on the dynasties of the Middle East, partly because modern education in Cairo, Constantinople and Beirut was largely in French. But the Hashemites depended on Britain and Abdulilah had been educated at the most famous British school in the Middle East, Victoria (now Victory) College in Alexandria. He loved Britain and the smart, sophisticated friends he made in London such as Chips Channon and Lady Cunard. British mechanics looked after the Rolls-Royce in his garage. Signed photographs of the British royal family, in silver frames, occupied pride of place on his mantelpiece. The palaces were furnished with British furniture — chintzes, flounces and pink silk shades — and the royal family acquired a house near Staines. Faisal II had a British nanny, governess and tutor. Since no school in the Middle East was thought good enough, he also went to a British prep school (Sandroyd) and public school (Harrow, which he enjoyed more than his father). His nanny, a sacred figure called Miss Borland who had helped deliver him, was able to induce asthmatic fits in the young King when his advisers suggested that he should get to know Iraq better and travel outside Baghdad.

British influence in Iraq was so strong that it was called Perownia, after the influential Oriental Counsellor at the embassy, Stewart Perowne. In 1943 a famous embodiment of Hashemite anglophilia, the Royal Harithiyah Hunt, was founded. Looking like an advertisement for Savile Row, wearing jodhpurs and a yellow polo-necked jersey under his hacking jacket, the Regent of Iraq hunted foxes and jackals on the plains of Mesopotamia with officers of the Royal Guard and Englishmen serving in Iraq. The hounds, which had been shipped from England, were kennelled near Qasr al-Zuhoor and fed on Iraqi army rations, despite traditional Muslim distaste for dogs. This royal anglophilia, which was equally strong on the political plane, created hatred and resentment which led to the revolution of 1958, in which the Iraqi royal family was butchered in front of its own palaces.

However, the Regent also loved his Arab heritage. He had a fine collection of Korans and enjoyed listening to the great Egyptian singer Oom Kalthoum. One of his favourite subjects of conversation, to which he returned with an exile's longing, was his lost homeland of the Hejaz.[11] For while Abdullah and Faisal were establishing monarchies in Transjordan and Iraq, the family power-base in the Hejaz had been eroded. In

The Proclamation of King Hussein of the Hejaz as Caliph at Shunat Nimrin, Transjordan, 1924
None of his fellow-monarchs acknowledged King Hussein as Caliph. When he was proclaimed Caliph, he was on a visit to his son Abdullah, who is on the right. Officers of Abdullah's Circassian Guard are saluting.

1919 their hated rival, Abdul Aziz al-Sa'ud, ruler of the eastern section of Arabia and leader of the puritanical Wahabi sect, had defeated Abdullah at the Battle of Turaba. In 1921 he conquered the territory of the al-Rashid tribe in Hail. Many people in London and Mecca feared, or hoped, that the Hejaz was next on the list. Despite the efforts of King Hussein's sons, his entourage and his wife, he refused to sign a treaty with Britain guaranteeing his possession of the Hejaz, since it would have meant recognising the British mandate for Palestine, established in order to create a national home for the Jews. If he had signed, there might still be a Hashemite Kingdom of the Hejaz today.

King Hussein was out of touch with what his son Faisal called 'bitter reality' and had dreams of replacing the Ottoman Sultan as the paramount monarch in the Middle East. During a visit to Transjordan, on 11 March 1924, one week after the expulsion of the Caliph Abdul Medjid from Turkey, King Hussein was elected Caliph by, in Abdullah's words, 'members of

Ex-King Ali of the Hejaz with Karim Thabet
After his brief reign in Jeddah in 1924 to 1925, ex-King Ali went to live at the court of his brother Faisal I in Iraq until his death in 1934. Karim Thabet was an important Egyptian journalist who later became one of King Farouk's most unpopular advisers.

his family and government, with certain Meccan notables'. In some Muslim countries, particularly in Syria, as well as in the Hashemite lands of Iraq, Transjordan and Hejaz, King Hussein was recognised as Caliph.[12]

However, he was less respected in his own kingdom than he was in the Arab world. He was an old-fashioned autocrat opposed to reforms. The annual pilgrimage or *hajj* of Muslims to Mecca and Medina was badly organised. In comparison even the puritanical Abdul Aziz al-Sa'ud seemed tolerable. On 3 October 1924, 140 Hejazi notables sent a message to King Hussein that 'the people of the Hejaz have decided to request your abdication and nominate Ali as King of the Hejaz. He will be supported by a constitution.' Thus, in the Hejaz as in other monarchies of the Middle East, many members of the ruling class no longer accepted a traditional monarchy. King Hussein abdicated to his eldest son Ali that day. He lived in Cyprus in a villa on Mount Troodos, an embittered exile, until his death in Amman in 1931.

Ali's kingdom soon shrank to the port of Jeddah. In the words of a British official: 'Poor, kind, gentle Ali is at his wits' end and is pulled hither and thither by the rogues who surround him. He has no money, no men and no kingdom.'[13] He finally left on 20 December 1925. The transition from Hashemite to Sa'udi rule in the Hejaz went remarkably smoothly. Already Sultan of Nejd since 1922, Abdul Aziz al-Sa'ud was proclaimed King of the Hejaz by the notables in January 1926.

Abdul Aziz al-Sa'ud was a genius who created a new country, Sa'udi Arabia, by force of personality as well as victory in battle. 'Anybody who met his Majesty, however briefly, could not fail to realise that he was in the presence of an utterly exceptional man, a born leader and a great monarch,' wrote a courtier from Iraq, Mohammed Almana. He was a mountain of a man and his charm was as overwhelming as his size. More than other monarchs of the Middle East, he continued to lead a traditional life in his desert capital Riyadh — a remote oasis totally different from the cosmopolitan Hashemite cities of Mecca and Jeddah.

His palace was a magnificent battlemented mud fort about 800 feet square. It contained a warren of rooms:

Waiting for the King, Riyadh, 1937
The variety of courtiers' costumes and footwear shows that King Abdul Aziz employed advisers from all over the Middle East.

139

Audience chamber in Hail, 1914
Hail was the capital of the powerful pro-Ottoman al-Rashid tribe in northern Arabia. Weakened by murderous internal feuds, it was conquered by Abdul Aziz al-Sa'ud in 1921.

A courtyard in the royal palace, Riyadh, 1935
It is 1935 and the King is returning from Friday prayers. His palace is still made of mud brick; but the troops presenting arms are in modern uniforms and there are motor-cars in the courtyard.

halls; staircases; courtyards; the palace mosque; store-rooms; the King's offices and his *majlis* or council chamber. One of the most important rooms was a huge kitchen which catered for the crowds of visiting bedouin as well as for the needs of the palace. It contained cooking pots eight and ten feet high, each of which was able to hold the meat of a whole camel. Every day the cooks prepared traditional meals of boiled rice and meat for at least a hundred bedouin guests. The coffee was excellent, prepared with cardamon and the residue of previous pots by a family with a secret recipe.

Each of three corner towers of the palace contained one of the King's wives. 'The fourth was kept vacant in case the King should desire to marry again' — as he frequently did. The palace seethed with activity. Every day the King gave judgement, received important visitors and held a general *majlis* of up to 130 people. 'Nobody who attended the *majlis* ever went away empty-handed', remembered Almana. Presents of food, clothes or money helped to reinforce their loyalty. The palace contained the entire central administration of the kingdom. There were sophisticated secretaries from Syria and Iraq, chamberlains, turbaned *ulema*, bedouin bodyguards, black guards and servants and, as a conversational partner for the King, Hajj Abdullah, otherwise known as St John Philby, the celebrated Arabist and father of Kim. As in Europe in the Middle Ages, the court was itinerant and followed the King around his kingdom.

Nevertheless, Abdul Aziz began to modernise his kingdom. By 1929 he had defeated and dissolved the

**King Abdul Aziz, Karim Thabet, and some of the King's
sons, Cairo, 1945**
*King Abdul Aziz created the Kingdom of Sa'udi Arabia by a
combination of tact and genius. In 1945 it was about to
become the richest country in the region.*

Visit of the Emir Sa'ud (future King Sa'ud of Sa'udi Arabia) to Sheikh Ahmad al-Jabir, ruler of Kuwait (1921–50), 1944
The al-Sa'ud and the al-Sabah had a tradition of friendship since the former took refuge with the latter during the occupation of Riyadh by the al-Rashid in the 1890s.

The ruler of Kuwait and his court, 1939
Like other rulers in the Gulf, the al-Sabah of Kuwait practised a more democratic form of monarchy than rulers in Cairo and Constantinople. They lived relatively simply and were accessible to all their subjects.

Visit of the Viceroy of India to Muscat
*The Viceroy was visiting Britain's allies in the Gulf in 1915, in order to raise morale at
the beginning of the First World War. In the background is one of the old forts of Muscat,
a port at the entrance to the Gulf which was capital of the Sultanate of Muscat.*

Sayyid Faisal bin Turki (left) and his son Sayyid Taimur bin Faisal (right)
They were Sultans of Muscat from 1888 to 1913 and 1913 to 1932 respectively. They are wearing the distinctive costume, dagger and head-dress of the ruling family. The present Sultan of Oman is grandson of Sayyid Taimur bin Faisal. A branch of their family were Sultans of Zanzibar until their expulsion in 1964.

puritan *Ikhwan* (Brothers), who had helped him create the country. They disapproved of the modern age so much that they hated cars and telephones and raided Kuwait, Iraq and Transjordan, spreading devastation as they went. Splendour began to appear at the court of Abdul Aziz al-Sa'ud. In 1932 he assumed the title of King of Sa'udi Arabia and Majesty. On the King's journeys in 1926 the women travelled in a large lorry; ten years later each woman had a car to herself. The servants and bodyguards in the palace began to wear special gowns with heavy gold embroidery from Bombay and Damascus, and members of the royal family began to build modern palaces outside the walls of Riyadh. By 1947 there were 450 cars in the royal garages.[14] For Americans had discovered oil and the revenues from the Arab American Oil Company enabled the royal family to live with increasing extravagance. Instead of being a distant country which occasionally sent officials and missionaries to the Middle East, America was now the principal ally of the richest monarch in the Middle East.

~9~

The Rise of the Pahlavis

Reza Shah and his Prime Minister Mr Djam

THE Hejaz was not the only country in the Middle East where one dynasty replaced another. During the First World War Persia sank deeper into chaos. British, Russian and Ottoman forces marched across its territory as if the Persian government and army did not exist. By the end of 1918 there were British troops along the Gulf (the South Persia Rifles) as well as the Russian frontier (Norperforce). British ships sailed the Caspian and Britain took over responsibility for the Cossack Brigade. It was spending about £30 million a year in Persia, including a pension of £60,000 to the Shah.

Sultan Ahmad, the last of the Qajars, was, in the words of his distant cousin the Aga Khan, 'an extremely intelligent young man, highly educated, with a wide knowledge of both Eastern and Western culture, and well read in history, politics and economic theory'. Unlike most Middle Eastern rulers, he was also a constitutional monarch with no desire to be absolute. However, surrounded by ambitious and unprincipled courtiers, he grew up unable to believe in himself or the future of his dynasty. He lived in a state of fear: fear of germs (he usually wore gloves), fear of his subjects, fear of the British, the Bolsheviks and the Bakhtiaris.

Thus he failed to inspire the respect necessary for effective government in Persia. The Aga Khan wrote: 'He did not much care about his crown... He concentrated on providing for his children and his mother and to a lesser extent for his brother.'[1] He represented one solution to the problem of Middle Eastern monarchs torn between East and West, for he was the first to prefer living in Europe to reigning in his own country. Hitherto, however European they had become in their way of life, the dynasties of the Middle East had kept their roots in their countries. Pierre Loti was dismayed to eat French meals, accompanied by French conversation, in the houses of Ottoman princes. He complained that the only sign that he was not in Paris was the fez on their heads. Nevertheless, the last Ottoman Sultans and princes were patriots who fought to save the Sultanate and the Caliphate.

The Egyptian reigning family was even more cosmopolitan. Prince Mohammed Ali, brother of the Khedive Abbas Hilmi, travelled throughout Europe and lived with a Frenchwoman. He boasts in his memoirs that on his drives through the Bois de Boulogne he did not stop one minute from nodding right and left to greet acquaintances. But he saw no contradiction between his love of Europe and his pride in his Middle Eastern heritage. He was also a pious Muslim who made his palace at Manyal on the Nile a monument to 'the revival of Islamic arts and their splendour'. In the same way King Faisal I of Iraq was a patriotic Arab, who had been brought up in the desert; but he spent every summer in Europe and liked champagne.

However, the last Qajar Shah preferred attending a costume ball in the Hôtel du Palais in Biarritz to holding a *salaam* in the Gulestan palace in Tehran. He loved Europe and European art, especially the surrealists, and after his first visit in 1919 he was determined to return. In January 1921 he said that he wanted to abdicate in favour of his brother, a tougher personality who, like previous Qajar heirs, was Governor of Azerbaijan.

Ruled by a monarch who hardly cared for his throne, and by weak and incompetent ministers, Persians felt a need for change. Britain's attempt to take charge by the treaty of 9 August 1919 (whose three principal signatories were paid a total of £131,147) had so outraged Persian public opinion, and the Shah himself, that the treaty had been shelved. The post-war economy drive made direct British involvement in Persian affairs difficult. Yet Britain was frightened of

146

Parade of Russian Cossacks and Bengal Cavalry in Isfahan on the Tsar's birthday, September 1916.
A banquet was later given by the Governor of Isfahan, and a telegram of congratulation sent to the Tsar. During the First World War, Persia was so weak that the wartime allies, Britain and Russia, could meet in the middle.

Ahmad Shah (1909–25) and Reza Khan (1925–41)
Ahmad Shah is surrounded by ministers, courtiers and Bakhtiari Khans. Like the others, Reza Khan stands respectfully behind his master. This is a unique photograph of the last Shah of the old dynasty with the man who was to supplant him.

Reza Shah at his coronation, 16 December 1925
The new Shah is wearing a new crown, the Pahlavi crown specially designed for him. Unlike previous Shahs he wears uniform beneath his pearl-studded blue cloak — a sign that the army was the basis of his power.

the spread of communism and there had been a Soviet-backed republic on the Caspian in 1918. Clearly a less expensive and less obvious way of installing a stable anti-Soviet regime in Persia was necessary.[2]

Although the exact sequence of cause and effect is hard to establish (nor is it made easier by the excision of documents from the relevant British files), the events of the next four years appear to follow a pre-ordained pattern. At the end of 1920 General Ironside, commander of Norperforce, took control of the Cossack Brigade, now about 6,000 strong. Against the Shah's wishes Russian officers were dismissed, and the Persian commander, Sirdar Homayoun, 'a useless little creature', was sent to visit his estates. Ironside believed, as he wrote in his diary for 14 January 1921, 'In fact a military dictator would solve all our troubles.' He found the perfect candidate in Reza Khan, an illiterate giant who had risen through the ranks of the Cossack Brigade. On 12 February Ironside recorded, 'I have interviewed Reza Khan and put him definitely in charge of the Persian Cossacks', and on 14 February, 'Better a coup d'état for us than anything else.' On 20 February the coup took place. The Cossacks occupied Tehran and arrested leading members of the elite. Reza Khan proclaimed his intention 'to cleanse and purify our capital of the idle pampered parasites without honour'. A pro-British journalist became Prime Minister and Reza Khan became Minister of War.[3]

The Qajar monarchy still had such prestige that, like Mustafa Kemal in Turkey, Reza Khan did not at first attack the monarch. The Shah, after expressing confidence in the new government, went on another prolonged tour of Europe until November 1922. His brother stayed behind as Regent. Reza Khan's appetite for power increased with his experience of office. In the next two and a half years, in the words of a British diplomat, the old politicians proved 'incapable of ruling this country' and the Shah and Reza Khan 'lost all confidence in each other'. Britain's involvement in the rise of the Pahlavis (the name adopted by Reza Khan) is shown by the British minister's role as intermediary in the appointment of Reza Khan as Prime Minister, and the departure of the Shah on what proved to be the longest of his trips to Europe in October 1923.[4]

In 1924 there was a movement, inspired by Reza Khan, in favour of a republic. But the mullahs were still the leaders of public opinion and associated a republic with the anti-Muslim policies of the republic installed in Turkey by Mustafa Kemal. Reza Khan decided to replace the monarch instead of the monarchy. However, even the anti-Qajar British minister reported that the country as a whole was not anti-Qajar, and that the Pahlavis would not be popular. In June 1925, on the insistence of Sayyid Hassan Modarres, a prominent mullah who remained a supporter of the Qajars until his murder in 1939, the government begged the Shah to return from Europe. But he hesitated and, reported the British minister, 'even the Qajar princes are losing confidence in the Shah'.[5]

On 29 October the British minister told Reza that Persia was 'absolutely free to settle her internal affairs' (in other words he could depose the Qajars), but in return Britain expected the questions of Persia's debts and a tariff dispute 'to be taken in hand and settled as soon as possible'. In November the Shah's announcement that he intended to return hastened the deposition of his dynasty. One of the four speakers in the Majlis against the motion was Mossadegh, a relation of the Qajars and the future popular hero of the oil crisis of 1952-3. Other people, even the mullahs, were too frightened to protest. On 12 December Reza Khan became Reza Shah, and on 25 April 1926 he crowned himself in Gulestan palace. He abandoned Persian traditions and based the uniforms, and much of the decoration of the ceremony, on English models. At the time Vita Sackville-West was visiting her husband Harold Nicolson, who was serving in the British embassy in Tehran, and offered advice to Reza's courtiers. She wrote of them: 'There was no point, however humble, on which they would not consult their English friends.'[6] It is hardly surprising that many Persians blame Britain for the Pahlavi dynasty.

The new Shah instituted a reign of terror in his country. Harold Nicolson wrote: 'There is no liberty in Persia today. There is fear, corruption, dishonesty and disease.' Reza Shah was a tyrant who whipped people in the street if they failed to salute him respectfully. Some Qajars shunned his court: a daughter of Muzafar al-din Shah became so poor that she scoured the tree-lined avenues of Tehran for kindling-wood. Others, however, were ready to serve their supplanter. Reza Shah's favourite minister Taymurtash, an aristocrat related to the Qajars, helped to teach him table manners and court etiquette. The Shah had him killed when he imagined Taymurtash was becoming too powerful. In 1927 a British diplomat wrote: 'The Shah has become most unpopular. He is one thousand times worse than Ahmet Shah in his love of money and land . . . He has amassed a huge, huge fortune.'[7]

**The Aga Khan
(1877–1960)**
*His traditional Persian court
costume shows that the Aga
Khan was a Persian noble as
well as a British knight, a
First Class Prince of the
Bombay presidency and head
of the Ismaili branch of Islam.
He was descended from the
early Qajar Shahs and his
ancestors had lived in Persia
until they moved to India
in 1846.*

Mohammed Reza with courtiers

Mohammed Reza, the Crown Prince and future Shah (1941–79), was educated in Iran and Switzerland. He grew up better informed, but weaker and less confident, than his awe-inspiring father. Courtiers' uniforms and hats are more modern than under the Qajars.

Reza Shah visiting a girls' school

Behind the Shah is his Prime Minister Mr Djam. Beside him is the Crown Prince. The Shah did more for education, including female education, than any of his predecessors. Even Harold Nicolson, who loathed him, admitted that he had 'a certain force and dignity' and 'fine eyes and chin'.

Reza Shah in exile
Deposed by Britain and Russia for his allegedly pro-German policies, Reza Shah was installed with his family in Johannesburg, where he died in 1944. His younger children are sitting around the table: his wives did not lunch with him.

Nevertheless Reza Shah, who disliked pomp and ceremony, lived very simply. His first wife Taj Malek and their children Mohammed Reza the Crown Prince and Princesses Shams and Ashraf lived in the Gulestan palace. To escape its associations with his predecessors, he built the much smaller Marble palace for himself and his second wife Ismat, a Qajar whom he had married before he ascended the throne. It was in a traditional Persian style, with walls encrusted with mosaic and mirrors. The Shah ate simple Persian food, meat and rice, and slept on a mattress on the floor. He was in his office by eight every morning.[8]

One of his greatest achievements was to give Persia a modern army, with many officers from the Cossack Brigade, who lacked the refinement of the upper classes and their ineffectiveness. Reza Shah was a military monarch, who spoke to ordinary conscripts and made sure they were well looked after. He used his army to suppress tribal separatism and imprison tribal chiefs. In contrast to the Qajars, Reza Shah did not come from a particular tribe or have a tribal power-base: it is said that he did not know the name of his own father. The powerful British protégé, the Arab Sheikh of Mohammerah, was taken prisoner while giving a drinking party for Persian officers during Ramadan on his yacht, the *Ivy*, out of sight of his own bodyguards. He died in custody in Tehran in 1936.

Reza Shah's court was so unsophisticated that it was said that only the servants knew how to behave. He was proud of the railways he built in Iran. But when Queen Nazli of Egypt brought her daughter Fawzia to marry the Crown Prince in 1939, she thought Iran was uncivilised. The electricity supply broke down and the water ran out on the train taking them to Tehran. There was a rush for places at the state banquet since the master of ceremonies did not know his job. Army officers had to take over.

Under Reza Shah Persia finally experienced the benefits and miseries of modernisation. He admired

Mustafa Kemal and one of Kemal's most daring and unpopular reforms, in 1925, had been to make it a crime to wear the fez, a symbol of the Ottoman Empire and religious conservatism. Reza Shah also took costume seriously. In 1928 he ordered all Persian males to wear European dress and the Pahlavi cap which had a brim, making prostration during prayer more difficult. In 1936 he went further. On 8 January Taj Malek and their daughters appeared with him unveiled and in European dress at Tehran high school. Thenceforth the veil was forbidden. Some old women, unable to bring themselves to appear in public without one, never left their houses again while Reza Shah remained on the throne.

His fall was sudden. He had risen to power as a British protégé; and in the summer of 1941 Britain turned on him. Britain and Russia were alarmed by the presence of three thousand Germans in Iran while German armies were at the gates of Moscow. The Shah wanted to remain neutral and refused to cooperate in the Allied war effort. When Britain and Russia invaded, the Shah knew resistance was useless and, to the relief of his subjects, abdicated. He drove down to Bander Abbas (now Bander Khomeini) on the Gulf; his car broke down and his baggage was plundered en route, although he managed to save a case which he had filled with Iranian soil. Like the last Ottoman Sultan he sailed away from his country on a British ship, to Bombay, Mauritius and finally Johannesburg, where he died in 1944.[9]

Some British officials thought of restoring the Qajars in the person of a nephew of Ahmad Shah who had served in the Royal Navy under the name of Lieutenant David Drummond; his father, the former Crown Prince, took him to lunch with Anthony Eden, the Foreign Secretary. However, he could not speak a word of Persian and the British minister in Tehran advised against the plan.[10] Reza Shah's son Mohammed Reza succeeded. In the first years of his reign he was a constitutional monarch content to observe, rather than command, events. The days of Persepolis, the 'fifth world power' and the Iranian imperial calendar were far away.

~10~
Central Asia

King Amanullah of Afghanistan in Paktya tribal dress

ONE reason for British supremacy in the Middle East after 1918 was the defeat of Germany and the eclipse of Russia (where it was involved, as in the supply of munitions to Mustafa Kemal, it could still inflict a major defeat on British policy). On 25 March 1918, during the Russian Civil War, the Soviet Union even recognised the independence of Khiva and Bokhara. However, a strong army was better protection than Soviet promises; and the Emir of Bokhara's army was, in the words of a British officer, 'unimpressive although profusely decorated with medals and orders'.

Clearly it was no match for the Red Army. The last Khan of Khiva was expelled from his capital in February 1920, and died a few months later in a Soviet prison hospital. Many people in Bokhara were opposed to the autocratic Emir, and supported the Soviet invasion in August 1920. On the night of 29 August the Emir fled from his palace disguised as a coachman. In the east of his emirate he rallied 2,500 soldiers and wrote to George V asking for the inclusion of Bokhara in the British Empire. But geography condemned central Asia to be controlled by Russia. In May 1921 the Emir finally fled to Afghanistan with his family and 500 followers. He was treated as the Emir of Afghanistan's guest and given an allowance, but in fact he was under close surveillance and lived by selling the jewels in the three crowns which he had managed to bring with him. The rest of his fortune, even when it had been deposited in European banks, found its way into Soviet hands.[1] He died in 1943. His family had to flee again after the Soviet invasion of Afghanistan in 1978 and now lives in Turkey.

The last incarnation of the independence of Bokhara was not its Emir but Enver Pasha. After 1918 he had led an adventurous life moving between Berlin and Moscow. Disappointed by Mustafa Kemal's continued success, he decided to play the Soviet card. In September 1920 he was the delegate of 'the revolutionaries of Tunisia, Algeria and Morocco' to the Council of the Peoples of the East in Baku. On 8 November 1921 he arrived in Bokhara, ostensibly to suppress resistance to the Soviets. Three days later he took to the mountains to lead the *basmatchis* or 'bandits' against his former employers. He knew little about central Asia and may have been driven to his last gamble by a desire to be worthy of his Ottoman wife, and by a feeling that he had come to the end of the road. The Emir appointed him commander of all Bokharan forces and he signed proclamations as 'Commander-in-Chief of all the forces of Islam, son-in-

Enver Pasha and Naciye Sultan in Berlin, 1920
Enver and his wife, still a devoted couple, lived in Berlin, where he had many German friends, until he moved to the Soviet Union in 1920.

Sayyid Mir Alim Kahn, last Emir of Bokhara (1910–20)
The last Emir was a traditional autocrat opposed to reforms. Some of his subjects supported the Soviet advance, and he died in exile in Afghanistan.

law of the Caliph and representative of the Prophet'. Using Ottoman titles and wearing an Ottoman uniform, he died leading a last heroic charge against the Soviets on 4 August 1922.[2]

Afghanistan also showed the importance of the Ottoman and Turkish bond to the monarchies of the Middle East. The Emir Habibullah, who had succeeded in keeping his country out of the First World War, was murdered in 1919, possibly at the instigation of his own son Amanullah, who took power after a struggle with Habibullah's brother Nasrullah. A brief war with Britain in 1919 secured Afghanistan's right to conduct its own relations with foreign powers.

Sardar Amanullah and his sisters, 1918
*Afghan princesses'
emancipation and love of
European dress later hastened
Amanullah's loss of his
throne.*

Thereafter Amanullah always remained if not anti-British, certainly different from those monarchs such as Reza Shah or Faisal 1 of Iraq, who owed their throne to British help. In 1921 he signed a treaty with the government of Mustafa Kemal in which Turkey was described as 'the guide of Islam' and 'the upholder of the Caliphate'. Turkish educational and military missions arrived to help modernise the country, and so many former Ottoman officers served in the Afghan army that they aroused resentment. In order to avoid British influence, Amanullah imported doctors and architects from Turkey, France or Germany rather than Britain or India.[3]

His main concern was the modernisation of his king-

Costume ball, Paghman, summer 1925
The ball takes place in the house of the Queen's sister Huriya (sitting on the floor, third from left) in the court suburb of Paghman. Among the guests are, third and fourth from left, sitting on chairs, King Amanullah and Queen Soraya, in Afghan and Bokharan dress respectively. Other guests are in Scottish, Afghan, Burmese and Japanese dress. This photograph shows that in 1925 the Afghan royal family and its friends thought, or pretended, that their own local dress was as exotic as Scottish or Japanese and therefore was suitable to wear at a costume ball.

dom. To this daunting task he brought impressive personal qualities. In 1922 a British diplomat wrote that 'His Majesty Amir [in 1923 as part of his policy of modernisation he became King] Amanullah Khan is himself probably the most interesting and complex character in his dominions... He has a tremendous appetite for work and except on the Friday holiday he is constantly employed from eight o'clock in the morning until midnight.'

For a time King Amanullah produced remarkable results. He founded many schools, usually named after himself or his beautiful wife Queen Soraya. In 1921 forty-five students, including the heir apparent, were sent to France. European costume was encouraged and even made compulsory in the court suburb of Paghman, and in certain districts of Kabul. At the beginning of his reign Amanullah roamed the bazaars in disguise to find out what his subjects were thinking. However, he gradually lost touch with public opinion, and his revolutionary changes and heavy taxation alienated the mullahs and the tribes.

He seemed to have lost all sense of proportion after his return from a tour of Europe and the Middle East in

June 1928. He failed to heed Reza Shah's advice to make sure of the loyalty of his army. Eight years before Reza Shah dared to attempt a similar measure in Persia, senior officials' wives in Afghanistan were compelled to unveil and wear European dress. Queen Soraya appalled her husband's subjects by her cloche hats, short skirts and scanty veil. In December 1928 a Tajik highwayman called Habibullah Ghazi Bacha-i-Saqao (Water Carrier's Son), took Kabul and assumed the title of Emir.[4] After attempting to resist in the provinces, Amanullah fled to India, and then to exile in Italy (chosen because the King of Italy had made him

Huriya, Khayriya and Soraya Tarzi, Kandahar, 1925
The Tarzi sisters brought back new ideas of dress and behaviour from their years in Europe and the Ottoman Empire. Queen Soraya was the first Muslim Queen to appear in public with her husband, before the Queens of Persia and Egypt, and wore a modern veil attached to the brim of her hat instead of a traditional veil. Her daring costume horrified most of her husband's subjects.

The Afghan state visit to Britain, March 1928
Left to right: King Amanullah; Queen Soraya; Mohammed Hassan Ziayi, aide-de-camp, cousin and brother-in-law of the King; Huriya, sister, and Abdul Wahab Tarzi, brother, of the Queen. King Amanullah returned from his visit to Europe determined to proceed even faster with the modernisation of Afghanistan.

Deputies at the Loya Jirgah, 2 September 1928
At the Loya Jirgah or assembly of tribal representatives, the King and Queen (top) are surrounded by subjects who have been made to wear European dress for the first time in their lives. Such compulsory modernisation was one cause of King Amanullah's overthrow a few months later.

Habibullah Ghazi, Kabul, 1 November 1929
Habibullah Ghazi had led the rising against King Amanullah. Shortly after this photograph was taken, he was shot in the moat around the erg in Kabul and his body was exposed in public.

King Zaher Shah, c. 1935
Modest and accessible, King Zaher Shah, a cousin of Amanullah, pursued a policy of modernisation, often against the wishes of the mullahs: hence fundamentalists' opposition to his possible restoration in 1988.

a Knight of the Annunziata, which gave him the title 'cousin of the King'). Like the late Shah of Iran, he failed because he lacked popular support and a secure power-base.

After ten months of chaos and looting, Habibullah was replaced by Amanullah's third cousin Nadir Shah. Nadir Shah practised a policy of cautious modernisation — even introducing a constitution in 1931 — until he was assassinated by a rival's servant in 1933, while distributing prizes to school-children. He was succeeded by his son Mohammed Zaher, who reigned until the proclamation of a republic in 1973 while he was abroad. He now lives in Rome, waiting to return to the throne.

~11~
The Fall of the Throne of Egypt

King Farouk, 1936

THE monarchy which replaced the Ottoman Empire as the most important in the Middle East was Egypt. At first this seemed unlikely, since in 1914 Britain disposed of the throne of Egypt as it pleased. It used the alleged pro-Ottoman sentiments of the Khedive Abbas Hilmi and his entourage to establish a protectorate and depose him while he was in Constantinople. Thereafter, he drifted between Constantinople, Switzerland and Vienna, a focus for fears and intrigues for years to come. He was replaced not by his son or his brother but by his uncle Hussein Kamil (1914–17) — known as *le père des fellahs* for his interest in agriculture — who took the title of Sultan.

However, there was a certain resilience in the House of Mohammed Ali. Its survival was partly due to the refusal of the ministers to serve 'under a throneless Protectorate'. The end of Ottoman suzerainty meant the end of restrictions on the size of the Egyptian army and navy. The ruler of Egypt could now award honours of his own instead of having to recommend his subjects for Ottoman honours. Since the Egyptian ruling class had as great an appetite for honours as any other, this gave the ruler a powerful weapon; and in 1915 Hussein Kamil created the Orders of Mohammed Ali and the Nile and designed a new court uniform.[1]

In 1917 he died after a banquet at Abdine palace. His son refused the succession out of personal distaste and respect for the rights of his brother-in-law Abbas Hilmi. In the end the throne went to the last surviving son of the Khedive Ismail, Prince Fouad, a short, fat man with an up-turned moustache. Brought up in Egypt, Italy, Constantinople and Paris, he was a man of the world, equally at home in Europe and the Middle East. He had served in the Italian army, had been considered for the throne of Albania and had earned the reputation of being 'everything which is Parisian, witty and amusing'. One of his chief amusements was gambling away his own, and part of his wife Shivekiar's, fortune. This so infuriated her brother that he shot at Fouad while Fouad was playing cards in the Mohammed Ali Club, the smartest in Cairo. Fouad was left with a bullet in his throat, and a voice like a barking dog, for the rest of his life.

When he succeeded to the throne in 1917, Britain tried to select his court as well as his government. Some of Fouad's ministers said that they wanted him to be 'a purely constitutional sovereign', while many members of his dynasty continued to regard the Khedive Abbas Hilmi as their *souverain légitime*, in the words of Princess Shivekiar, whom Fouad had since discarded.[2]

Nevertheless, helped by his splendid palaces and elaborate court, Fouad soon increased the power and prestige of the monarchy. As early as 1918 a British official reported that 'the etiquette of a reigning sovereign or something like it has been introduced at Abdine'. It is recorded in a lavish book of protocol issued by the Cabinet du Grand Chambellan in 1947, which codifies the practice of previous reigns. At the Egyptian court an elaborate order of precedence, with eighty-two categories, placed the Private Doctor of His Majesty and the First Chamberlain before senators and deputies, and required all officials to wear an *habit de cour*. A special etiquette governed the King's hunts and tea-parties, his visits to the mosque or the opera, and the award of royal decorations and audiences. The atmosphere of the court of Egypt was so deferential and so pervasive, and the monarch's palaces were so magnificent (unlike the Hashemites' humble residences in Baghdad and Amman), that it was difficult for him not to inspire respect.[3]

Moreover, Egypt was at the time a deferential, monarchical country. When a movement for independence from British control began at the end of the war, it is typical that it originated from a suggestion made by Prince Omar Toussoun, a cousin of Fouad, to Sa'ad Zaghloul at a tea-party at Ras el-Tine palace on 9 October 1918, that he form a *wafd* or delegation to ask for independence.[4] This movement was at first supported by the Sultan and many princes of the ruling family. As it grew more extremist, and violence against the British became more widespread (in 1919 a few republics were established in the Egyptian countryside), its relations with the monarchy deteriorated. But the monarchy was the principal beneficiary of the partial independence which the Wafd (now an organised political party) helped win from Britain in February 1922.

Fouad was proclaimed King of Egypt on 15 March 1922. Thereafter, although British troops remained in Cairo, and the High Commissioner retained the power to veto or suggest ministers, King Fouad dominated Egyptian politics. In 1922 a British diplomat wrote: 'The prestige of the King has risen since the Declaration of Independence. He still presides over the Council of Ministers' — a practice he maintained until his death.

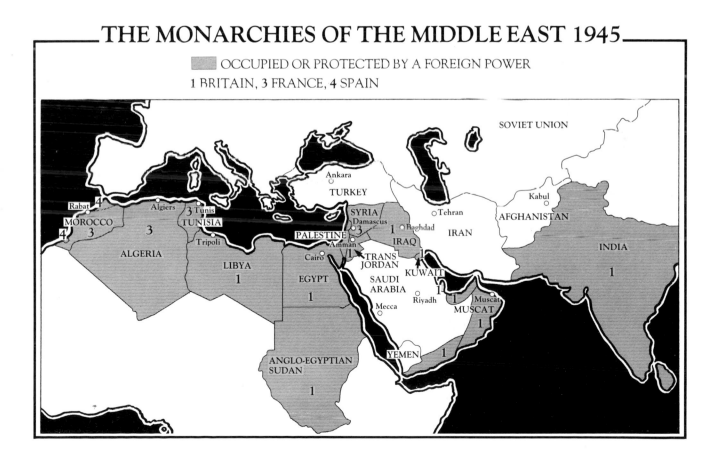

THE MONARCHIES OF THE MIDDLE EAST 1945

OCCUPIED OR PROTECTED BY A FOREIGN POWER
1 BRITAIN, 3 FRANCE, 4 SPAIN

Safiya Zaghloul
Sa'ad Zaghloul's wife Safiya was a pasha's daughter with close connections with the court. She was almost as popular as her husband and was called 'the mother of the Egyptians'.
Although after 1925 most upper-class Egyptian women went unveiled, they still wore a yashmak and long train for formal court occasions.

Adly Yeghen Pasha
A cousin of the King and an opponent of Zaghloul, Adly Yeghen Pasha was an important member of the 'Turkish' ruling class of Egypt. Three times Prime Minister, he was called 'the gentleman' for his negotiations with the British. He was President of the Senate and the Mohammed Ali Club when he died in 1933.

The 1922 constitution stated that 'the nation is the source of all power' and, in part because politicians could play the British residency and the palace against each other, Egypt had the freest parliament in the Middle East. However, King Fouad despised parliaments and would have preferred to behave as a traditional Muslim autocrat (if possible, Caliph as well). In 1923 the constitution was modified to increase the King's powers, and Lord Allenby wrote: 'All the Ministers were selected personally by the King.'[5] Even when there was a popular government in 1924 under Sa'ad Zaghloul, leader of the Wafd, a British diplomat wrote of Fouad: 'No appointment, however subordinate, was made without his consent.'[6] A figure such as Hassan Nachat Pasha, Director of the Royal Cabinet, 'young, dark, arrogant, and charming', and other members of the court, were crucial players in the political game, under the orders of their royal master. Although he was never popular, the King was able to ignore or change the constitution almost as he wished. In 1934 the British High Commissioner complained of 'the Palace's growing absorption of all power'.[7]

King Fouad grew rich as well as powerful. He had

King Fouad with princes and ministers

Although the occasion is informal, since the King is in a lounge suit, he is accompanied by princes and ministers in habits de cour. On the King's right is Mohammed Mahmoud, a Prime Minister whose dark skin once caused him to be expelled from the Gezireh Club. Behind the King is a master of intrigue, Ali Maher, future Director of the Royal Cabinet, Prime Minister and architect of the fall of King Farouk. On the King's left is his cousin Prince Omar Toussoun, historian, art-collector and uncrowned King of Alexandria, flanked by his sons Prince Said and Prince Hassan Toussoun. Their physical appearance is quite different from that of the native Egyptian on the right.

The Caliphate Conference, Cairo, 1926

After the abolition of the Caliphate by Mustafa Kemal in 1924, many Muslims felt like Catholics without a pope. This conference was secretly financed by King Fouad in the hope that it would support his ambitions to be Caliph. His candidature was unpopular and the institution lapsed.

been in debt when he ascended the throne but died a millionaire owning some of the finest land in Egypt.[8] He also strengthened his control over his own dynasty. At first Abbas Hilmi, 'the Khedive over the water', was as much a problem to him as 'the King over the water' had been to the Hanoverians in Great Britain. In 1924 he is described as 'a source of anxiety amounting to obsession'. No Egyptian politician who met Abbas Hilmi in Europe could expect to hold office under King Fouad in Egypt. The rhyme *Allah hai/Abbas gai* ('as God is alive, so Abbas will come back') was repeated everywhere. However, ruined by the crash of 1929, the ex-Khedive had to make terms. By a treaty in French and Arabic signed in 1931 he affirmed his loyalty to King Fouad and renounced his claims in return for 30,000 Egyptian pounds a year.[9]

One of the most cultivated kings of his day, King Fouad also devoted himself to raising the educational

Ladies and diplomats at the investiture of King Farouk
Queen Nazli and the princesses are on the left of the upper tier; below are ambassadors and their wives. Women of the royal family were still segregated at official ceremonies. The unveiled woman in the middle is Madame Mihalla, a Syrian Christian lady-in-waiting. The royal family had relations with so many Europeans that it employed Christian or Jewish ladies-in-waiting.

Investiture of King Farouk in parliament, July 1937
The princes of the dynasty are to the left, ministers to the right, of the throne. At the insistence of the Prime Minister Nahas Pasha, leader of the Wafd, who is reading a speech, the King's investiture was a modern and constitutional, rather than a traditional and Islamic, ceremony. Instead of receiving the homage of his subjects, the King swore an oath to observe the constitution.

level of his country. As a prince he had helped to found a modern university in Cairo in addition to the traditional Muslim university at the mosque of al-Azhar. As a king he founded innumerable charitable or cultural organisations, such as the Oeuvres d'Industrie Féminine and the Académie Royale Arabe. King Fouad also has the distinction of being the last great royal patron of history. He commissioned and subsidised monuments of erudition and fine printing, not all of them uncritical of his ancestors, such as the Grand Rabbi of Egypt's edition of Ottoman decrees concerning Egypt, and innumerable collections of diplomatic documents. Published in Cairo in French, they are an appropriately intelligent and cosmopolitan monument to King Fouad and his dynasty.

Like many products of the Ottoman world, King Fouad was abrupt with Egyptians, and behaved in a peremptory manner towards the enormous entourage of ministers, courtiers and under-secretaries who followed him wherever he went. His bad Arabic cannot have helped. Towards the end of his reign, however, an Englishman granted an audience could report that, although 'H.M.'s opinion of Egyptian officials did not seem high, [he did feel that there was] an improved standard among the young men [and that] the most efficient and hard-working officials and students were usually sons of poor men, relations of Pashas and Ministers being generally useless.'[10]

One of the native Egyptians whom he trusted most was his First Chamberlain Hassanein Pasha, who had been educated at Oxford and had married into the royal family. It was into Hassanein's care that King Fouad bequeathed his son Farouk when he died in 1936.

Posterity remembers Farouk as an obese debauchee who choked to death at the age of forty-four in a Rome restaurant. Contemporaries believed that he was full of promise. For many years after his accession, young, handsome and fluent in Arabic, King Farouk was even more popular with his subjects than King Ghazi of Iraq. They did not cheer, they danced for joy when he drove past in one of the red cars from the palace. Sheikh al-Maraghi, rector al-Azhar, called him 'the first King of Egypt who has direct contact with the people'. Sir Ronald Campbell, British ambassador from 1946 to 1950, found him 'very intelligent and quick' with 'a good deal of dignity of demeanour...an audience with him was usually stimulating if unproductive'. After

being received in audience, General de Gaulle called the King 'prudent, well informed, quick-witted'.[11] Praise from such a source cannot be solely due to the bond of shared anglophobia.

Moreover, King Farouk was interested in politics, and was able to maintain almost as much power as his father. Like King Fouad he was always surrounded by ministers, courtiers and photographers recording his activities. He dismissed Wafd ministries which he disliked in 1938 and 1944 and ministers who displeased the King soon resigned. The Director of the Royal Cabinet frequently became Prime Minister and the King's personal servants, such as a Sudanese called Idris, could be small dictators. 'Every prime minister had to have a good relation with the servants,' remembers one of the King's former ADCs. The King also helped to launch Egypt as leader of the Arab world. In 1945 Cairo became headquarters of the Arab League, and it was on King Farouk's personal initiative, despite his government's reluctance, that Egypt fought in the first Arab-Israeli war in 1948.

The Egyptian monarchy appeared so splendid, powerful and popular that King Farouk's ignominious end seems inexplicable. Many people have retreated into a personal explanation of events and place the blame on individuals or foreign powers. It is true that the King was surrounded by some overpowering personalities.

Ali Maher Pasha was a prominent and subtle

King Farouk and his household, 1937
Left to right: Edward Ford, the King's tutor, Mourad Mohsen Pasha, the King, Ahmed Hassanein Pasha, Raafat Bey. Standing: doctors and chamberlains. Hassanein was one of the most influential figures in the palace under King Farouk. The King never found enough time to study with his English tutor.

Wedding Banquet of King Farouk, Abdine palace, 1938
*Left to right: Princess Nimet (looking left), Queen Nazli and
two daughters, Queen Farida, King Farouk, Sultane Melek.
After the death of King Fouad the court of Egypt became more
modern, as the presence at this banquet of both male and
female members of the royal family suggests. Queen Farida
bore King Farouk three daughters. The marriage ended in
divorce in 1948.*

politician who used his influence over the King and his position as Director of the Royal Cabinet to make the palace, rather than the Wafd, the centre of political life. He deliberately kept the King away from English influences, such as Edward Ford, the tutor the English ambassador had hired to turn the King of Egypt into an English gentleman. Ali Maher, on the other hand, hoped to make King Farouk into an Islamic monarch, and even Caliph, by frequent lessons with Sheikh al-Maraghi and unofficial visits to mosques — without his ministers, so that only the King received applause. He also forged links between the palace and the Muslim Brotherhood, the powerful secret society which led the Muslim revival of the 1930s.

The British ambassador Sir Miles Lampson had been so pro-Arab that he had been called 'Let 'em have it Lampson'. At first he described Farouk as 'A nice simple boy — talks English well'. However, although they maintained appearances, he and King Farouk grew to detest each other. He continued to call Farouk 'the boy' after he became King and as early as 1937 talked of his deposition. After the outbreak of the Second World War, although officially neutral, Egypt was expected to help the British war effort. Ali Maher's government hedged its bets, and there were leaks of information from Egyptian sources to the Axis.

In the end in June 1940, despite a personal appeal to George VI, King Farouk was forced by Lampson to dismiss his own Prime Minister: no British monarch showed sympathy with any Middle Eastern monarch in this period. King Farouk's alleged pro-German lean-

Banquet in honour of the Crown Prince of Iran, Abdine palace, 1939

Left to right: Iranian chamberlain, Lady Lampson, Crown Prince of Iran, King Farouk, unidentified ambassadress, the British ambassador Sir Miles Lampson. The Crown Prince, the future Mohammed Reza Shah (1941–79), was in Cairo to marry the King's sister Fawzia. King Farouk looks bored and ill at ease, perhaps because of the proximity of the overbearing British ambassador.

Queen Nazli

Forceful and charming, Queen Nazli preferred the novels of Elinor Glyn to the traditions of the Egyptian ruling family. She broke with King Farouk in 1950 over her daughter's marriage to a Christian.

ings, which alarmed Lampson so much, were limited to assurances of goodwill by Egyptian to German diplomats in neutral capitals.[12] Germany regarded Abbas Hilmi, or another cousin Prince Abbas Halim, rather than Farouk, as its candidate for the throne of Egypt.

However, Lampson wanted a purge of the palace and a Wafd government headed by his friend Nahas Pasha, the most popular politician in Egypt. On the evening of 4 February 1942 three British tanks took up position in the courtyard of Abdine palace. Since the King thought resistance was useless, the Royal Guard stayed in its barracks. The ambassador arrived in his Rolls-Royce, escorted by armoured cars. Leaving a group of British officers, armed to the teeth, outside, Lampson brushed past the Grand Chamberlain, stormed into the King's study and handed him a letter of abdication (since no clean paper was available in the British embassy in wartime, it was dirty). The King was ready to sign, but was stopped by the words whispered by Hassanein: 'Think what you are doing.' Farouk agreed to let Nahas form an entirely Wafd government which imposed restrictions on his power. Lampson kept Farouk on the throne to check the Wafd and to prevent trouble in the Egyptian army. He wrote to the Foreign Secretary that he could not have enjoyed the evening more.

King Farouk, however, felt defeated: he was shown to be, in the end, a pawn in the hands of the British. In retrospect the events of 4 February 1942 seem to supporters of the monarchy to have been 'the beginning of the end of Egypt'; for they helped persuade Nasser and the Free Officers to plan the coup d'état which overthrew King Farouk in 1952. One of the Free Officers, the future President Sadat, wrote: 'Up till now the King had been symbolic with the patriotic idea and the violation of the royal palace was regarded by all patriotic Egyptians as an outrage against Egypt herself.'[13]

Another humiliation for the King came from his adored mother Queen Nazli. Charming and intelligent, she had been kept in the harem by King Fouad while other women of her class led increasingly emancipated lives. King Fouad and Queen Nazli had innumerable quarrels over her clothes, his servants, Farouk's nanny Mrs Naylor, whom the Queen detested, and her desire to lead a modern life. After his death she went wild. 'You see, Mr Ford, I have never known the love of a man,' she hissed to her son's tutor while they were visiting England in 1937. She

intended to make up for her lack of experience.

She tried in vain to be discreet but her lovers included Hassanein Pasha (who may have been her second husband). She consulted the future through table-turning — a decision-making process which suited her daughters since they could usually fix the tables. When she allowed her daughter Fathia to marry a Christian in San Francisco in 1950, the King expelled them both from the royal family. Queen Nazli died in California in 1978, after Fathia had been murdered by her ex-husband and she herself had (allegedly) turned Catholic.

Queen Nazli was not the only problem which his own family posed for Farouk. He had no son and the heir to the throne was his much older cousin Prince Mohammed Ali, younger brother of the Khedive Abbas Hilmi. The prince tried to give good advice but, as Edward Ford recorded: 'It is said that he has strong views when talking with other people but that face to face with the boy he crumples and becomes like the rest of the courtiers.' At this time Prince Mohammed Ali was a forceful man of the world of sixty-two; Farouk was only sixteen and had been King for under a year.[14]

Although Prince Mohammed Ali was pro-British, he was the most respected member of the royal family. He knew and received everyone of prominence, sheikhs, journalists, and leaders of the Wafd. Although Suzanne Hémon, the Frenchwoman he kept secluded in his splendid palace of Manyal, would hardly have been a suitable consort for a Muslim monarch, Prince Mohammed Ali thought that as a younger son, rather than a nephew, of Khedive Tewfik, he had a better claim to the throne than Farouk (as the King noticed, on his sole visit to Manyal, neither he nor his father were represented among the family portraits which lined the walls of Prince Mohammed Ali's throne-room). He grew to hate and despise the King: in 1944 he was complaining to Lampson 'that the young Monarch was definitely vindictive and cracked'.[15]

As the King became wilder and less popular after 1945, Manyal became a rival to Abdine; and Prince Mohammed Ali and his relations discussed the King's deposition with mounting desperation. However, like the cousins of Nicholas II before the Russian Revolution, they could not agree on a precise *modus operandi*. Some people believe that, if they had, there would still be a king in Egypt today.

Prince Mohammed Ali in the garden of Manyal
*Prince Mohammed Ali was heir to the throne until the birth of
Ahmad Fouad, King Farouk's only son, in 1952. He died in
exile in Switzerland in 1955.*

Queen Farida
At first her marriage to King Farouk was happy. The court of Egypt was so modern that the Queen looked like a Hollywood star.

Queen Farida and Nabila Ayesha Hassan (a great-granddaughter of Khedive Ismail) in uniform
The Queen of Egypt is going to a ceremony of the murshidette or Egyptian girl-guides, wearing their uniform. This was the first time that she attended an official ceremony without the yashmak. Despite her concern over the public's reaction, she was cheered in the streets of Cairo.

King Farouk epitomised and exaggerated the problems of a Middle Eastern monarch. Even more than the last Ottomans and Qajars, he was torn in different directions by having too many parts to play. He was expected to be both a modern monarch and an Islamic ruler. He inherited the autocratic instincts of his father, but had to operate within the framework of a constitution. He was head of an independent country, but it contained more British than Egyptian troops. He wanted to be the hero of the Arabs as well as King of Egypt. He loved his people and told Churchill of his eagerness to improve the condition of the poor. But he did not do much about it. He was surrounded by courtiers who encouraged him to enjoy himself and flattered him day and night — 'He would have been very, very good if he had good people around him,' remembers one of his ADCs. Torn between East and West, old and new, the mosque and the nightclub, he

was a monarch in search of an identity.

Trapped in such a jungle, it is not surprising that the King took refuge in pleasure. It was easy to find, for Cairo under King Farouk was one of the most cosmopolitan and sophisticated cities in the world, 'better than London or Paris' insist survivors. It became the Hollywood, the Fleet Street and the Oxford of the Arab world and, after the establishment of the Arab League in Cairo in 1945, its political capital as well. In the Second World War it was also an Allied headquarters and the centre of the air routes of the world. Every European language, except German, could be heard in its streets. Every statesman passed through, from Chiang Kai Shek to King Abdul Aziz al-Sa'ud. Freya Stark wrote in her memoirs: 'No one can forget the gaiety and the glitter of Cairo while the desert war went on.'

In the middle of a world war the court of Egypt rein 1938, they 'received the whole country'. Such official receptions were strictly segregated and in the palace (although no longer outside) women still wore an elegant white yashmak over the lower half of their faces. A first night at the Cairo opera was more splendid than anything rationed and devastated Europe could offer. The white yashmaks of the ladies added to the glamour of the occasion. Three beautiful Ottoman princesses who had married into the Egyptian royal family barely threw a glance at their in-laws.

However, Queen Farida helped ensure that at the court of Egypt women began, on certain occasions, to be entertained at the same time as men. The handsome young King and Queen gave parties which over-

The sisters of King Farouk, Lake Geneva, 1937
Left to right: Princess Fathia, Princess Fawzia, Princess Faika and Princess Faiza. The first was murdered by her husband; the second became Empress of Iran; the third devoted herself to good works; and the fourth was equally tireless in attending parties and opening hospitals. Like their brother, the princesses were given names beginning with F to commemorate Feryal, the adored mother of their father King Fouad.

captured the splendour and panache of the reign of the Khedive Ismail. It was run by Zulficar Pasha, an impeccable Grand Chamberlain, with an unrivalled knowledge of court protocol, who had served for fifty years in the palace, under five different rulers of Egypt. When he was lying on his death-bed in 1942, his last words were to dictate a change in the order of precedence at a banquet in Abdine palace.

The King's beautiful, popular and intelligent first wife Queen Farida remembers that, after their wedding

The Empress Fawzia of Iran
The most beautiful of King Farouk's sisters, the Empress Fawzia disliked life at the court of Tehran and returned to Egypt looking like a skeleton in 1947. She still lives there, with her second husband Ismail Shirin.

Nabila Ayesha Hassan and her governess Miss Machray
Miss Machray was one of the many British governesses employed in the courts of the Middle East. She had been a lady-in-waiting of Nabila Ayesha Hassan's aunt before helping to bring her up.

Princess Nimet Moukhtar and Princess Hadidja Abbas Halim visiting a workshop founded by the Khediva Emina, 1 June 1940
Princess Nimet Moukhtar, a daughter of the Khedive Ismail, was one of the most respected members of the royal family and had frequently reconciled King Fouad and Queen Nazli. Here she is with her niece, a daughter of the Khedive Tewfik.

The *galerie des ancêtres*, Palais Shivekiar, Cairo
The House of Mohammed Ali was immensely proud of its history. Princess Shivekiar placed a colossal statue of King Farouk, whom she often entertained in this palace, at the end of a gallery lined with busts of their ancestors.

whelmed such visitors as Princess Ashraf, daughter of Reza Shah, on her way back from Johannesburg. She wrote: 'Egyptian court life evoked the glitter and splendour of the oriental fairy tales with perhaps a soupçon of Versailles...I thought the women of the Egyptian court very lovely and fashionable.'[16]

Cairo seethed with parties: '...and they were always exquisite... At one time we had five kings at our parties', remembers one survivor (Greece, Albania, Yugoslavia, Bulgaria and Egypt). Princesses danced all night. A party given by one of the King's beautiful

sisters lasted a week. In the magical Ottoman-Italian palace of Choubra, where the great Mohammed Ali had watched ladies of his harem swimming in the pool, his descendants performed in *tableaux vivants* for the benefit of the Mohammed Ali Foundation.

Princesses competed as to who gave the party where the King stayed longest. The most hospitable was his father's first wife, the legendary Princess Shivekiar. She had since consoled herself with a succession of handsome young husbands and gave a huge party every year in honour of King Farouk on his birthday in her

A ball in Cairo

It is Cairo in wartime: British officers and Egyptian princesses are at a ball given by a cousin of King Farouk, Princess Emina Toussoun. The woman in a black dress, Princess Fatima Toussoun, was linked with King Farouk but left Egypt and married a Brazilian prince.

palace in Cairo. In 1945 at a dance for eight hundred people, Sir Miles Lampson, now Lord Killearn, wrote that it was '...as always, beautifully done. I do not think one could see anywhere a collection of prettier women or more magnificent jewels. Our hostess was resplendent in an emerald necklace of colossal size.' Every guest received a silver paper-knife engraved with the date. Princess Shivekiar was so fond of parties that at her last ball, when she was very ill, she had her bedroom door left open, so that she could listen to the sounds of revelry below. At such balls it is said that the King acquired his taste for gambling and seduction, occupations which soon took up much of his time.

King Farouk began to try to live like other people. So royal and dignified when receiving the British ambassador or the Prime Minister of Egypt, on other occasions he behaved quite differently. He often dropped in on friends in the RAF or spent the night at the Auberge des Pyramides (the Lampsons were sometimes at the next table) or on the roof of the Semiramis Hotel. One evening he flung coloured pompoms at the occupants of the nearby tables; 'the stuffier the people the more he roared with laughter'.

A stronger character, like his own father or King Faisal I of Iraq, might have surmounted the temptations and problems of the throne of Egypt and reigned with success. However, Farouk was less intelligent and forceful and had become king when he was only sixteen. He had no real friends and preferred the company of servants, such as Pulli, the Italian electrician in the palace. He was not a bad man: Queen Farida remembers him as 'very, very lonely'. They were divorced in 1948, long after he had ceased to be faithful to her. His second wife Queen Narriman, an Egyptian girl he married in 1951 in an attempt to restore his popularity, found the King kinder and simpler than the engineer who later became her second husband.

Yet out of the contradictions in Farouk's character

King Farouk on a shoot
The King became increasingly fat after a serious car accident in 1943. He enjoyed shooting, and lying about the number of birds he killed.

King Farouk welcoming King Victor Emmanuel III of Italy, Alexandria, 1946
The King of Italy has lost his throne and come to live in Egypt. The two dynasties had a tradition of exchanging hospitality. King Farouk's father Fouad had been sheltered in Italy by King Victor Emmanuel's father King Umberto; and King Farouk himself went to live in Italy after he lost his throne in 1952.

and position a monster emerged. Even when he was sixteen, his tutor Ford had noticed that he stayed in bed half the morning and that 'his showmanship and his sense of possession are perhaps the two strongest parts of his make-up'.[17] As he grew older, his sense of possession became a mania. He acquired thousands of gold boxes, match-box labels, Fabergé objects, sticks, coins, stamps, guns and swords. His visits to private houses were as dreaded as Queen Mary's. It took two weeks for Sotheby's to sell his collections (and many of his ancestors' possessions) in 1954. Where he had not inherited a palace, he built a 'rest-house', even in the middle of the Second World War.

Food had always been one of the chief pleasures of the monarchs of the Middle East. King Farouk ate voraciously between meals as well as after them. He soon became one of the fattest kings in history.

In the end he was so unhappy that he wanted to go. Like other threatened monarchs he turned to Europe. Once a source of danger for the monarchs of the Middle East, Europe was now their second home. Exile held few terrors for monarchs who spoke French as a second language, ate European food, read European books, consulted European doctors and had accounts in European banks. The last Qajars amd Ottomans chose France; the Regent of Iraq wanted to retire to England; the Afghan royal family preferred Italy; later exiles have settled in America.

King Farouk knew French, Italian and English as well as Arabic: he had had an English nanny and spoke English with his sisters. He began to lose interest in Egypt and to take holidays in Europe: the *Mahroussa* spent the summer on the Côte d'Azur rather than the coast of Egypt. The King knew about the Free Officers' plans for a coup. Indeed, just as Mehmed VI helped to engineer his own downfall by promoting Mustafa Kemal, so the origin of the Free Officers who overthrew Farouk lies in the secret society, the Ring of Iron, created by Ali Maher to prevent officers being attracted by the Wafd and to draw them around the throne. The King's former tutor Aziz Ali al-Masri was their inspiration, Ali Maher (who was to hand the King his letter of abdication) their chief political ally.

When the coup d'état took place in 1952, it seemed almost as much of a relief to the King as it was to his people. Farouk said: 'You have done what I always intended to do myself.'[18] He led a life of pleasure and loneliness in Italy, abandoned by most of his friends (except his two faithful Albanian bodyguards); Pulli did not telephone when he visited Italy. King Farouk had been his own worst enemy and the architect of his own downfall. The coup of 1952 led to dictatorship in Egypt and revolutions in much of the Middle East. Yet sitting in a flat in Kensington a survivor of his court remembers: 'He could be terrible but sometimes he was a darling. Poor Farouk!'

Conclusion

New Monarchs for Old

THE history of the Middle East between 1869 and 1945 is largely the history of its monarchs and dynasties. If by 1945 Egypt and Turkey were more advanced, and Morocco and Persia more backward, than their neighbours, this was partly due to the attitude of their dynasties towards modernisation. The contribution of the Hashemites to Arab nationalism was immeasurable. King Abdul Aziz al-Sa'ud created Sa'udi Arabia, as his hated rival King Abdullah did Jordan.

The ruling dynasties were important in part because they had such vigour. In Europe most dynasties were exhausted stocks, unable to produce more impressive figures than Nicholas II or George V. In India most princes were frivolous or powerless. It was a different story in the Middle East. No European dynasty in this period produced a monarch with the subtlety of Abdul Hamid, the drive of Reza Shah, the political skill of King Faisal of Iraq or the genius of Abdul Aziz al-Sa'ud. Whatever their personal defects, such figures had immense impact on the lives of their subjects. One reason was that in the Middle East the court and the government were still intertwined. The monarch's palace — Yildiz, Gulestan or the *erg* in Kabul — was still the centre of power, and contained the offices which administered the country. Even when there was a parliament and a constitution, as in Egypt and Iraq, the monarch and his court officials still wielded enormous power.

The fate of peoples without a monarchy shows its importance in the Middle East. Algerians and Palestinians suffered more than Tunisians and Jordanians, whose ruling dynasties protected them from extreme forms of imperialism such as annexation or colonisation. Indeed, from the point of view of the dynasties which reigned in the Middle East, imperialism was a potentially useful passing phase. However distasteful the presence of an imperialist power might be, it could be used to modernise the power-base of the monarchy. Both the Egyptian and Moroccan monarchies emerged from their occupation, by Britain and France respectively, stronger than before. But for British support, neither the Hashemites nor the Pahlavis would have acquired a throne.

However, the fall of the most important dynasty in the Middle East, the Ottomans, was due in part to the Sultan's miscalculation about the power and determination of the British Empire. With the end of the Ottoman Empire the monarchies of the Middle East lost their supreme model. It was to the Ottoman Empire that leaders from Tunisia to Afghanistan had turned for guidance and protection when faced with the incursions of the modern age and European imperialism.

Years later, the most anti-Ottoman of the Hashemites, King Abdullah of Jordan, came to regret the Arab Revolt which he had helped to launch. In his memoirs he blamed Arabs for 'turning blindly towards the West', and wrote of the Turks, 'at least they remained Turks in everything'. That is to say, the political, religious and cultural heritage of the Ottoman Empire was so strong that European ideas and customs became less European and more Ottoman when practised in the Ottoman Empire. By definition the Ottoman Empire (unlike some of its successors) could never be an imitation of, or feel inferior to, Europe. Even its official architectural style was more distinctive than that of its successors. At the coronation of George VI, attended by potentates from every corner of the British Empire, Abdullah remarked that it was just like the *Selamlik*, when the Padishah went to mosque every Friday.

For the people of the Middle East the loss of the Ottoman Empire was hardly less serious. In retrospect it was a better champion of Arab unity than subsequent Arab regimes. The structure of the Ottoman Empire was sufficiently solid, and jobs in its service sufficiently attractive, to prevent a catastrophic emigration of talent such as the Middle East has experienced since 1945. The loss of Constantinople deprived the peoples of the Middle East (not only Turks and Arabs, but also Afghans, Bokharans and Persians) of a great international capital where leaders were educated, books and newspapers published, ideas exchanged and careers advanced, on a scale equal to any city in the world. No lasting substitute has since emerged, except for Cairo in the decades before 1952.

The power of the monarchs of the Middle East in this period suggests that the great Arab historian, Ibn Khaldun, was correct when he wrote that 'royal authority is an institution that is natural to mankind'. Subsequent events have confirmed his analysis. Since 1945 many countries of the Middle East have endured the installation, under the name of republics, of regimes which are parodies of monarchy. In many 'republics' of the Middle East the cult of the ruler's personality, the concentration of power in his hands, the influence of his family and the intensity of his security precautions are greater than in any conventional monarchy. Oppressed by forms of tyranny inconceivable to an earlier age, many subjects of these modern monarchs miss their former masters.

Courtiers in the Golden Hall, Manyal
*Built on an island in the Nile, in a variety of neo-Islamic styles,
and filled with treasures inherited or collected by Prince
Mohammed Ali, Manyal still evokes the vanished splendour of
the courts of the Middle East.*

Notes

After first reference, books are referred to by the author's name in italic type.

Introduction

1. Franz-Josef, *Briefe . . . an Kaiserin Elizabeth*, 2 vols, Wien 1966, 1, 122, 125 Franz-Josef to Elizabeth, 15, 20 November 1869; Eugène de Fromentin, *Voyage en Egypte*, 1935, p.127.

2. Roger Owen, *The Middle East in the World Economy 1800-1914*, 1983, p.105; Jean Ganiage, *L'Expansion Coloniale de la France sous la Troisième République*, 1968, p.65; Firuz Kazemzadeh, *Russia and Britain in Persia 1864-1914*, New Haven, 1968, p.15.

3. A. Farley, *The Decline of Turkey*, 1870, p.27, Fouad Pasha to Sultan Abdul Aziz, 3 January 1869.

4. Anne K.S. Lambton, *Theory and Practice in Medieval Persian Government*, 1980, pp.420, 424, 433, 436.

1 Long Live our Padishah!

1. Hon. Mrs William Grey, *Journal of a Visit to Egypt, Constantinople, etc.*, 1969, p.170; W.H. Russell, *A Diary in the East during the Tour of the Prince and Princess of Wales*, 1869, p.119.

2. Carter V. Findlay, *Bureaucratic Reform in the Ottoman Empire 1789–1922*, Princeton, 1982, p.386; Roderic H. Davison, *Reform in the Ottoman Empire*, Princeton, 1963, p.242; King Abdullah, *Memoirs*, 1950, p.40.

3. Sir Henry F. Woods, *Spunyarn from the Strands of a Sailor's Life*, 2 vols, 1924, II,12.

4. Ismail Kemal Bey, *Memoirs*, 1920, p.93.

5. *Woods*, II, 224; A Consul's Daughter, *The Peoples of Turkey*, 2 vols, 1878, I, 247; *Grey*, p.162.

6. Pierre Crabitès, *Ismail the Maligned Khedive*, 1933, pp.175, 201, reports by Abraham of 8.7, and 29.10.1871; Gordon Waterfield, *Layard of Nineveh*, 1963, p.373.

7. *Crabitès*, p.197, report by Abraham, 18.9.1871.

8. Ali Haidar Midhat, *The Life of Midhat Pasha*, 1903, p.67.

9. Charles Mismer, *Souvenirs du Monde Mussulman*, 1892, p.105; Marcel Colombe, 'Une Lettre d'un Prince Egyptien du XIXe Siècle au Sultan Abdul Aziz', *Orient*, V, 1958, pp.26, 35, 37; for a striking example of Ottoman freedom of language see W.S. Blunt, *Gordon at Khartoum*, 1911, p.307, conversation with Ahmed Vefyk, 20.10.1884.

10. Sir Henry G. Elliot, *Some Revolutions and Other Diplomatic Experiences*, 1922, p.231, despatch of 25.5.1876; A. Gallenga, *Two Years of the Eastern Question*, 2 vols, 1877, II, 87, 89; *Midhat*, p.86; *Ismail Kemal*, p.119.

11. *Gallenga*, II, 126; Sir Charles Eliot, *Turkey in Europe*, 1900, p. 365, cf. Sir Harry Luke, *Cities and Men*, 3 vols, II, p.57.

12. A.D. Alderson, *The Structure of the Ottoman Dynasty*, Oxford, 1956, p.13; *Midhat*, pp.97,104; Elizabeth Longford, *Victoria R.I.*, 1976, pp.515-7.

13. *Davison*, p.403.

14. Anna Bowman Dodds, *In the Palaces of the Sultan*, 1904, p.63; William Crown Prince of Germany, *Memoirs*, 1921, p.50; *Waterfield* p. 372; Arminius Vambéry, *The Story of my Struggles*, 2 vols, 1904, II, p.373.

15. *Ismail Kemal*, pp.219, 269; *Waterfield*, p.438; Nikki Keddie, *Sayyid Jamal al-din 'al-Afghani'*, Los Angeles, 1981, p.151; Pierre Bardin, *Algériens et Tunisiens dans l'Empire Ottoman de 1848 à 1914*, Marseille, 1979, pp.92, 128, 149.

16. Vambéry, 'Personal Recollections of Abdul Hamid and his Court', *Nineteenth Century and After*, June 1909, CCCLXXXVIII, p.989; *Findlay*, p.276.

17. PRO FO 800/32 f. 104 report by Vambéry, June 1980; M.A. Griffiths, 'The Reorganisation of the Ottoman Army under Abdul Hamid II 1880–1897', (unpublished Ph.D. thesis), UCLA, 1966, pp.vii, 39, 45, 42, 45, 57, 103-4, 109.

18. *Waterfield*, pp.414-5; *Bardin*, p.257, despatch of Paul Cambon, 25 January 1892; *Eliot*, p.146; Théodore Blancard, *Les Mavroyennis*, 2 vols, 1909, II, p.440.

19. H. Thorossian, *Histoire de l'Arménie et du Peuple Arménien*, 1957, pp.134-40; Sir Telford Waugh, *Turkey Yesterday, Today and Tomorrow*, 1930, p.49.

20. *Ismail Kemal*, p.234; Stanford, J. and Ezel Kural Shaw, *History of the Ottoman Empire and Modern Turkey*, 2 vols, Cambridge, 1975-7, II, 230.

21. *Eliot*, p.134; Colin L. Smith, *The Embassy of Sir William White at Constantinople 1886–1891*, 1957, p.157, despatch of 4.7.1885.

22. Mrs, Max Muller, *Letters from Constantinople*, 1897, pp.53, 57; George Dorys, *Abdul Hamid Intime*, troisième èdition 1903, pp.109-10; interview with Prince Osman Nami Osmanoglu, July 1984; *Dodds*, p.70.

23. *Eliot*, p.92; *Findlay*, p.230.

24. Full description of the *Selamlik* can be found in *Woods*, II, 224-33; *Muller*, pp.94, 191; Frances Eliot, *Diary of an Idle Woman in Constantinople*, 1893, pp.216-20; William J.J. Spry, *Life on the Bosphorus*, 1895, p.51; *Dodds*, pp.35-52; cf. HRH Prince Nicholas of Greece, *My Fifty Years*, 1929, p.201.

25. G.F. Abbott, *Turkey in Transition*, 1909, p.239; Bernard Lewis, *The Evolution of Modern Turkey*, 1961, p.191; Aubrey Herbert, *Ben Kendim*, 1919, p.257; George Stitt, *A Prince of Arabia*, 1948, p.97.

26. Feroz Ahmad, *The Young Turks*, Oxford, 1969, p.28; *Abbott*, pp.172, 245.

27. Sir W.M. Ramsay, *The Revolution in Constantinople and Turkey*, 1909, pp.69, 71, 91, diary for 22 April 1909; *Abbott*, pp.252, 260; PRO FO 800/32 f. 103 report by Vambéry, June 1890; *Woods*, II, p.112; Lord d'Abernon, *Portraits and Appreciations*, 1931, p.203.

28. AH 48/160 report from Rashid Mumtaz, 1908; Maurice Baring, *Letters from the Near East*, p.49, letter of 2 May 1909.

29. M. Izzedin, 'Le Palais sous les deux derniers Sultans', *Revue de l'Ecole Nationale des Langues Orientales*, 1965, p.181; *Stitt*, p.151; Liman von Sanders, *Five Years in Turkey*, Annapolis, 1928, p.4.

30. AH 46/172, 248 reports by Rashid Mumtaz, 2 May 1910, 10 October 1911; AH 48/61, 68 reports by Rashid Mumtaz, 1912; AH 67/57 Damad Ferid to Abbas Hilmi, 3 September 1912.

31. AH 70/83 report by Sakakini Bey, 9 May 1912; William I. Shorrock, *French Imperialism in the Middle East*, Madison, 1976, p.168; AH 41/324, 344 Zeki Pasha to Abbas Hilmi, 8 December 1912, 28 March 1913.

32. *Ahmad*, pp.135, 139; Margaret Fitzherbert, *The Man who was Greenmantle*, 1983, pp.83, 126; James Goldberg, *The Foreign Policy of Sa'udi Arabia*, Cambridge Mass., 1986, p.106; AH 195/83 Jelal al-din Pasha to Abbas Hilmi, 31 March 1914.

2 Khedives and Pashas

1. *Crabitès*, p.154.

2. J.C. McCoan, *Egypt as it is*, New York, 1877, p.56; Alexander Schölch, *Egypt for the Egyptians*, Oxford, 1981, pp 107-09.

3. *McCoan*, p.91; *Grey*, pp.19, 147; Emine Foat Tugay, *Three Centuries*, 1963, p.191.

4. Alfred J. Butler, *Court Life in Egypt*, 1888, pp.13, 203; Edwin de Leon, *The Khedive's Egypt*, 1877, pp.337-9; William Howard Russell, *The Prince of Wales's Tour*, 1877, p.57.

5. *Tugay*, pp.257-8; *Grey*, p.26; 'One who knows them well', *Khedives and Pashas* 1884, pp.5, 7, 11; *de Leon*, p.172; Jacques Berque, *Egypt, Imperialism and Revolution*, 1972, p.49.

6. John Marlowe, *Spoiling the Egyptians*, 1974, pp.119, 135; *de Leon*, p.175.

7. F. Robert Hunter, *Egypt under the Khedives 1805-1879*, Pittsburgh, 1984, pp. 65, 181, 183; *Crabitès* p.154.

8. *Owen*, pp.135, 140; Paul Cambon, *Correspondance*, 3 vols, 1940-6, I, 353, Cambon to his mother, 27.12.1891; *Blunt, Gordon at Khartoum*, p.547, Arabi to Blunt, 2.6.1884.

9. *Schölch*, p.33; AH 133/3 memoirs by Abbas Hilmi.

10. *Schölch*, passim.

11. *Schölch*, p.23.

12. *Blunt, Secret History*, pp.159-60; *Schölch* pp.163, 186; Ronald Robinson and John Gallagher with Alice Denny, *Africa and the Victorians*, 1961, p.100.

13. *Blunt, Secret History*, p.172; *Schölch*, pp.172, 311, 241; Hassan Adali, 'Documents pertaining to the Egyptian Question in the Yildiz Collection in the Başbakanlik Arşivi', in P.M. Holt ed., *Political and Social Change in Modern Egypt*, 1968, pp.55, 57.

14. *Blunt, Gordon at Khartoum*, p.36, Arabi, 'Memorandum', 12.1882. p.547, Arabi to Blunt 2.6.1884; M.E. Chamberlain 'The Alexandria Massacres of June 1882 and the British Occupation of Egypt', *Middle Eastern Studies*, XII, pp.16, 23 suggests that Tewfik was an instigator of the massacres; *Berque*, p.111.

15. *Robinson and Gallagher*, p.131, Baring to Granville, 9.10.1883; Robert Tignor, *Modernisation and British Colonial Rule in Egypt 1882-1914*, Princeton, 1966, p.65, Baring to Granville, 7 January 1884; *Berque*, p.124.

16. Berque, p.152; John Marlowe, Cromer in Egypt, 1970, p.149.

17. Francis Adams, The New Egypt, 1893, p.144; AH 133/9 memoirs of Abbas Hilmi.

18. Tignor, p.155; Cromer to Lord Salisbury, 15 April 1892; Philip Magnus, Kitchener, p.84.

19. Tignor, p.160; Marlowe, Cromer in Egypt, p.106; Lutfi al-Sayyid Marsot, Egypt under Cromer, 1968, p.139.

20. Agatha Christie, An Autobiography, 1977, p.168.

21. Butler, pp. 64, 124-6; Tugay, p. 227; Arthur Goldschmidt jr., 'The Egyptian National Party 1892-1919' in Holt, Political and Social Change in Modern Egypt, pp.170-1.

22. Magnus, p.272.

3 Beys and Sultans

1. Mougi Smida, Khéreddine, Tunis 1970, pp.370, 387; Jamil M. Abun-Nasir, A History of the Maghrib, second edn, Cambridge, 1975, p.273.

2. Herbert Vivian, Tunisia and the Modern Barbary Pirates, 1899, p.11.

3. N.A. Ziadeh, Sanusiya, Leiden, 1958, pp.62-3.

4 Jean Miège, Le Maroc et l'Europe, 4 vols, 1961-3, IV, p.176; H.M.P. de La Martinière, Morocco,1889, p.325n.

5. Walter B. Harris, The Land of an African Sultan, 1889, p.196; Miège, III, 198, 200n; Eugène Aubin, Le Maroc d'Aujourd'hui, 1904, p.173.

6. Aubin, p.134; Philip Durham Trotter, Our Mission to the Court of Morocco in 1880, Edinburgh,1887, p.99; Budgett Meakin, The Moorish Empire, 1899, pp.194, 199.

7. Aubin, pp.178, 195-208.

8. Aubin, p.170; Trotter, pp.115-17.

9. Harold Nicolson, Lord Carnock, 1930, pp.117-18; Veyre, pp.71, 85.

10. Arthur Leared, Morocco and the Moors, second edn, 1891, p.239.

11. Alan Scham, Lyautey in Morocco, Berkeley 1970, pp.54, 58, 193, 210; G.H. Selous, Appointment in Fez, 1956, p.170.

12. Scham, p.224; André Maurois, Marshal Lyautey, 1931, p.180; Pierre Lyautey, Lyautey l'Africain, 4 vols, 1953-7, IV, 18, 81, Lyautey to the Président du Conseil, 24.10.1920, to Gouraud, 23.7.1920; Jean Lacouture, Cinq Hommes et la France, 1961, p.183.

4 Shahs and Mullahs

1. PRO FO 800/32 f. 101 report by Vambéry, June 1890.

2. S.G.W. Benjamin, Persia and the Persian Question, 1887, p.191; E.Y. Yarshater, 'Observations on Nasser al-din Shah' in Edmund Bosworth and Carole Hillenbrand eds, Qajar ran from 1800 to 1925, Edinburgh, 1984, p.7.

3. Iraj Afshar, 'Some Remarks on the Early History of Photography in Iran', in Bosworth and Hillenbrand, p.276, diary for 10 January 1890.

4. James Bassett, Persia the Land of the Imams, New York, 1886, pp.1,3,4; Jennifer Scarce, 'The Royal Palaces of the Qajars, a survey', in Bosworth and Hillenbrand, pp.339-40; V.B. Meen and A.D. Tushingham, Crown Jewels of Iran, Toronto, 1968, pp.84, 140.

5. C.J. Wills, In the Land of the Lion and the Sun, 1883, pp.51-2; Benjamin, pp.199-200; Hon. George N. Curzon, Persia and the Persian Question, 2 vols, 1892, I, 313-25; Eustache de Lorey and Douglas Sladen, Queer Things about Persia, 1907, pp.177-8, cf. Hon. J.M. Balfour, Recent Happenings in Persia, 1922, p.60, for a description of a salaam under Ahmad Shah.

6. Wills, pp.52-3; Count C. Mijatovich, The Memoirs of a Balkan Diplomatist, 1917, p.261.

7. Curzon, Persia, I, 396.

8. Firuz Kazemzadeh, Russia and Britain in Persia 1864-1914, New Haven, 1968, passim, especially pp.165, 210, 217, 297.

9. Yarshater, p.9; Curzon, Persia, I, 400; Dr Feuvrier, Trois Ans à la Cour de Perse, seconde édition, 1906, p.160.

10. Afshar, p.9; General T. E. Gordon, Persia Revisited, 1896, p.34; Yarshater, p.10.

11 Algar, p.218; Kazemzadeh, p.285, Sir Frank Lascelles to Lord Salisbury to 9 November 1892; Edward G. Browne, The Persian Revolution of 1905-1909, 1910, pp.30, 82, interrogation of Mirza Riza, 10-11 August 1896.

12. Kazemzadeh, p.296; PRO FO 800/32 f. 213 report by Vambéry, 28 September 1900; Shaul Bakhash, 'The Failure of Reform: the Prime Ministership of Amin al-Dowleh 1897-8' in Bosworth and Hillenbrand, pp.15,27; Stephen Gwynn, The Letters and Friendships of Sir Cecil Spring-Rice, 2 vols, 1929, I, 290, letter of 15 September 1899, p.296, letter of 30 November 1899.

13. Algar, pp.226, 228, 230; Kazemzadeh, pp.387, 393, memorandum by Grahame, 23 February 1902.

14. F.R.C. Bagley, 'New Light on the Constitutional Movement' in Bosworth and Hillenbrand, p.51; Browne, p.217, letter from a Persian, 29 December 1906, p.135.

15. J.M. Hone and Page L. Dickinson, Persia in Revolution, 1910, p.104; Eugène Aubin, La Perse d'Aujourd'hui, 1908, pp.131-43.

16. Kazemzadeh, pp.521-44.

17. W. Morgan Shuster, The Strangling of Persia, 1912, p.210.

18. Kazemzadeh, pp.312, 410, 428-9, 597, 604; Peter Avery, Modern Iran, 1964, pp.146, 170-1.

5 Khans and Emirs

1. Mary Holdsworth, Turkestan in the Nineteenth Century, Oxford, 1959, p.60; Fitzroy Maclean, A Person from England, 1984 edn, p.197.

2. Arminius Vambéry, Sketches of Central Asia, 1868, pp.88-93; Fred Burnaby, A Ride to Khiva, 1985 edn., p.307; Emil Olufsen, The Emir of Bokhara and His People, Copenhagen, 1911, p.199; Henir Moser, A Travers l'Asie Centrale, 1885, p.255.

3. Andrew D. Kalmykov, The Memoirs of a Russian Diplomat, New Haven, 1971, p.167.

4. Moser, pp.154-5; Olufsen, pp.156-7; Hon.George N. Curzon MP, Russia in Central Asia in 1889 and the Anglo-Russian Question, 1889, p.200.

5. Olufsen, pp.576-7; Kalmykov, pp.168-70.

6. Serge A. Zenkovsky, Pan-Turkism and Islam in Russia, Harvard, 1960, pp.81, 87-8; William Eleroy Curtis, Turkestan 'the Heart of Asia', 1911, p.141-2.

7. Maclean, p.303.

8. Vartan Gregorian, The Emergence of Modern Afghanistan, Stanford,1969, p.43.

9. Davison, p.274.

10. Emir Abdul Rahman, The Life of. . .GCB, GCSI, 2 vols, 1900, II, 81.

11. Lord Curzon, Tales of Travel, 1923, p.52; Abdul Rahman, II, 5, 251n.

12. Abdul Rahman, II, 44.

13. Angus Hamilton, Afghanistan, 1906, pp.348-50; A.H. Grant, 'A Winter at the Court of an Absolute Monarch', Blackwoods Magazine, CLXXX, November 1906, p.604.

14. Abdul Rahman II, 81-8, 91-2; John Alfred Gray, At the Court of the Amir, 1895, pp.192, 211.

15. Gray, p.523; Gregorian, p.185; Ludwig W. Adamec, Afghanistan 1900-1923, Berkeley, 1970, p.81.

16. Hamilton, pp.434-5, Sir Percy Sykes, The Right Hon. Sir Mortimer Durand, 1926, p.217; Adamec, p.95.

6 Harems

1. Leila Hanoum, Le Harem Impérial et les Sultanes au XIXe Siècle, 1925, p.121; Pars Tuglaci, The Ottoman Palace Women, Istanbul, 1985, p.156; Tugay, p.107.

2. Dr Comanos, Souvenirs, n.d., pp.51,62; Meakin, p.202.

3. E.R. Toledano, 'The Imperial Eunuchs of Istanbul: from Africa to the Heart of Islam', Middle East Studies, XX, 3 July 1984, p.381; Hanoum, p.130; Princess Musbah Haidar, Arabesque, 1946, p.185.

4. Hanoum, p.27; interview with Prince O.N. Osmanoglu, 7.1984.

5. Hanoum, pp.37, 43; Toledano, pp.379-90.

6. Hanoum, p.181.

7. Hanoum, p.XV; Papiers Secrets Brûlés dans l'Incendie des Tuileries, Bruxelles, 1871, pp.124, 126, Empress Eugénie to Napoléon III, 16, 17.10.1869.

8. Tuglaci, pp.161, 345.

9. Lott, II, 25, 31; E. Chennells, *Recollections of an Egyptian Princess*, 2 vols, 1893, I, 222-49.

10. *Olufsen*, pp.326, 436; *Yarshater*, p.8; *Harris*, p.206.

11. *Lott*, II, 290; Gerald de Gaury, *Three Kings in Baghdad*, 1961, p.134.

12. *Hanoum*, p.216; *Alderson*, p.89; *Eliot*, p.119; *Tuglaci*, p.339.

13. *Lott*, II, 232-3, 239.

14. *Yarshater*, p.5; *Keddie*, pp.35, 81; interview with Malekeh Mansur, 5 May 1984.

15. *Baer*, p.42; *Tugay*, pp.287-8.

16. AH 120/167, 212 intercepted police reports of 20 October, 18 December 1923; PRO FO 141/482/338/3A report of 5 March 1934.

7 The End of the Ottomans

1. PRO 800/32 f. 301 report by Vambéry, 7 May 1894; Alan Bodger, 'Russia and the End of the Ottoman Empire' in Marian Kent ed., *The Great Powers and the End of the Ottoman Empire*, 1984, pp.96-7.

2. *Avery*, p.141.

3. Commandant M. Larcher, *La Guerre Turque dans la Guerre Mondiale*, 1926, pp.44-7.

4. Albert Hourani, *Arabic Thought in the Liberal Age*, Oxford, 1970, p.269; Gerald de Gaury, *Rulers of Mecca*, 1951, p.161.

5. *Hourani*, pp.267-8; Blunt, *Gordon at Khartoum*, p.492, diary for 8 October 1885; *Keddie*, '*Al-Afghani*', p.375, ambassador to Amin as-Sultan, 1 October 1892; Elie Kedourie, *Arabic Political Memoirs and Other Studies*, 1974, p.108.

6. For the best discussion of the Hashemites' relations with the Ottoman government, see C.E. Dawn, *From Ottomanism to Arabism*, Urbana, 1973, passim esp.pp.48, 50; King Abdullah of Transjordan, *Memoirs*, 1950, ed. Philip Graves, p.58.

7. Hanna Batatu, *The Old Social Classes and the Revolutionary Movement in Iraq*, Princeton, 1978, p.322; Majid Khadduri, '*Aziz Ali al-Masri and the Arab Nationalist Movement*', *St. Anthony's Papers*, 1965, pp.140, 144; *Abdullah*, pp.105-06.

8. *Abdullah*, p.129; Kedourie, *In the Anglo-Arab Labyrinth*, Cambridge 1976, pp.28-32; Frank G. Weber, *Eagles on the Crescent*, 1970, p.182.

9. *Dawn*, p.82; Princess Musbah Haidar, *Arabesque*, 1946, pp.19, 124; Randall Baker, *King Hussein and the Kingdom of the Hejaz*, 1979, pp.114, 116.

10. *Zenkovsky*, pp.259-60; PRO FO 371/4227 Mehmed VI to Grand Vizir, 19 May 1919.

11. PRO FO 371/6469, Annual Report for 1920, 27 April 1921; *Ryan*, p.128; Paul Dumont, *Mustafa Kemal*, Bruxelles, 1983, pp.25, 27.

12. Michael Llewellyn Smith, *Ionian Vision. Greece and Asia Minor*, 1973, pp.72, 213; Martin Gilbert, *Sir Horace Rumbold*, 1973, p.233; *FitzHerbert*, p.235.

13. Gwynne Dyer, 'The Turkish Armistice of 1918, I', *Middle East Studies*, 8, 1972, p.158.

14. *Shaw*, II, pp.341-2; *Dumont*, pp.42, 45.

15. *Dumont*, p.52.

16. PRO FO 371/4162 Summary of Intelligence, 2 January 1920; *Dumont*, pp.67-9, 77.

17. PRO FO 371/4227 letter of Abdul Medjid enclosed in despatch of 18 June 1919; memorandum by Admiral Calthorpe, 30 July 1919; PRO FO 371/5178 reports from Constantinople, 12 August 1920, 25 October 1920; PRO FO 371/6469 Sir Horace Rumbold to Lord Curzon, 29 April 1921, 5 May 1921.

18. *Gilbert*, p.236, Rumbold to Curzon, 23 March 1921; PRO FO 371/7912/12647 Rumbold to Curzon, 7 November 1922; *Gilbert*, p.278, Lady Rumbold to her mother, 6 November 1922.

19. PRO FO 371/13234/12790 Nevile Henderson to Curzon, 17 November 1922, George V to Mehmed VI, 28 November 1922.

20. *Bernard Lewis*, p.252; Aziz Nesim, *Istanbul Boy*, Part I, Austin 1977, p.68; *Aga Khan*, p.153; Edward Mortimer, *Faith and Power*, 1982, pp.137, 195.

21. Lord Kinross, *Ataturk. The Rebirth of a Nation*, 1964, pp.348-56; *Stitt*, p.267, Diary of Princess Fatma Haidar, 29 February 1924; Constantine Brown, 'The Tragi-comic Exit of the Osmanli Dynasty', *Asia*, June 1924, pp.449-50.

22. Interviews with Prince O.N. Osmanoglu, 30 July 1984, with Taha Toros, 20 May 1984; Anne Freemantle, *Loyal Enemy*, 1938, p.424; AH 198/51 Abdul Medjid to Emperor of Japan, 10 July 1942 (copy).

23. *Ryan*, p.275; Eric Macro, *Yemen and the Western World*, 1968, p.48.

8 Kings of the Arabs

1. Zeine N. Zeine, *The Struggle for Arab Independence*, Beirut, 1960, pp.33, 51, 139.

2. *Storrs*, p.431; *King Abdullah*, pp.190-02.

3. King Abdullah of Transjordan, *My Memoirs Completed*, 1978, p.73; Aaron S. Klieman, *Foundations of British Policy in the Arab World. The Cairo Conference of 1921*, Baltimore, 1970, pp.208-11.

4. Sir Alec Kirkbride, *A Crackle of Thorns*, 1956, p.29; Cecil Beaton, *Near East*, 1943, p.115; Neville Mandel, the Arabs and Palestine before World War I, Berkeley, 1971, p.11.

5. Helmut Mezcher, *Imperial Quest for Oil. Iraq 1910-1928*, Oxford, 1976, p.76, Churchill to Lloyd George, 14 March 1921; Stephen Longrigg, *Four Centuries of Modern Iraq*, Oxford, 1925, p.312n; Winstone, *Gertrude Bell*, 1980 edn, p.236, Cox to Churchill, 11 April 1921.

6. *Klieman*, pp.147, 154.

7. *Batatu*, p.324, High Commissioner to Secretary of State, 16 August 1921; Mohammed A. Tarbush, *The Role of the Military in Politics. A Case Study of Iraq to 1941*, 1982, p.17.

8. Mrs Steuart Erskine, *King Faisal of Iraq*, 1933, p.5.

9. Gerald de Gaury, *Three Kings in Baghdad*, 1961, pp.39, 57, 102-06, 110.

10. Interview with Julian Pitt-Rivers, 2 February 1988.

11. Desmond Stewart and John Haylock, *Young Babylon*, 1957, p.27; interview with Major Yussuf Salim, 3 December 1987.

12. Suleiman Mousa, 'A Matter of Principle: King Hussein of the Hejaz and the Arabs of Palestine', *International Journal of Middle East Studies*, September 1978, pp.183-94; *Abdullah*, 1950, p.213n.

13. *Baker*, p.205; Gilbert Clayton, *An Arabian Diary*, Berkeley, 1969, p.132, entry for 4 November 1925.

14. Mohammed Almana, *Arabia Unified. A Portrait of Ibn Saud*, 1980, pp.171-4, 177, 183, 187, 247; Gerald de Gaury, *Arabia Phoenix*, 1946, passim.

9 The Rise of the Pahlavis

1. Sir Denis Wright, *The English amongst the Persians*, 1977, p.179n; *Aga Khan*, p.276.

2. PRO FO 641/621/221, Norman to Curzon, 12 January 1921; PRO FO 371/6422/550 Norman to Curzon, 7 January 1921.

3. Major-General Sir Edmund Ironside, *Diaries*, 1972, pp.147-8; *Wright*, pp.181-4 and notes, for what appears to be a fuller version of Ironside's diary; *Avery*, pp.229-30.

4. PRO FO 371/3684 Norman to Curzon, 25 March 1921; PRO FO 371/9025/10452 Sir Percy Lorraine to Curzon, 24 October 1923; PRO FO 371/10512 Loraine to Curzon, 26 October 1923.

5. PRO FO 371/10840/6390 Loraine to Chamberlain, 11 November 1925; ibid/3980 Loraine to Chamberlain, 16 June 1925.

6. PRO FO 371/10840/E6649 Loraine to Chamberlain, 11 November 1925; ibid/6185 Loraine to Chamberlain, 10 October 1925; ibid/6930 Loraine to Chamberlain, 11 November 1925; V. Sackville-West, *Passenger to Tehran*, 1926, p.140.

7. Harold Nicolson, *Curzon: The Last Phase*, 1934, p.148; interview with Iran Taymurtash, 5 May 1984; Waterfield, *Professional Diplomat*, pp.81, 138, Havard to Loraine, 31 December 1927.

8. Donald N. Wilbur, *Riza Shah Pahlavi*, Hicksville 1975, pp.86, 107, 227, 230; interview with General Djam, 13 January 1988.

9. *Avery*, pp.292, 330.

10. Denis Wright, *The Persians amongst the English*, 1985, p.214.

10 Central Asia

1. *Becker*, p.289; *Zenkovsky*, pp.238, 316; *Maclean*, pp.311, 334, 343; Lieutenant-Colonel P.T. Etherton, *In the Heart of Asia*, 1925, p.170; interview with Professor Nasrullah el-Terazi, son-in-law of the last Emir of Bokhara, Istanbul, 26 July 1984.

2. *Maclean*, pp.343, 356; Joseph Castagné, *Les Basmatchis*, 1925, pp.48-51.

3. Leon B. Poullada, *Reform and Rebellion in Afghanistan 1919-1929*, pp.45, 113, 233; *Gregorian*, p.228.

4. *Gregorian*, pp.239, 242; *Poullada*, pp.51, 60-3, Sir H.C. Dobbs to Viceroy of India, 9 January 1921, note by M. Fouchet, 1924; Khalilullah Enayat Seraj and Nancy Hatch Dupree, The KES Collection of Vintage Photographs, *Asia Society Afghanistan Council, Occasional Papers*, no. 17, Spring 1979, passim.

11 The Fall of the Throne of Egypt

The section on King Farouk is also based on interviews in 1984-8 with courtiers and relations of King Farouk who prefer to remain anonymous.

1. Lieutenant-Colonel P.G. Elgood, *Egypt and the Army*, Oxford, 1924, pp.90-1.

2. *Guerville*, p.136; PRO FO 141/620/5635 Sir William Brungate to Sir R. Wingate, 3 October 1917; Wingate to Balfour, 18 October 1917; AH 50/57 Princess Shivekiar to Abbas Hilmi, 3 July 1922.

3. *Kedourie*, 1970, p.87 letter of Sir Milnes Cheetham, August 1918; Cabinet du Grand Chambellan, *Protocole*, Le Caire, 1947.

4. Janice J. Terry, *The Wafd*, 1982, pp.75-6, 103.

5. PRO FO 371/4437 Ernest Scott to Curzon, 23 April 1922; PRO FO 371/8961/3188, 4589 Allenby to Curzon, 18 March, 23 April 1923.

6. PRO FO 371/10022/9549 Clerk-Kerr to Macdonald, 24 October 1924.

7. Laurence Grafftey-Smith, *Bright Levant*, 1970, p.100; Sir David Kelly, *The Ruling Few*, 1952, p.226; PRO FO 141/482/338/25, Sir Miles Lampson to Foreign Secretary, 1 March 1934.

8. Lord Killearn, *Diaries*, 1972, p.60, entry for 13 November 1935; Gabriel Baer, *A History of Landownership in Modern Egypt*, 1962, p.135.

9. PRO FO 371/10022/9549 Clerk-Kerr to Macdonald, 24 October 1924; AH 123/11 treaty of 12 May 1931.

10. Gabriel Fehmy Pasha, *Souvenirs*, 2 vols, Le Caire 1935, II, pp.41, 87; Major C.S. Jervis, *Desert and Delta*, 1938, p.107; PRO FO 141/482/338/20 Mr Payne 'report on conversation with King Fouad', 11 June 1934.

11. Barrie St Clair McBride, *Farouk of Egypt*, 1967, p.68; Mansel Papers, Sir Ronald Campbell, 'Note on H.M. King Farouk', c.1950; General de Gaulle, *Salvation*, 1960, p.61.

12. Charles Tripp, 'Ali Mahir Pasha', (unpublished Ph.D. thesis, London 1984), pp.36, 66, 162, 301, 340, 356; *Killearn*, p.59, entry for 6 October 1935.

13. Major A.W. Samson, *I Spied Spies*, 1958, p.94; *McBride*, pp.121-3; *Terry*, p.251; *Killearn*, p.213, entry for 4 February 1942; George Bilainkin, *Cairo to Riyadh Diary*, 1950, p.61.

14. Interview with Sir Edward Ford, 1985; Diary of Edward Ford, January 1937.

15. *Killearn*, pp.276, 295, diaries for 3 January, 19 April 1944.

16. Freya Stark, *Dust in the Lion's Paw*, 1961, p.56; Duncan Fallowell, 'Brittle Glories', *Harpers & Queen*, January 1987, p.149; Ashraf Pahlavi, *Faces in the Mirror*, 1980, p.56.

17. *Killearn*, p.319, diary for 11 February 1945; diary of Edward Ford, January 1937.

18. Barbara Skelton, *Tears before Bedtime*, 1987, p.63; *Tripp*, pp.279, 293; *McBride*, p.199.

Manuscript Sources

1. Public Record Office (PRO) Foreign Office Papers (FO) 371/4227, 4162, 5178, 6469, 6497, 6526, 6573, 7962, 7916, 7912, 7870, 9135, 10217, 5285, 8946, 6454, 5171, 5172, 5170, 10840, 6422, 6409, 10157, 7733, 4437, 7731, 12296, 8959, 8961, 8963, 10022, 10023, 10089, 11294 Despatches from Constantinople 1908-24.

FO 881/7028, 60/522 Despatches from Tehran 1923-5
800/32, 33 Vambéry Papers
141/620, 726, 471, 684, 482 Correspondence of the Cairo Residency 1914–34.

2. Papers of the Khedive Abbas Hilmi, Durham University (AH), consulted by kind permission of the Mohammed Ali Foundation
AH 46, 50, 41, 67, 70, 84 agents' reports and miscellaneous correspondence 1900–31
AH 120 intercepted police reports, 1923–4
AH 133 memoirs of the Khedive Abbas Hilmi.

3. Edward Ford, 'Journal of a Journey up the Nile with H.M. King Farouk', 1937, Ford papers.

4. Sir Ronald Campbell, 'Note on H.M. King Farouk', c. 1950, Mansel papers.

Bibliography

Unless otherwise stated, all books in English were published in London and all books in French were published in Paris.

Abbott, G.F., *Turkey in Transition*, 1909.
Abdullah, King, *Memoirs*, ed. Philip Graves, 1950, *My Memoirs Completed*, 1978.
Abdul-Rahman, Emir, *The Life of*, 2 vols, 1900.
Abun-Nasir, Jamil M., *A History of the Maghrib*, second edn, Cambridge, 1975.
Adamec, Ludwig W., *Afghanistan 1900–1923*, Berkeley, 1970.
Adams, Francis, *The New Egypt*, 1893.
Adle, Chahyar, avec la collaboration de Yahya Zoka, 'Notes et documents sur la Photographie Iranienne et son Histoire', *Studia Iranica*, tom. 12, fasc. 32, 1983.
Aga Khan, The, *Memoirs*, 1955.
Ahmad, Feroz, *The Young Turks*, Oxford, 1969.
Alderson, A.D., *The Structure of the Ottoman Dynasty*, 1956.
Algar, Hamid, *Religion and State in Iran*, Berkeley, 1969.
Almana, Mohammed, *Arabia Unified*, 1980.
Al-Sayyid Marsot, Lutfi, *Egypt under Cromer*, 1968.
Ashmead-Bartlett, C., *The Passing of the Shereefian Empire*, 1910.
Atasoy, Professor Dr Nurhan, 'Istanbul Kutuphanesi Universitesi', *Istanbul Universitesi Belletin*, Temmuz 1977, sayyi 5, pp. 30-32, Kazim 1978, sayyi 9, pp.243-5, Mart 1979, sayyi 10, pp.16-17, Temmuz 1979, sayyi II, pp. 30-32, Kazim 1979, sayyi 12, pp. 30-32.
Aubin, Eugène, *Le Maroc d'Aujourd'hui*, 1904, *La Perse d'Aujourd'hui*, 1908.
Avery, Peter, *Modern Iran*, 1964.
Azan, Colonel, Paul, *L'Expédition de Fez*, 1924.
Baer, Gabriel, *A History of Landownership in Modern Egypt*, 1962.

Bailey, Lieutenant-Colonel F.M., *Mission to Tashkent*, 1946.
Baker, Randall, *King Hussein and the Kingdom of the Hejaz*, 1979.
Balfour, Hon. J.M., *Recent Happenings in Persia*, 1922.
Baring, Maurice, *Letters from the Near East*, 1909.
Bassett, James, *Persia, the Land of the Imams*, New York, 1886.
Batatu, Hanna, *The Old Social Classes and the Revolutionary Movement of Iraq*, Princeton, 1978.
Becker, Seymour, *Russia's Protectorates in Central Asia: Bokhara and Khiva 1865–1924*, Cambridge Mass., 1968.
Benjamin, S.G.W., *Persia and the Persian Question*, 1887.
Berggren, G., *Photographic Views of the Bosphorus and Constantinople*, Stockholm, 1984.
Berque, Jacques, *Egypt, Imperialism and Revolution*, 1972.
Blancard, Théodore, *Les Mavroyennis*, 2 vols, 1909.
Blunt, W.S., *Gordon at Khartoum*, 1911, *Secret History of the British Occupation of Egypt*, 1907.
Bosworth, Edmund and Carole Hillenbrand eds., *Qajar Iran 1800–1925*, Edinburgh, 1984.
Brown, Constantine, 'The Tragicomic Exit of the Osmanli Dynasty', *Asia*, June 1924, pp.449-53, 492-4.
Browne, Edward G., *The Persian Revolution of 1905–1909*, 1910.
Buisseret, Cte. Conrad de, *A la Cour de Fez*, Bruxelles, 1907.
Busch, Burton Cooper, *Mudros to Lausanne, Britain's Frontier in Western Asia 1918–1923*, Albany, 1976.
Butler, Alfred J., *Court Life in Egypt*, 1888.
Caillard, Mabel, *A Life in Egypt*, 1935.
Castagné, Joseph, *Les Basmatchis*, 1925.
Chennells, Miss, *Recollections of an Egyptian Princess*, 2 vols, 1893.
Chamberlain, M.E., 'The Alexandria Massacres of 1882 and the British Occupation of Egypt', *Middle East Studies*, XII, 1977, pp.12-25.
Clayton, Gilbert, *An Arabian Diary*, Berkeley, 1969.
Cleveland, William R., *Islam against the West: Shakib Arslan and the Campaign for Islamic Reform*, 1985.
Colombe, Marcel, 'Une Lettre d'un Prince Egyptien du XIXe Siècle au Sultan Abdul Aziz', *Orient*, V, 1958, pp.25-39.
Crabitès, Pierre, *Ismail, the Maligned Khedive*, 1933.
Curzon, Hon. George N., *Russia in Central Asia*, 1889, *Persia and the Persian Question*, 2 vols, 1892, *Tales of Travel*, 1925.
Davison, Roderic C., *Reform in the Ottoman Empire*, Princeton, 1963.
Dawn, C.E., *From Ottomanism to Arabism*, Urbana, 1973.
De Gaury, Gerald, *Arabia Phoenix*, 1946, *Three Kings in Baghdad*, 1961.
De Leon, Edwin, *The Khedive's Egypt*, 1877.
De Lorey, Eustache and Douglas Sladen, *Queer Things about Persia*, 1907, *The Moon of the Fourteenth Night*, 1910.
Dodds, Anna Bowman, *In the Palaces of the Sultan*, 1904.
Dumont, Paul, *Mustafa Kemal*, Bruxelles, 1983.
Dupree, Nancy Hatch, 'Behind the Veil in Afghanistan', *Asia*, July/August 1978, pp.10–15 'Early Twentieth-Century Afghan adaptations of European Architecture', *Art and Archaeology Research Papers*, II, June 1977.
Dyer, Gwynne, 'The Turkish Armistice of 1918 I', *Middle East Studies*, VIII, 1972, pp.143-78.
Elgood, Lieutenant-Colonel P.G., *Egypt and the Army*, Oxford, 1924.
Eliot, Charles, *Turkey in Europe*, 1900.
Eliot, Frances, *Diary of an Idle Woman in Constantinople*, 1893.
Elliot, Sir Charles, *Some Revolutions and Other Diplomatic Experiences*, 1922.

Erskine, Mrs Steuart, *King Faisal of Iraq*, 1933.
Etherton, Lieutenant-Colonel P.T., *In the Heart of Asia*, 1925.
Farley, A., *The Decline of Turkey*, 1870.
Fehmy Pasha, Gabriel, *Souvenirs*, 2 vols, Cairo, 1935.
Feuvrier, Dr, *Trois Ans à la Cour de Perse*, seconde édition 1906.
Findlay, Carter V., *Bureaucratic Reform in the Ottoman Empire 1789–1922*, Princeton, 1982.
Franz-Joseph, Kaiser, *Briefe . . . an Kaiserin Elizabeth*, 2 vols, Wien-München, 1966.
Freemantle, Anne, *Loyal Enemy*, 1938.
Fromentin, Eugène de, *Voyage en Egypte*, 1935.
Furlonge, Geoffrey, *Palestine is my Country: The Story of Musa Alami*, 1969.
Gallenga, A., *Two Years of the Eastern Question*, 2 vols, 1877.
Ganiage, Jean, *L'Expansion Coloniale de la France sous la Troisième République*, 1968.
Gilbert, Martin, *Sir Horace Rumbold*, 1973.
Gordon, General Sir T.E., *Persia Revisited*, 1896.
Grafftey-Smith, Laurence, *Bright Levant*, 1970.
Graham-Brown, Sarah, 'Snapshots for a Sultan', *The Middle East*, August 1984, pp.45-54.
Grand Chambellan, Cabinet du, *Protocole*, Cairo, 1947.
Grant, A.H., 'A Winter at the Court of an Absolute Monarch', *Blackwoods Magazine*, CLXXX, November 1906, pp.587-612.
Gray, John, *At the Court of the Amir*, 1895.
Gregorian, Vartan, *The Emergence of Modern Afghanistan*, Stanford, 1969.
Grey, Hon. Mrs William, *Journal of a Visit to Egypt, Constantinople etc.*, 1869.
Griffiths, M.A., 'The Reorganisation of the Ottoman Army under Abdul Hamid II 1880–1897' (unpublished Ph.D. thesis), UCLA ,1966.
Guerville, A. B. de, *New Egypt*, 1905.
Haidar, Princes Musbah, *Arabesque*, 1946.
Hanoum, Leila, *Le Harem Impérial et les Sultanes au XIXe Siècle*, 1925.
Hamilton, Angus B., *Afghanistan*, 1906.
Harris, Walter B., *The Land of an African Sultan*, 1889.
Hirszowicz, L. 'The Sultan and the Khedive 1892–1908', *Middle East Studies*, VIII, 1972, pp.285-301.
Holdsworth, Mary, *Turkestan in the Nineteenth Century*, Oxford, 1959.
Holt, P.M. ed., *Political and Social Change in Modern Egypt*, 1968.
Hone, J.M. and Page L. Dickinson, *Persia in Revolution*, 1910.
Hourani, Albert, *Arabic Thought in the Liberal Age*, Oxford, 1970.
The Emergence of the Modern Middle East, 1981, *Europe and the Middle East*, 1981.
Hunter, F. Robert, *Egypt under the Khedives*, Pittsburgh, 1984.
Ironside, Major-General Sir Edmund, *Diaries*, 1972.
Izzedine, M., 'Le palais sous les deux derniers Sultans, Mehmet V Reşad et Mehmet VI Vahdeddine', *Revue de l'Ecole Nationale des Langues Orientales*, 1965, pp. 175-98.
Jarvis, C.S., *Desert and Delta*, 1938.
Kalmykov, Andrew D., *The Memoirs of a Russian Diplomat*, New Haven, 1971.
Kamil Pasha, Mustafa, *Lettres Egyptiennes*, n.d.
Kazemazadeh, Firuz N., *Russia and Britain in Persia 1864–1914*, New Haven, 1968.
Keddie, Nikki, *Roots of Revolution*, 1981, *Sayyid Jamal al-din 'al-Afghani'*, Los Angeles, 1972.
Kedourie, Elie, *The Chatham House Version and Other Middle Eastern Studies*, 1970, *Arabic Political Memoirs and Other Studies*, 1974, *In the Anglo-Arab Labyrinth*, Cambridge, 1976.
Kelly, Sir David, *The Ruling Few*, 1952.
Kemal Bey, Ismail, *Memoirs*, 1920.

Kent, Marian ed., *The Great Powers and the End of the Ottoman Empire*, 1984.

Khadduri, Majid, 'Aziz Ali Al-Masri and the Arab Nationalist Movement', *St. Anthony's Papers, Middle East Affairs*, 1965, pp.140-63.

Kinross, Lord, *Ataturk: The Rebirth of a Nation*, 1964.

Kirkbride, Sir Alec, *A Crackle of Thorns*, 1956.

Klieman, Aaron S., *Foundations of British Policy in the Arab World. The Cairo Conference of 1921*, Baltimore, 1970.

La Martinière, H.M.P. de, *Morocco*, 1889.

Lambton, Ann K.S., *Theory and Practice in Medieval Persian Government*, 1980.

Larcher, Cdt. M. *La Guerre Turque dans la Guerre Mondiale*, 1926.

Leared, Arthur M., *Morocco and the Moors*, second edn 1891.

Lewis, Bernard, *The Evolution of Modern Turkey*, 1960.

Liman von Sanders, *Five Years in Turkey*, Annapolis, 1928.

Lloyd, Lord, *Egypt since Cromer*, 2 vols. 1933-4.

Longrigg, Stephen, *Four Centuries of Modern Iraq*, Oxford, 1925,
Iraq 1900–1950, 1953,
Oil in the Middle East, 1964.

Lott, Emmeline, *Harem Life in Egypt and Constantinople*, 2 vols, 1866.

Luke, Sir Harry, *Cities and Men*, 3 vols, 1953-4.

Lyautey, Pierre, *Lyautey l'Africain*, 4 vols. 1953-7.

Maclean, Fitzroy, *A Person from England*, 1984.

Macro, Eric, *Yemen and the Western World*, 1968.

Magnus, Philip, *Kitchener*, 1958.

Marlowe, John, *Cromer in Egypt*, 1970.
Spoiling the Egyptians, 1974.

Martin, Frank A., *Under the Absolute Amir*, 1907.

Maurois, Andre, *Marshal Lyautey*, 1931.

McCoan, J.F., *Egypt as it is*, New York, 1877.

Meakin, Budgett, *The Moorish Empire*, 1899.

Mezcher, Helmut, *Imperial Quest for Oil, Iraq 1910-1928*, Oxford, 1976.

Midhat, Ali Haidar, *The Life of Midhat Pasha*, 1903.

Miège, Jean, *Le Maroc et l'Europe*, 4 vols. 1961-3.

Mismer, Charles, *Souvenirs du Monde Mussulman*, 1892.

Moore, Frederick, *The Passing of Morocco*, 1908.

Mortimer, Edward, *Faith and Power*, 1982.

Moser, Henri, *A Travers l'Asie Centrale*, 1885.

Mousa, Suleiman, *T.E. Lawrence: An Arab View*, 1966,
'A Matter of Principle: King Hussein of the Hejaz and the Arabs of Palestine', *International Journal of Middle East Studies*, September 1978, pp.183-94.

Muller, Mrs Max, *Letters from Constantinople*, 1897.

Nicolson, Harold, *Lord Carnock*, 1930,
Curzon, the Last Phase, 1934.

Nizam al-Mulk, *The Book of Government or Rules for Kings*, 1978.

Olufsen, Emil, *The Emir of Bokhara and his People*, Copenhagen 1907.

One who knows them well, *Khedives and Pashas*, 1884.

Owen, Roger, *The Middle East in the World Economy 1800–1914*, 1983.

Piemontese, Angelo M. 'The Photograph Album of the Italian Diplomatic Mission to Persia (Summer 1862)', *East-West*, New Series, Vol.XXII, Nos 3-4, September-December 1972.

Porch, Douglas, *The Conquest of Morocco*, New York, 1983.

Poullada, Leon B., *Reform and Rebellion in Afghanistan 1919–1929*, 1973.

Ribeyre, Félix, *Voyage de Sa Majesté l'Impératrice en Corse et en Orient*, 1870.

Robinson, Ronald and John Gallagher with Alice Denny, *Africa and the Victorians*, 1961.

Rush, Alan, *Al-Sabah*, 1987.

Russell, W.H., *A Diary in the East during the Tour of the Prince and Princess of Wales*, 1869,
The Prince of Wales's Tour, 1877.

Ryan, Sir Andrew, *The Last of the Dragomans*, 1951.

Saray, Mehmet, 'The Russian Conquest of Central Asia', *Central Asian Survey*, I, 2/3 November 1982, pp.1-30.

Scham, Alan, *Lyautey in Morocco*, Berkeley, 1970.

Schölch, Alexander, *Egypt for the Egyptians!*, Oxford, 1981.

Seraj, Khalilullah Enayat and Nancy Hatch Dupree, 'The KES Collection of Vintage Photographs', *Asia Society, Afghanistan Council, Occasional Papers*, No. 17, Spring 1979.

Shorawi, Hoda, *Harem Years*, 1986.

Shorrock, William I., *French Imperialism in the Middle East*, Madison, 1976.

Shuster, W. Morgan, *The Strangling of Persia*, 1912.

Sinderson, Sir Harry, *Ten Thousand and One Nights*, 1973.

Smida, Mougi, *Khereddine*, Tunis, 1970.

Smith, Colin L., *The Embassy of Sir William White at Constantinople 1886–1891*, 1957.

Smith, Michael Llewelyn, *Ionian Vision, Greece and Asia Minor*, 1973.

Spry, William J.J., *Life on the Bosphorus*, 1891.

Stitt, George, *A Prince of Arabia*, 1948.

Storrs, Ronald, *Orientations*, 1943 edn.

Tarbush, Mohammed A., *The Role of the Military in Politics: A Case Study of Iraq to 1941*, 1982.

Tcharykov, N.V., *Glimpses of High Politics through War and Peace*, 1931.

Terry, Janice J., *The Wafd*, 1982.

Thorossian, H., *Histoire de l'Arménie et du Peuple Arménien*, 1957.

Tignor, Robert, *Modernisation and British Colonial Rule in Egypt 1882–1914*, Princeton, 1966.

Toledano, Edward J., 'The Imperial Eunuchs of Istanbul: from Africa to the Heart of Islam', *Middle East Studies*, XX, 3, July 1984.

Toledano, Ehad, *The Ottoman Slave Trade and its Suppression 1840–1890*, Princeton, 1982.

Tugay, Emine Foat, *Three Centuries. Chronicles of Family Life in Turkey and Egypt*, 1960.

Tripp, Charles, 'Ali Mahir Pasha', (unpublished Ph.D, thesis), London, 1984.

Trumpener, Ulrich, *Germany and the Ottoman Empire 1914–1918*, Princeton, 1968.

Tuglaci, Pars, *The Ottoman Palace Women*, Istanbul, 1985.

Vambéry, Arminius, *Sketches of Central Asia*, 1868,
The Story of my Struggles, 2 vols, 1904,
'Personal Recollections of Abdul Hamid and His Court', *Nineteenth Century and After*, June 1909, CCCLXXXVIII.

Veyre, Gabriel, *Au Maroc dans l'Intimité du Sultan*, 1904.

Vivian, Herbert, *Tunisia and the Modern Barbary Pirates*, 1899.

Waterfield, Gordon, *Layard of Nineveh*, 1963,
Professional Diplomat, 1973.

Waugh, Sir T., *Turkey, Yesterday, Today and Tomorrow*, 1930.

Weber, Frank G., *Eagles on the Crescent*, 1970.

Wilbur, Donald N., *Riza Shah Pahlavi*, Hicksville, 1975.

William, Crown Prince of Germany, *Memoirs*, 1921.

Wills, C.J., *In the Land of the Lion and the Sun*, 1883.

Wilson, Mary Christian, 'King Abdullah of Jordan: A Political Biography', (unpublished Ph.D. thesis), Oxford, 1984.

Winstone, H.V.F., *Gertrude Bell*, 1980 edn.

Wolff, Sir Henry Drummond, *Rambling Recollections*, 2 vols, 1908.

Woods, Sir Henry F., *Spunyarn from the Strands of a Sailor's Life*, 2 vols, 1924.

Wright, Sir Denis, *The English amongst the Persians*, 1977,
The Persians amongst the English, 1985.

Zeine, Zeine N., *The Struggle for Arab Independence*, Beirut, 1960.

Zenkovsky, Serge, *Pan-Turkism and Islam in Russia*, Harvard, 1960.

Ziadeh, N.A., *The Sanusiyah*, Leiden, 1958.

List of Photographs

This list gives sources and, in brackets, the photographer's name where known.

End-papers: Official tribune at the opening of the Suez Canal. Association des Amis du Souvenir de Ferdinand de Lesseps et du Canal de Suez (W.Hammerschmidt).
Half-title page: Abdullah Frères advertisement. Author's collection.
Title page: Dolmabahçe palace. Royal Geographical Society (Sebah and Joailler).

Introduction: The Opening of the Suez Canal.

1 Official Tribune at the Inauguration of the Suez Canal. Association des Amis du Souvenir de Ferdinand de Lesseps et du Canal de Suez (W.Hammerschmidt).
2 Khedive Ismail. Royal Archives, Windsor.
3 Procession opening the Suez Canal. Association des Amis du Souvenir de Ferdinand de Lesseps et du Canal de Suez.

I Long Live Our Padishah!

1 Abdul Hamid II. Military Museum, Cairo.
2 Panorama of Constantinople. Royal Geographical Society (Abdullah Frères).
3 Dolmabahçe palace. Deutsches Archaeologisches Institut Istanbul (henceforward DAII) (Sebah and Joailler).
4 Throne-room, Dolmabahçe. (Sebah and Joailler).
5 The Sultan's bathroom, Dolmabahçe. DAII (Berggren).
6 Omar Pasha. Coll. C.Gülersoy.
7 Sultan Abdul Aziz. Royal Archives, Windsor.
8 Beylerbey palace. DAII (Abdullah Frères).
9 Staircase in Beylerbey. DAII (Sebah and Joailler).
10 The Sultan's Dwarf. Military Museum, Cairo.
11 Midhat Pasha. Military Museum, Cairo.
12 Murad V. Sutherland Papers, Stafford County Record Office.
13 Park in Yildiz. DAII (Berggren).
14 Salon in Yildiz. DAII (Sebah and Joailler).
15 Dining room in the Chalet pavilion. Yildiz Collection.
16 Library in Yildiz. Yildiz Collection.
17 Ceremonial Saloon in the Chalet pavilion. Yildiz Collection.
18 Regimental Fête. Yildiz Collection.
19 *Selamlik* at Yildiz. Coll. Brinsley Ford.
20 Abdul Hamid driving to a *Selamlik*. Coll. Prince O.N. Osmanoglu.
21 Mehmed V. Coll. C. Gülersoy.
22 Mehmed V in Salonica. Coll. Taha Toros.
23 Procession of the *mahmal* in Mecca. Imperial War Museum (henceforward IWM).
24 Sheikh Mubarak al-Sabah, ruler of Kuwait. India Office Library (henceforward IOL).
25 Pupils from the School of Nomadic Tribes. British Library (Abdullah Frères).
26 Ottoman Prince. Yildiz Collection (Kargopoulo).
27 Ahmed Nihad Effendi and his son. Coll. Prince Osman Vassib.
28 Naciye Sultan and Enver Pasha. Coll. Mahpeyker Enver.

2 Khedives and Pashas

1 Khedive Tewfik. Coll. Badr al-Hajj.
2 Abdine palace. Kamiliya Books (Zangaki).
3 The Buffet, Abdine palace. Private collection (Kerop).
4 Gezireh palace, Cairo. Kamiliya Books (P.Sebah).
5 Ras el-Tine palace, Alexandria. National Army Museum.
6 Sherif Pasha. Coll. A.Sabit.
7 Sayyid Jemal al-din 'al-Afghani'. Beit al-Umma.
8 Arabi Pasha. Coll. Badr al-Hajj.
9 Place des Consuls Alexandria before the British bombardment. Kamiliya Books (Bonfils).
10 Alexandria after the bombardment. Kamiliya Books.
11 General Gordon. Mansell Collection.
12 The Khedive Abbas Hilmi. Durham University, Sudan Archive.
13 Prince Hassan Toussoun and Mustafa Pasha Fahmy. Coll. Prince Aziz Toussoun.
14 Inauguration of the Asyut-Girgeh Line. Mohammed Ali Foundation.
15 Palace of the Khedive of Egypt on the Bosphorus. Société de Géographie Française.
16 Running footmen or *sayces*. Kamiliya Books.
17 The Opening of the Legislative Council. Mohammed Ali Foundation.
18 Meeting of the Khedive and George V. Royal Commonwealth Society.
19 Queen Mary and the Grand Vizir. Royal Commonwealth Society.

3 Beys and Sultans

1 The Bardo palace, Tunis. Coll. Sirot-Angel.
2 Ali Bey of Tunis. Roger Viollet (Albert).
3 The Bey al-Mahalla with a prince. Coll. Sirot-Angel. Universal Photos.
4 Visit of President Loubet to the Bey of Tunis. Bibliothèque Nationale.
5 The Bey of Tunis and his ministers. Société de Géographie Française.
6 Visit of Sidi Mohammed el-Habib to President Millerand in Paris. Roger Viollet.
7 Ahmad Pasha. Coll. King Reshad of the Tunisians.
8 Moulay Abdul Aziz. Royal Palace, Rabat.
9 Moulay Hafid. Royal Palace, Rabat.
10 Moulay Youssef. Coll. Hasna Dauda.
11 Moulay Youssef on a journey. Roger Viollet.
12 Mohammed V and Crown Prince Hassan in Paris. Roger Viollet.
13 Mohammed V and Crown Prince Hassan going to Friday prayers. Roger Viollet.
14 Mohammed V. Coll. Hasna Dauda.
15 Mohammed V, Crown Prince Hassan and Moulay Abdullah at a Circumsion Feast, 13 July 1942. Archives de l'Ambassade de France, Rabat.

4 Shahs and Mullahs

1 Nasser al-din Shah in front of the Peacock Throne. Freer Gallery of Art, Smithsonian Institution (Sevruguin).
2 The Shah on a shoot. Freer Gallery of Art, Smithsonian Institution (Sevruguin).
3 Muzafar al-din and advisers, 1862. Biblioteca Marciana, Venice (Luigi Montalbone).
4 The Shah's camp. Société de Géographie Française (Dr Feuvrier).
5 Courtyard in Gulestan palace. Metropolitan Museum of Art, Gift of Charles Wilkinson (Luigi Pesce).
6 The *khabga* or palace of sleep in the women's quarters of Gulestan. Société de Géographie Française (Dr Feuvrier).
7 *Salaam* in Gulestan. Freer Gallery of Art, Smithsonian Insitution (Sevruguin).
8 The Museum in Gulestan. Freer Gallery of Art, Smithsonian Institution (Sevruguin).
9 Group at Hatfield House. Royal Archives, Windsor.
10 Zill as-Sultan. Edinburgh University Library.
11 Mirza Mohammed Reza. Edward G. Browne, *The Persian Revolution of 1905–9*, 1910.
12 Muzafar al-din Shah. Royal Archives, Windsor.
13 Muzafar al-din Shah and Edward VII. Royal Archives, Windsor.
14 Deputies to the first Majlis. Edward G. Browne, *The Persian Revolution of 1905–9*, 1910.
15 Mohammed Ali Shah. Private collection.
16 The Cossack Brigade. W. Morgan Shuster, *The Strangling of Persia*, 1912.
17 Turcoman chiefs' heads. W. Morgan Shuster, *The Strangling of Persia*, 1912.
18 Sultan Ahmad Shah. Roger Viollet.
19 *Salaam* in a provincial court. Qajar family collection.

5 Khans and Emirs

1 Abd al-Ahad, Emir of Bokhara. Archives Photographiques (Paul Nadar).
2 A notable of Samarkand. Musée de l'Homme, Paris.
3 Mohammed Rahim, Khan of Khiva. Franz von Schwarz, *Turkestan*, Berlin, 1900.
4 Throne of the Emir of Bokhara. National Museum, Copenhagen (Olufsen).
5 Entrance to the *erg* or citadel, Bokhara. Société de Géographie Française. La Baume-Pluvinel.
6 The Emir Sher Ali of Afghanistan on a visit to the Viceroy of India, Ambala, 1869. India Office Library.
7 The Emir Abdul Rahman of Afghanistan with the Viceroy of India, 1885. India Office Library.
8 The Emir Habibullah at a review. Khalilullah Enayat Seraj Collection (henceforward KES).
9 The Emir Habibullah on a hunting expedition. KES.
10 Wedding of Sardar Enayatullah. KES.
11 Mahmoud Beg Tarzi with his daughter and grandson. KES.
12 An Afghan prince in Scottish dress. KES.

6 Harems

1 Corridor leading to the harem, Çiragan palace, Constantinople. Galerie Texbraun.
2 Princes, pages and eunuchs at the court of Persia. Biblioteca Nazionale Marciana, Venice (Luigi Montalbone).
3 Princesses with a eunuch. Mohammed Ali Foundation.
4 Princess Nimet Moukhtar and her eunuch. Private collection.
5 A lady of the Ottoman harem. Royal Archives, Windsor (H. Quaas).
6 Mehmed Nazim Effendi and his sisters. Coll. Prince M. Nazim.
7 Nevzut, wife of the last Ottoman Sultan, Mehmed VI. *Milliyet*.
8 The wives of Suleiman Effendi. Coll. R. Eldem.
9 Inge Hanoum. Manyal Palace Museum.
10 Princess Chafak Nour. Private collection.
11 Sultane Melek. Private collection.
12 Princess Nazli Fazil. Sutherland papers, Stafford County Record Office.
13 The family of the Khedive Ismail. Private collection.
14 Malekeh Jehan. Coll. Prince Hamid Qajar.
15 The family of the Khedive Tewfik. Dar al-Hillal.
16 Emir Habibullah of Afghanistan and fourteen *surati*. KES.

7 The End of the Ottomans

1 Abdul Medjid II. Coll. Nedjla Gerrmann.
2 Group photograph in front of the Kasino. Askeri Müze Istanbul (henceforward AMI).
3 The Niedermayer Expedition in Kabul. AMI.
4 The Kaiser greeting the Sheikh al-Islam. IWM.
5 The Emperor and the Sultan leaving the station. Coll. C.Gülersoy.
6 Habsburg, Bourbon and Ottoman. Coll. C.Gülersoy.
7 Sayyid Mohammed Idris al-Senussi. Royal Archives Windsor.
8 Osman Fouad Effendi. Coll. Nedjla Gerrmann.

9 Proclamation of Sherif Hussein as Sherif and Emir of Mecca. Royal Palace, Amman.
10 Group at Jeddah. IWM.
11 Emir Faisal and French officers. Royal Palace, Amman (Section Photographique de l'Armée Française).
12 Nuri al-Said. IWM.
13 Inauguration of Mehmed VI. Private collection.
14 Allied Battleships in the Bosphorus. IWM.
15 Mustafa Kemal Pasha. Milliyet.
16 Visit of Abdul Medjid Effendi and Omar Farouk Effendi to a Turkish Hearth, 1920. Coll. C. Gülersoy.
17 Princes at the Lycée Impérial de Galataseray. Coll. Prince Osman Vassib.
18 Arrival of Mehmed VI in Malta. Hürriyet.
19 Jemal Pasha and King Amanullah of Afghanistan. KES.
20 The former Ottoman Vali of the Yemen. E.F.Jacob, Kings of the Arabs, 1926.

8. Kings of the Arabs
1 Emir Abdullah, 1942. IWM (Cecil Beaton).
2 Emir Abdullah in Jerusalem. IWM.
3 Meeting in Amman. IWM (G.E.Matson).
4 Palace antechamber, Amman, 1942. IWM (Cecil Beaton).
5 At home with Gertrude Bell, 1920. University of Newcastle (Gertrude Bell).
6 Installation of Emir Faisal as King of Iraq. St Antony's College, Oxford (Kerim).
7 Opening Ceremony, Alward Refinery. BP Archives.
8 King Faisal I on the SS Esperia. Coll. Lody Cordahi (Pianchi).
9 King Ghazi. Coll. Badr al-Hajj (J.S.Hoory).
10 King Faisal II on his throne, 1942. IWM (Cecil Beaton).
11 King Faisal II in front of Qasr al-Zuhoor, 1942. IWM (Cecil Beaton).
12 King Faisal II with the Regent Abdulilah, 1942. IWM (Cecil Beaton).
13 The first meeting of the Royal Harithiya Hunt. Royal Geographical Society.
14 King Hussein of the Hejaz at Shunat Nimrin. EMI Pathé.
15 Ex-King Ali of the Hejaz with Karim Thabet. Private collection.
16 Waiting for the King, Riyadh, 1937. Steineke coll. Aramco.

17 Audience Chamber at Hail, 1914. University of Newcastle (Gertrude Bell).
18 Courtyard in the royal palace, Riyadh. Royal Geographical Society (Gerald de Gaury).
19 King Abdul Aziz and Karim Thabet, 1945. Private collection.
20 Visit of the Emir Sa'ud to the Ruler of Kuwait, 1944. Coll. H.W.Y.P. Dickson.
21 The Ruler of Kuwait and his court. Coll. Gerald de Gaury (Gerald de Gaury).
22 Visit of the Viceroy of India to Muscat, 1915. Hardinge Papers, Kent County Archives.
23 Sayyid Faisal bin Turki, Sultan of Muscat and Sayyid Taimur bin Turki. Private collection.

9 The Rise of the Pahlavis
1 Reza Shah and his Prime Minister Mr Djam. Coll. General Djam.
2 Parade of Russian Cossacks and Bengal Cavalry, Isfahan, 1916. IWM.
3 Ahmad Shah and Reza Khan. Qajar family collection.
4 Reza Shah at his coronation, 16 December 1925. Barnaby's Picture Library.
5 The Aga Khan. Private collection. (Vandyk).
6 Mohammed Reza with courtiers. Coll. General Djam.
7 Reza Shah visiting a girls' school. Coll. General Djam.
8 Reza Shah in exile. Coll. General Djam.
9 Mohammed Reza Shah and his first wife Fawzia. IWM (Cecil Beaton).

10 Central Asia
1 King Amanullah in Paktya tribal costume. KES.
2 Said Alim Khan, last Emir of Bokhara. Coll. Professor Terazi.
3 Enver Pasha and Naciye Sultan in Berlin, 1920. Coll. Mahpeyker Enver.
4 Sardar Amanullah and his sisters, 1918. KES.
5 Costume Ball, 1925. KES.
6 The King of Afghanistan on a state visit to Britain, 1928. Royal Archives, Windsor.
7 The Tarzi sisters, 1925. KES.
8 Habibullah Ghazi. KES.
9 Loya Jirgah deputies, 1928. KES.
10 King Zaher Shah. Coll. Princess Miriam.

11 The Fall of the Throne of Egypt
1 King Farouk. Coll. Sir Edward Ford. (Riad Chehata).
2 Sa'ad Zaghloul with admirers. Beit al-Umma, Cairo.
3 Safiya Zaghloul. Beit al-Umma.
4 Adly Yeghen Pasha. Coll. Mrs Zulficar-Mohsen.
5 King Fouad, princes and ministers. Al-Ahram. (Riad Chehata).
6 Caliphate Conference, 1926. Roger Viollet.
7 Investiture of King Farouk. Popperfoto.
8 Ladies and diplomats at the investiture of King Farouk. Popperfoto.
9 King Farouk and his household. Coll. Sir Edward Ford (Edward Ford).
10 Wedding banquet of King Farouk. Mohammed Ali Foundation.
11 Banquet in honour of the Crown Prince of Iran. Popperfoto.
12 Queen Nazli. Mohammed Ali Foundation. (Albani).
13 Prince Mohammed Ali. IWM. (Cecil Beaton).
14 Queen Farida. Private collection. (Riad Chehata).
15 Queen Farida in uniform. Private collection. (Riad Chehata).
16 The sisters of King Farouk. Coll. Sir Edward Ford. (Edward Ford).
17 The Empress Fawzia of Iran. Coll. General Djam.
18 Nabila Ayesha Hassan and her governess. Private collection.
19 Princess Nimet Moukhtar and Princess Abbas Halim. Private collection.
20 The galerie des ancêtres, Palais Shivekiar, Cairo. Coll. Gaston d'Angélis.
21 Ball in Cairo. Private collection. (Servatch).
22 King Farouk on a shoot. Coll. Max Rodenbeck.
23 King Farouk welcoming King Victor Emmanuel III of Italy, Alexandria, 1946. Coll. Max Rodenbeck.
24 Courtiers in the Golden Hall, Manyal. IWM (Cecil Beaton).

Index